POLITICAL CONFLICT, POLITICAL DEVELOPMENT, AND PUBLIC POLICY

POLITICAL CONFLICT, POLITICAL DEVELOPMENT, AND PUBLIC POLICY

Edited by
Eduard A. Ziegenhagen

Westport, Connecticut
London

Library of Congress Cataloging-in-Publication Data

Political conflict, political development, and public policy / edited
by Eduard A. Ziegenhagen.
    p. cm.
  Includes bibliographical references and index.
  ISBN 0–275–94174–4 (alk. paper)
  1. Government, Resistance to. 2. Political development.
  3. Political persecution. I. Ziegenhagen, Eduard A., 1935– .
  JC328.3.P633   1994
  323.6'5—dc20   93–15350

British Library Cataloguing in Publication Data is available.

Library of Congress Catalog Card Number: 93–15350
ISBN: 0–275–94174–4

First published in 1994

Praeger Publishers, 88 Post Road West, Westport, CT 06881
An imprint of Greenwood Publishing Group, Inc.

Printed in the United States of America

The paper used in this book complies with the
Permanent Paper Standard issued by the National
Information Standards Organization (Z39.48–1984).

10 9 8 7 6 5 4 3 2 1

Copyright Acknowledgment

Excerpts from C. Taylor and D. Jodice, *World Handbook of Political and Social Indicators*,
third edition (New Haven: Yale University Press, copyright © 1983), appear by permission
of the publisher.

CONTENTS

TABLES AND FIGURES

TABLES

FIGURES

PREFACE

Substantially diverse and sometimes contradictory findings reported in the systematic study of political behavior have led to a degree of despair tinged with regression in our discipline. Isn't knowledge of political phenomena the aggregate of numerous, irrefutable findings based on paired comparisons? And once these findings are determined, can we not move on to establishing the nature of other relationships of interest? An unqualified positive response to such propositions sometimes contributes to the conclusion that all attempts to understand political phenomena are innately futile or that some modes of investigation or measurement are to be established over others, therefore contributing, possibly, to greater consistency in results.

The comparative study of political conflict and, to a lesser extent, of political development seems to have more than its share of these contentions, perhaps due to the voluminous literature produced during the last four decades. Without addressing the undesirable effects of entirely abandoning systematic investigations, or accepting the a priori selection of some measures over others, it seems reasonable to perceive our modes of investigation as well as our findings as essentially tentative, exploratory, and subject to reinterpretation and elaboration, as is the case, for that matter, of all scientific investigation. Perhaps every generation of researchers needs to be reminded that only ideology promises immutable certainty, while scientific investigation generates clarifying propositions for investigation. In an evolving scientific enterprise such as our own, encouraging investigation on a broad front is our proper priority, as vexing and unassuring as that may be.

The contributions to this volume are based upon this premise, although there is often an effort to draw upon a common perspective, that of general systems theory, and address specific research questions, namely, what are the relationships among political conflict, political development, and public policy, and how do these relationships contribute to system change? These areas of inquiry are familiar to most social scientists and have received substantial attention historically as well as intensive scrutiny through the use of empirically based statistical analysis during the last three decades. Most attention has been focused on definitional issues, operationalization, taxonomy, and the identification of behavior associated with each of these phenomena individually. If linkages exist, most investigations have been based upon the assumption of one-way causal relationships.

The unidirectionality of causation is an artifact of Western traditional thought about the nature of the physical world, transferred to the study of social and political behavior. This orientation has been combined with preoccupation with taxonomy rather than with transformation and change. Until very recently, the social sciences, especially political science, have been notoriously deficient in the formulation and testing of propositions about change. This book is composed of research strategies and findings addressing this process.

INTRODUCTION

This collection of research is based upon the premise that political conflict, political development, and public policy—especially policy of a repressive nature—are interrelated and that any single behavior can be best accounted for in the context of the others. Political conflict and its disruptive and costly effects preoccupy policy makers, regardless of whether they represent nation states or multinational corporations, much as denial of human rights through repressive policies is the continuing concern of various localized or worldwide humanitarian organizations. The fact that such behaviors are interrelated and are linked to the capacity of a political system to develop and cope with local and global problems tends to be overlooked. Demands are made for changes in the behavior of governments often without reference to why particular actions are taken or omitted. Why are regimes repressive? Why do opponents of governments, as well as governments themselves, engage in disruptive and violent acts? How do some political systems escape both repression and political conflict? Such questions, although of ancient origin, are as timely as ever. Knowing why particular behavior occurs can contribute to informed choices as to what can be done to preserve or modify prevailing patterns.

Readers acquainted with the literature that lies at the basis of this investigation may be struck by its familiarity; political conflict and political development are concepts that have been explored empirically by social scientists for at least three decades, and political repression, although less systematically explored, is hardly an unfamiliar notion. It is equally true that the proliferation of the meanings of these concepts has led to arguments for their abandonment. However, familiarity and the increasingly specialized meanings assigned to their variation eventually contribute to an integrated understanding of several areas of behavior.

Most theorists concede that political processes, including those noted above, are inherently dynamic, but they tend to represent them as endpoints in a dynamic process rather than explore the processes that contribute to particular system states. For example, political scientists have endorsed the notion of cyclical change, as indicated by work such as Modelski's (1987) on long range cycles, but how such cycles function is not addressed directly. More often, change is described in terms of stages of political development or revolution without addressing the process of transformation. Reluctance to proceed in the direction of dynamic models is understood and appreciated given the powerful intellectual tradition of reliance on taxonomy and cause and effect models.

THEORETICAL ORIENTATION

The theoretical guidance for many of the contributions to this book is drawn from general systems theory and, more specifically, cybernetics. Cybernetics is usually thought of as an area appropriate to machine technology resulting in products such as computers, robots employed in manufacturing, and the machines used in the exploration of space. Closer attention will disclose applications in a wide variety of human endeavors including mental health, city planning, economics, and, more recently, political behavior. Initially cybernetics was concerned with understanding relationships that preserve equilibrium through feedback mechanisms. The process by which a thermostat maintains a constant temperature in one's home or office is a commonly used example.

The deceptively simple notion of positive and negative feedback can contribute to formulation of propositions and the understanding of relationships in a manner which departs substantially from previous efforts. For example, in the 1960s, indigenous populations of developing nations realized that living conditions are subject to improvement through political and economic change. This realization was identified as the revolution of rising expectations by observers in the West. Increasing expectations were associated with enhanced receptivity of governments to respond in some respect. Governmental response increased expectations, closing the positive loop. If this process were to continue unimpeded, no limits to government responsiveness are conceivable. However, governments often do not or cannot respond to the expectations of their citizens. Eventually, citizens learn that a government's ability to satisfy a rapidly expanding level of expectations is limited by the availability of resources and the willingness of fellow citizens to accept redistribution of their share of whatever resources exist. Decreasing returns contribute to a reduced level of expectations and a lessened governmental responsiveness, dampening the growth of the upward spiral. Applied to political development, conflict, and public policy, the concept of positive and negative feedback requires researchers to specify and test propositions of interest. Will increases in repression contribute to lessening conflict and provide an environment in which governments can develop democratic institutions and eventually lessen repression? Or does repression contribute to the emergence of repressive institutions and continuous repression, which prevents the emergence of democratic institutions?

By reference to cybernetic concepts such as this, it is possible to change the nature of the research questions being addressed from what is the proper classification of a particular political practice at some point in time, to a description of how various system features interact to produce behavior of interest and, finally, to the question of what can be done to change behavior in desired directions. Most of the research reported in this book addresses why particular behavior emerges, although the capability of identifying what can be done to secure desired behavior is at least implied at this stage of development.

PROCEDURES

In order to address issues of substantial complexity and changing relationships, it is necessary to employ statistical procedures that are capable of measuring relationships among many variables that change simultaneously. Although these procedures are employed less frequently in political science than in some of our fellow disciplines in the social sciences, they are utilized by many of the contributors to this volume. Propositions that were once investigated individually can now be considered collectively and interactively by virtue of the increasing maturity of substantive and methodological theory in concert with vastly increased access to data and the capability to manage it efficiently and effectively.

This effort entails risks and reduces the number of prospective readers who are acquainted with these procedures. This also enters an area of vastly greater technical demands on data and data management procedures. Special care has been taken to lessen these difficulties and to communicate the procedures as clearly as possible.

ORGANIZATION AND PERSPECTIVE

This book is divided into two parts. Part one is devoted to particular area- and nation-based research. Here the emphasis is on systems in rapid transition, characterized by comparatively high rates of change often involving persisting political violence, repressive governmental policies, and the collapse and regeneration of political institutions.

Christian, Davenport, and Arat all explore conflict behavior, political development, and public policy on a regional level. Christian turns her attention to exploring the extent to which world economic structure is related to political conflict in Latin American states and the policies they employ in attempts to control conflict. This outlook is based on the assertion that the behavior of dependent Third World nations is determined by the demands of economically developed nations located at the core of the world economic system. Accordingly, core nations impose unfavorable economic and political practices on dependent states through trade agreements, economic and military aid, and loans. These devices perpetuate reliance on extractive industries, labor, and agriculture in dependent states and maintain the position of core states as centers of manufacturing. Political structure and the policies of dependent states are designed to protect and advance the interests of core states, given this perspective. Christian moves beyond static description of relationships, however, and poses questions central for understanding the implications of dependency as a dynamic system. What behavior can be expected in dependent states when changes in the structure of the world economic system occur? Do the rate and type of political conflict change as dominant members of the core decline and competitors emerge? Do periods of relative decline in the dominance of particular core states provide opportunities for economic development? How do local elites respond to variation in political conflict structurally and in terms of public policy? For example, is the military elite likely to emerge as the primary tool in the implementation of repressive policies to control political conflict?

Christian addresses these questions by drawing on time series data for the United States and the nations of Latin America for the period of 1945 to 1982. Behavior of interest is modeled in the form of cybernetic paradigms of the world economic system with provisions for the measurement of economic features of core periphery relations as well as linkages of dependent states' policies to political conflict.

Davenport is concerned with external threats to the state in concert with internal conflict as predictors of militarization of governments, repressive policies, and political conflict in Third World systems. That external threats may be responsible for the application of force inside the system is a hypothesis of long standing. Additionally, those societies that lack resources to satisfy the demands of discontented populations have few options other than the use of force if a regime is to remain in power. Davenport carries the investigation several steps further. He focuses attention on the repression of domestic forms of political conflict, in this case mass protest behavior. He also links military capability to external threats and the repression of conflict by measuring increased state resources for the military, growth in the size of the military apparatus, and the direct representation of the military in high-level, decision-making positions in the government. The military, in such circumstances, not only has a large and well-financed organization, but it is capable of advocating the use of force as a remedy to political conflict at the highest levels of government. The application of force takes the form of repressive measures, most commonly censorship of the media and all forms of political expression, restriction on organization and assembly for political purposes, and the use of political executions to eliminate persons considered to be politically undesirable. Davenport draws on data for twenty-two nations from 1945 to 1982 to test a variety of hypotheses based on the considerations noted above.

Arat also investigates linkages of political conflict to repressive policies and the decline of democratic governments. In her chapter she explores governmental responses to political conflict in the context of the world economic system. Rather than confining the investigation to a single nation, region, or type of conflict, Arat classifies all nations in existence from 1947 to 1982 according to world system status as core, centrally planned (socialist), semiperiphery, and periphery. Arat argues that position in the world system and, accordingly, the relative development of each member determine the type and level of political conflict in each nation. For example, nations located at the periphery of the world system are the least industrialized and less likely to have an organized labor force that is capable of using general strikes as antigovernmental tactics. Furthermore, when types or rates of political conflict are unacceptable to a regime, executive reorganization and repression are more likely to be used as a response in dependent nations than in core states, mainly because economic and social options are not available in nations of limited resources. Given this perspective, the conflict tolerated in political systems as well as governmental responses to it may be a function of a system's capacity to draw on social resources. Resources available to social systems and their governments coincide with the relative position occupied in the world economic system.

Changing the focus from consideration of behavior across nations, Çarkoğlu and Koutsoukis consider political conflict, development, and policy within individual nations, in this instance Turkey and Greece.

The Turkish experience with military regimes is the focus of Çarkoğlu's investigation. The search for how to account for successive advances and declines in democratic governments has led to a broad range of explanations including socioeconomic development, modernization, and political conflict. Economic development and modernization have been identified previously as primary sources for the advance or the collapse of democratic regimes but may be less compelling explanations when compared to the predictive power of political conflict and, conjointly, a habituation hypothesis. Political conflict, including a broad range of indicators such as riots, government crises, antigovernment demonstrations, assassinations, and guerrilla warfare, may be seen as a threat to state authority beyond the capability of civilian governments to prevent or regulate. The military intervenes, given this perspective, to preserve state authority or at least to prevent the collapse of the state. Political conflict alone has been a strong predictor of military intervention but may be insufficient as a sole explanation for it. Types of conflict rather than merely rates of conflict may be associated with intervention or lessen its likelihood. For example, elite conflict involving assassination and guerrilla warfare, rather than mass conflict of a protest variety, may be more likely to precipitate military intervention. Furthermore, military coups occuring during periods of political conflict may contribute to the likelihood that this type of solution is incorporated into a political system's problem-solving memory. Once it is incorporated, military intervention is invoked repeatedly during conflict periods. Just as successful coups contribute to the probability that they will be reintroduced in conflict situations, unsuccessful military interventions diminish reliance on this coping strategy. These propositions are investigated employing time series data from 1950 to 1986.

Koutsoukis focuses on the attributes of economic and political development in combination with those of political elites in Greece in identifying linkages between political conflict and political development. In the case of Greece, both authoritarianism and democratic development were experienced since Greece achieved independence. The structure and linkages of development and conflict are not explicit, although during the years in which political institutions functioned comparatively well, the likelihood that guerrilla war and purges would occur decreased. Economic development in Greece, often viewed as a prerequisite for political development, is indeed associated with political participation but seems less associated with political effectiveness than it does to a particular form of political conflict—in this case general strikes. In short, economic development may have advanced levels of political participation in Greece through voting but may also have increased the likelihood of mass protest behavior in the form of general strikes. These changes did not necessarily contribute to the emergence of political institutions that could accommodate increased levels of participation.

Part two of this book is focused on the universality of system components and linkages. Interest lies less in national or regional structure or behavior and more in exploring the range of common human experience. Although the focus remains on political conflict, development, and public policy, different theoretical perspectives of the precursors of conflict, the policies employed, and the results secured are investigated.

Both Hou and Dillon address the nature of the relationship of repression and political conflict, a feature of system behavior included in all of the preceding considerations of political development, conflict, and public policy. Although the question of how effective repression is as a policy tool for the regulation of political conflict has received substantial attention, the issue is not resolved to the complete satisfaction of researchers. Some difficulties in resolving the issue reside in the different conceptualization and measurement strategies utilized by researchers to investigate the relationship between repression and conflict, as well as major methodological differences related to cross-sectional and time series research. All researchers appear to agree that repressive measures and conflict influence each other to some extent but that the form of the relationship is particularly elusive.

Although both Hou and Dillon investigate relationships among repressive measures and political conflict, each employs a different approach. Hou notes that repression is most often reported to be a policy response of regimes to political conflict. Repression is employed to eliminate or at least reduce a perceived threat to the regime by challengers. However, observation of behavior also reveals that challengers respond to repression by increased levels of conflict and varieties of conflict behavior. The level of repression employed also seems important in determining conflict-repression relationships, as moderate levels of repression can increase conflict while highly repressive behavior eventually reduces conflict. For those regimes that employ the latter policies, one would expect that a curvilinear relationship of repression to conflict in the form of an inverted U would persist, although there are many instances in which this relationship does not exist. A seemingly positive loop appears to exist in many political systems repressing conflict, sometimes ending in the collapse of a regime or the entire state apparatus. Hou introduces political development as an additional element responsible for the repression and conflict linkage. Exploration of these relationships in the context of the greater political and social system is undertaken drawing on 434 conflict episodes from 64 nations for the period 1945 to 1982.

Dillon also notes that the form and direction of the relationship of repression to conflict remains an item of some speculation, although most researchers agree that they are related in some respect. An exact specification of the relationship is pursued by reference to two major explanations, one based on frustration-aggression theory and the other on rational-choice theory. Dillon notes that proponents of frustration-aggression theory as an explanation of conflict-repression relationships emphasize the cumulative effect of frustration and its discharge in aggressive behavior, that is, conflict. However, frustration also can be lessened through displacement and deflected through inhibition when regimes employ repressive policies. Proponents of rational-choice explanations argue that potential participants in political conflict consider possible benefits, for example, the acquisition of goods from looting, compared to costs, such as arrest or injury. In addition to the construction of measurement models having close correspondence to complex theoretical propositions, it is also necessary to disentangle cause and effect relationships. Dillon introduces a variety of models pertinent to these issues and employs time series analysis based upon daily event data for sixteen European nations for the period 1948–1982.

Ziegenhagen integrates previous findings from the areas of political development, political conflict, and public policy through the development and testing of a dynamic model. This effort represents a departure from assumptions that are unique to equilibrium-based models and requires attention to how systems are transformed from one state to another as well as what form those states assume at each point in the process. He relies on many of the hypotheses provided by empirical findings and translates them into propositions that define relationships among model components. The components themselves are familiar—political development, political conflict, and sanctioning apparatus—but the manner in which they are associated—that is, a series of input-output functions and positive and negative feedback loops—makes it possible to consider dynamic elements of the process.

PART ONE

NATIONAL AND REGIONAL POLITICAL JURISDICTIONS AS ENVIRONMENTS FOR SYSTEMIC CHANGE, CONFLICT, AND PUBLIC POLICY

1

THE EFFECTS OF U.S. HEGEMONIC DECLINE ON POLITICAL CONFLICT IN LATIN AMERICA

Cindy M. Christian

After World War II, a number of theories arose as a direct challenge to conventional perspectives on the positive relationship of international trade to economic development. Initially, these new conjectures emerged from the Economic Commission for Latin America (ECLA) but were later revised through the "*dependencia* theories" of Latin American scholars such as Dos Santos (1970) and Cardoso and Faletto (1979). The arguments of *dependencia* theorists represent a "broadly based critical perspective on development and underdevelopment" in peripheral societies of the capitalist world system (Duvall et al., 1981:312).[1] In this chapter an attempt is made to model the linkage of that economic world system to the origin and regulation of political conflict within a subset of the system's peripheral nations—that is, Latin America.

Essentially, the major research questions are, to what extent do structural manifestations of the international economic system affect the level and type of political conflict within Latin American states, and how do they affect the manner in which governments control that conflict? The relationship between governmental policies and political conflict requires examination. Do the hypothesized effects of structural inequality and economic dependence in the world system contribute to political conflict in Latin America? Do these same effects, as they are altered by changes in the international economic system, provide for more authoritarian and coercive responses to political conflict over time, for example, through an increased role for the military? Do such governmental policies increase or decrease the level and intensity of conflict within the nation; and, concurrently, does political conflict generate certain types of intervention by the government? Finally, do cycles of economic growth and decline in core nations, specifically in the hegemonic leader, alter the connections between the center and the peripheral nations?

To answer these questions, this chapter is divided into several sections. The first deals with the development of the literature and its exposure of the relevant relationships among theories of *dependencia*, political conflict, the role of the military, and world systems analysis. In the second section, an explanatory model and its assumptions are discussed. In the third section, a research design to test the model and the hypotheses derived from it are proposed. Finally, a series of regression equations are analyzed to demonstrate the validity of the model and to test its propositions.

DEPENDENCIA, ECONOMIC DEVELOPMENT, AND POLITICAL CONFLICT

Since their inception, *dependencia* theories have been concerned with explaining the development problems of Third World nations as caused by their relationships with more advanced nations. They are differentiated from other theories of development "by the emphasis placed upon articulation of the structure of social, political, and economic development, the relationship of developmental structure, especially economic, to alternative policy options, and the assertion that the problematic aspects of development can be attributed to the intrusion of foreign nations" (Ziegenhagen, 1986:21). The historical role of imperialism and the process of unequal exchange among and within nations are critical to explanations of underdevelopment and economic, social, and political distortions in the periphery.

Formal imperialism, which often required invasion of one country by another to install cooperative regimes, and, later, informal imperialism, which granted indirect control through aid, loans, and trade agreements, allowed core nations to dictate economic policies to peripheral nations. Peripheral states were forced to base their indigenous economic development on the production of raw materials and agricultural commodities. These were to be traded for manufactured products from the core. The periphery, therefore, provided the input for the development of the industrialized core and a market for the core's finished products.

These policies were based on the theory of comparative advantage, the cornerstone of the world's liberal trading system, which emerged under British hegemony. Within this system, each nation would specialize in providing, for trade on the world market, only those goods it could produce more efficiently than other nations. Each would be able to exchange its products for those it did not specialize in, and all would prosper equally from their contribution to the world economy. Unfortunately, the raw materials, agricultural products, and labor, which the peripheral nations were compelled to offer, were of less value on the world market than were the manufactured products of the core.[2] The result was a system of unequal exchange where the peripheral nations consistently received less foreign exchange for their exports and were paid more for their imports (Emmanuel, 1972). This left peripheral nations with few investment resources or opportunities for their own development.

In a 1957 assessment of the contradictions between the motivation behind imperialism and the economic development of backward nations, Baran stated that, "what is decisive is that economic development in underdeveloped countries is profoundly inimical to the dominant interests in the advanced capitalist countries" (Baran, 1966:28). The ECLA reasserted this pronouncement through its finding that international trade created an international division of labor that benefitted the core over the periphery (ECLA, 1963). Prices for goods produced by peripheral nations were lower and open to greater fluctuations on the world market than were those sold by core nations. When prices of their products decreased, peripheral nations were left with trade deficits, which further limited their financial ability to develop an indigenous manufacturing base. This process led to the severe debt crisis, which continues to this day, faced by many Third World nations, especially those in Latin America, whose governments borrowed heavily to invest in development. In addition, in recent decades, this has meant the provision of cheap labor for unskilled, labor-intensive manufacturing controlled by the core's multinational enterprises. Underdevelopment, therefore, continued in the periphery while the core expanded its technological and industrial development through the utilization of the periphery's resources; through infiltration of the periphery's markets, which were free from domestic competition; and through the profits gained from more favorable terms of trade. Without economic development, peripheral nations would remain plagued by a lack of social and political development.

In 1967, Frank proposed a model of underdevelopment that incorporated these conceptions of the dominant international structure into four general propositions: first, peripheral nations have been incorporated into the capitalist system since early colonial periods; second, these nations have been transformed into capitalist nations because of their incorporation; third, integration of the periphery into the capitalist system is necessary given its established relationship with the core where all surplus goes to the center; and, finally, the weakening of the core-periphery link would allow for the possibility of local development (Frank, 1967). For these theorists, improved development and a move toward greater self-sufficiency for the periphery meant economic growth, an increase in the domestic industrial base, and improved socioeconomic welfare for the general population. Those states adopting communism/socialism are excluded from Frank's analysis because their choice of this economic system protects them from capitalist incorporation and allows them to develop independently.

Frank's propositions typify the field of *dependencia* (Cardoso and Faletto, 1979; Dos Santos, 1970), which developed separately from dependency theories (Wallerstein, 1976; Galtung, 1971). The major difference between *dependencia* and *dependency* revolves around the former's limitation of the cause of dependency to the capitalist system. For dependency theorists, certain conditions result from relationships to world powers that are not necessarily capitalist. Furthermore, advanced capitalist nations may also be dependent, to different degrees, on each other. *Dependencia* relates the underdevelopment of the periphery solely to the capitalist world system (Ziegenhagen, 1986:22).

This difference certainly holds implications for the type of nations that might be examined in any analysis of such theories; however, there is basic agreement between the two areas that an international economic structure was produced by the unequal development of nations, which still affects the progression of those same nations. In addition, the international structure plays a role in the establishment of the internal economic, political, and social structure of those nations (Cardoso and Faletto, 1979; Galtung, 1971; Dos Santos, 1970). For example, certain sectors of the less developed nations advance more than others because of the orientation to meet the needs of the core. As Dos Santos states, "the unequal and combined character of capitalist development at the international level is reproduced internally in an acute form" (Dos Santos, 1970:234). Furthermore, elites within the nations of the periphery will unite with the controlling interests in the center at the expense of the remaining populations (Galtung, 1971). The role those elites play in the formulation of policy becomes critical to maintaining their nation's place in the world system and in the determination of their local political and economic system.

Very few empirical evaluations of the theories of development proposed by these two schools of research have been conducted. An exception is the work of Duvall, Jackson, Russett, Snidal, and Sylvan (1981). In their work, these authors provide a mathematical model of dependency and several measures of the major components of such theories, though they never actually test them. Within the framework they present, Duvall and associates hypothesize a linkage between the effects of the international economic system (trade sector distortions, internal economic distortions, sociopolitical distortions) and sociopolitical conflict (Duvall et al., 1981: 316). Using several of these measures, Ziegenhagen (1986) tests for the relationship of these variables to the regulation of political conflict through such policy interventions as negative sanctions.

The theoretical connection of the world system to conflict has been discussed by dependency and *dependencia* theorists (Zolberg, 1981; Cardoso and Faletto, 1979; Portes, 1976; Galtung, 1971). The general contention is that "nations that are dependent on international markets and foreign capital are likely to experience comparatively high levels of political instability" (Ziegenhagen, 1986:22). Penetration of a nation by external forces causes instability because of the resulting uneven economic development, economic inequality, and the establishment of authoritarian governmental structures to maintain the order necessary for economic exploitation by the core.

As suggested, political conflict may be directly determined by the effects of the international economic system on internal structures. Alternatively, the system may influence conflict only indirectly through the internal governmental structures it causes. The question, then, is not simply one of systemic impacts on the initiation of political conflict but also one of the regulation of that conflict once it exists. The causes of political conflict, both of a mass and an elite nature, have been so widely discussed that it would be futile to list them all here. Socioeconomic development, political development, state building, a historical precedent for violent collective action, and a response to political repression are a few of the hypothesized determinants of political conflict (Lichbach, 1987; Gurr and Lichbach, 1986; Gurr, 1986a; Gurr, 1986b; Cohen et al., 1981; Hibbs, 1973; Huntington, 1965; Lieuwen, 1961). However, the work of Ziegenhagen (1986) represents the only empirical analysis of the regulation of political conflict.

As Ziegenhagen states, "regulation implies the capability to maintain behavior within desirable or known limits of variation" (Ziegenhagen, 1986:1). The ability to maintain acceptable levels and forms of political conflict has usually required a coercive capacity on the part of the state. In dependency terms, the state would need to protect and promote the interests of the core nations. For this reason the role of the military in suppressing political conflict has been widely examined (Huntington, 1957; Janowitz, 1964; Johnson, 1962; Putnam, 1967). However, the military may also contribute to the level of political conflict as it competes for the allocation of resources with other institutions in the society (Putnam, 1967; Hibbs, 1973). Furthermore, political conflict may be so disruptive as to increase the size of and allocations to the military. In either case, the military serves as the major instrument through which the state controls political conflict.

The model presented in this chapter is based on the theoretical implications of *dependencia* theories, the linkages between structural factors to the causes and regulation of political conflict as presented by Ziegenhagen, and the variables constructed by Duvall and associates. However, this model also examines the direct effects of economic movements within the core on those within the periphery and their connection to political conflict. Specifically, the decline of the major economic power in the system, the hegemon, is examined. Cyclical notions of the evolution of the world economic system are based on well-established theories of short business cycles and the longer-term Kondratieff waves of growth and decline.

The basis for this additional component comes from world system analysts as well as *dependencia* theorists (Modelski, 1987b; Wallerstein, 1976).

Frank suggests that because of the interrelated development of the core and the underdevelopment of the periphery, economic decline in the core permits advancement of the periphery (Frank, 1967). Alternatively, world systems analysts suggest that imperial powers resort to more formal means of exploitation of underdeveloped countries when competition within the core is more intense and when the hegemon faces decline (Bergesen, 1980; Bousquet, 1980; Gordon, 1980). Still others maintain that cycles in political conflict follow economic waves so that the basis for new forms of conflict materialize during an upswing and then manifest in a subsequent decline (Cronin, 1980).

This crucial aspect of world system, dependency, and *dependencia* analyses has been overlooked to date. The contention of these theories is that the core advances economically at the expense of the periphery. Therefore, the decline of the center should change its relationship to internal developments in the periphery. Through this model, the structural impact of the world economic system can be formulated and tested not only for its indirect effects on political conflict through internal changes but also through its direct linkage.

THE MODEL AND ITS ASSUMPTIONS

The proposed model is represented in Figure 1.1. The logic of the model is based on general systems theory, which assumes that all political phenomena are the result of the operation of a highly structured system. More specifically, the model reflects the assumptions of cybernetic theory where control and regulation become the primary functions of the system and, therefore, determine the output of that system's operation in terms of political, economic, and social events. As Ziegenhagen suggests, because the state acts to regulate political conflict, a cybernetic model is appropriate (1986). Cybernetic models depend on the identification of the crucial components of the system that encases the phenomenon of interest. They also require the specification of the relationship between those components.

The regulator is the key and must allow the system to respond and change given disturbances either from outside or within the system. Disturbances influence outcomes through regulation and through the environment in which the system is found. In the model presented here, the components of the system are more difficult to determine but are still discernible. Government policy serves to regulate the impact of disturbances from the environment of the international economic system on the level and degree of political conflict. The disturbances include fluctuations in the economic position of the hegemon as well as the internal distortions caused by the world system. Essentially, changes in the relationship between the core and the periphery are posited to have an effect on the variations between political conflict and governments' regulation of that conflict.

Figure 1.1
Cybernetic Model of Economic World System Effects on Political Conflict in the Periphery

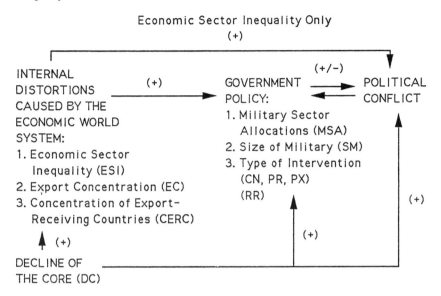

CN: censorship; PR: political restrictions; PX: political execution; RR: relaxation of restrictions.

In this sense the world system serves as both the environment and a set of disturbances because both manifestations are allowed to have a direct effect on political conflict along with an indirect effect through the regulator. Political conflict is an outcome but may also serve as a disturbance affecting regulation by the state. To summarize with an example, pressure from the declining hegemon, the United States, could lead any number of Latin American nations to increase resource allocations to their militaries so that they might better maintain order in the society. Greater order would allow the hegemon to more easily extract additional resources from those nations' economies to delay its own decline. The increased use of repressive measures by the military, reinforced by greater allocations, would then affect the degree and type of political conflict. Opposition groups, or the population at large, might react with more intense conflictual activities to counter the military measures. Conversely, governmental repression may serve to decrease political conflict through effective regulation and deterrence. In either case, the resulting degree of political conflict then influences the response of the government. The direction of the relationship between these components is indicated by the arrows in Figure 1.1.

More specifically, the model presented here proposes a set of relationships based on the tenets of *dependencia* theory. The concern is with the effects of the capitalist economic system. The major assumption of this model is that a world economic system exists that is hierarchically structured to the advantage of the most developed nations at the expense of less advanced nations. As discussed above, this is the major theoretical supposition of *dependencia* theories. The second assumption is that this international system affects the internal structure and societal behavior of the less developed nations. These propositions are characterized by a highly structured set of interactions with repetitive and predictable outcomes as suggested by the model's cybernetic formulation.

The actual relationships specified by the model can be explained within this larger framework. To begin with, the world system is apparent in underdeveloped or less developed nations through factors like the three listed in the model: economic sector inequality, export concentration, and a concentration of export-receiving nations.[3] While these have initially been used to explain underdevelopment, they have direct implications for the initiation of political conflict and its regulation. *Dependencia* theorists believe that one manifestation of the world capitalist system is the uneven development of various sectors of the peripheral societies. Usually this involves "the development of extractive and industrial sectors at the expense of lagging development of agricultural and service sectors" (Ziegenhagen, 1986:23). This inequity between sectors would have a direct effect on political conflict as one group, such as those involved in industrial or infrastructure development, is advanced without concern for the needs of other groups, such as peasants and small farmers. Furthermore, the development of the favored sectors is so closely tied to foreign interests that little surplus capital remains for the development of indigenous industries. The resulting uneven development leads to divided social and political classes that compete for control of the state. The military often emerges to regulate the resulting conflict in favor of a continuation of the uneven process of development and the maintenance of order; simply note the historical increase in military regimes throughout Latin America as evidence.

Export concentration indicates the prominence of trade practices by the periphery that favor the core. One indication of this internal distortion is the domination of a small number of exports in the trade profile of a peripheral nation. This factor affects the underdevelopment of the periphery in the most crucial ways. Specifically, it leads to dependency on fluctuating international markets for those particular commodities. Its relationship to political conflict is probably indirect and carried through political structures. This is consistent with the arguments of *dependencia* theorists who contend that the peripheral states represent the economic interests of the core. Following that logic, political conflict would result from the allocation of resources to the military for the protection of foreign and local elite interests and the maintenance of a stable environment for capitalist exploitation rather than appropriations to alleviate the harsh effects of dependence on a small number of exports. The size of the military, allocations to the military, and the use of repressive intervention techniques are the result of export concentration and, in turn, affect political conflict. A concentration of export-receiving nations would render the same relationship because the political structures of the periphery would represent the political and economic needs of that dominant trading partner instead of less favored sectors of its own society.

The expected impact of the relationships among these variables is represented in parentheses in Figure 1.1. The positive relationships between most of the variables in this model are based on the hypothesis that the decline of the core leads to even greater distortions or further underdevelopment in the economies of peripheral nations because core states seek to counter their own economic problems through greater exploitation of the periphery. The decline of the core and the resulting distortions lead to an increase in dissatisfaction, which is expressed through conflictual behavior, by affected groups in the periphery. Governments then must respond by increasing their use of repressive policies to maintain order. Of course, the inclusion of hegemonic decline in the model might also reverse the impact of the endogenous variables. The resulting negative relationships would be consistent with *dependencia* suppositions that economic decline in core states releases peripheral nations from their position of dependency and allows them to develop internally, at least until the core reasserts itself and begins an economic upswing. During such a decline, internal distortions in the periphery would decrease, coercive measures by increasingly authoritarian regimes would relax, and political conflict might decrease.

The exact relationship between government policy and political conflict is more difficult to determine. One could sensibly predict that greater allocations to the military and a larger military itself would decrease the level of conflict by its prevalent use of coercion. In this case, the assumption is that the cost of violent collective action would become too great for the civilian masses or opposition groups. Their utility for such action would become negative. Alternatively, an increase in repressive responses by the government could lead to an increase in political conflict. In this case, one would assume that the utility of continuing the conflictual activity remains positive or even increases compared with the negative utility of surrendering to oppression. This is true particularly if the conflict results from competition over the allocation of resources (Ziegenhagen, 1986:8). The relationship between political conflict and governmental policy may be nonrecursive. Not only might the regulatory policies of the state affect conflict, but conflict itself may lead to an increase in the coercive nature of that regulation. Because of the variety of possible outcomes, this relationship remains unspecified in the model.

RESEARCH DESIGN[4]

The connections among the components of the model and their impact upon one another represent the set of relevant relationships that should be tested. To do so, a pooled, cross-sectional analysis is conducted. Seventeen Latin American nations are examined for various years between 1946 and 1982. These nations include Bolivia, Brazil, Chile, Colombia, Costa Rica, Cuba, Ecuador, El Salvador, the Dominican Republic, Guatemala, Haiti, Honduras, Mexico, Nicaragua, Paraguay, Peru, and Venezuela. The United States will serve as the representative of the core because of its role as the hegemonic leader of the system since World War II. This will also permit a more precise measurement of decline.

Latin American nations and the United States were chosen to represent the two poles of the international economic system because of their historical relationship to each other. The United States has long been the dominant trading partner with Latin America and has intervened consistently in most Latin American affairs since the independence of those nations, particularly the nations of Central America due to their proximity to the United States. *Dependencia* theories originated as an attempt to explain the exploitative nature of this very relationship.

Furthermore, this close connection permits a more precise examination of the economic decline of the core without the threat of the effects of an alternative rising power within the center. In other words, although the United States may have been declining since the early 1970s, another core power—Japan—may have been experiencing an upswing. This newly emerging power could possibly replace the old in maintaining underdevelopment and dependency in the periphery. The relationship between Latin America and the United States has been so close, however, that the replacement with a new hegemon would probably not occur in the relatively short time period studied. While the influence of the United States has been declining, it has not yet been replaced within its own sphere of influence.

Data for the measurement of each of the variables considered in the model are obtained from Banks's *Cross-National Time-Series Data Archive* (1979) and *World Handbook of Political and Social Indicators* (1983), compiled by Taylor and Jodice. Political conflict serves as the ultimate dependent variable. The measurement of conflict utilized here is referred to as "dominant variety" (DV) conflict. Dominant variety reflects the degree to which conflict episodes exhibit variety. Conflict episodes are periods of time, usually measured as a duration of years, which are bounded by periods relatively free of conflict activity. They represent the units of anal-

Table 1.1
Examples of Dominant Variety Political Conflict for Conflict Episodes

Country	Episode	Years	Dominant Variety	Event
Chile	2202	1952-1958	39.90	Riots
	2203	1960-1961	40.00	No Dominance
	2204	1963-1963	54.55	Cabinet Change
	2205	1965-1967	55.56	Riots
	2206	1969-1976	17.28	Assassination
Haiti	4902	1948-1965	29.24	Coups
	4903	1967-1971	34.90	Guerilla War
	4904	1973-1973	100.00	Cabinet Change
	4905	1976-1976	76.92	Assassination
	4906	1978-1980	54.00	Purge
Honduras	5001	1947-1949	66.67	Revolutionary Acts
	5002	1951-1951	100.00	Cabinet Change
	5003	1954-1960	31.98	Revolutionary Acts
	5004	1963-1963	54.11	Coups
	5005	1965-1965	100.00	Cabinet Change
	5006	1969-1969	60.00	Antigovernment Demonstrations
	5007	1971-1972	40.18	Constitutional Change
	5008	1975-1975	63.81	Coups
	5009	1977-1978	76.00	Coups

ysis within which political conflict is measured. As Ziegenhagen describes it, a conflict episode is "a sequential ordering of temporally adjacent conflict events bounded by periods of political quiescence. . . . Its empirical definition is derived from the sequential distribution of conflict indicators along a time dimension" (1986:58). The dominant variety measure of conflict, then, is the degree to which a single conflict event type occurs in an episode relative to other events. The score for the dominant variety is "calculated by summing the frequencies of each type of event and dividing the total sum of each event by the summed total of all events" (Ziegenhagen, 1986:65). The resulting percentage represents the degree to which the most frequent event type, that is, the dominant variety, occurs with respect to all other events. The higher the dominant variety score, the greater the proportion is for a single event type relative to all events which take place in the episode. If several events exist in equal proportions, an episode is characterized as displaying "no dominance" (Ziegenhagen, 1986:65). Table 1.1 provides examples of dominant variety scores and types in temporal order for Chile, Haiti, and Honduras.

In terms of the cybernetic model incorporated in this analysis, the successful regulation of political conflict must be interpreted in relationship to the degree to which a single conflict event or a variety of events dominate an episode. Consistent with the logic of general systems theory, a regulator,

Figure 1.2
Cybernetic Model of Economic World System Effects on Political Conflict in the Periphery: Revised

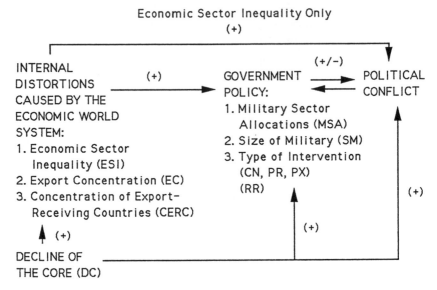

CN: censorship; PR: political restrictions; PX: political execution; RR: relaxation of restrictions.

in this case the Latin American governments, can respond to a narrow range of events more easily than it can to a broader variety. The governments can develop responses to only a few conflict events and incorporate those responses more easily into their output options. However, if the range and frequency of events increases, the governments cannot immediately alter their policies in response. The system must learn to cope with the increase in conflict and must develop responses over time. Because of this, an increase in the dominant variety measure of political conflict from one episode to the next indicates a decrease in the overall level of political conflict. It also suggests that government policies have been successful in regulating political conflict because the variety of activities has remained limited. Conversely, a decrease in the dominant variety score suggests that government regulation has failed and the scope and frequency of conflict activity has increased—that is, political conflict has increased. Figure 1.2 represents the expected relationships between the variables in the model given this revised interpretation of political conflict. For example, in Figure 1.1, the decline of the core (DC) and economic sector inequality (ESI) in the peripheral nations are hypothesized to lead to an increase in political conflict, that is, a decrease in the dominant variety of conflict as indicated in Figure 1.2.

The three internal distortions of the international economic system are measured in a more straightforward manner. ESIs are measured as Gini coefficients based on product per worker across agricultural, industrial, and service sectors. Export concentration (EC) is based on the degree to which commodity exports fall within a small number of categories. The smaller the number of export categories and the greater the value of the largest categories, the greater the EC coefficient. The measurement for the concentration of export-receiving countries (CERC) is defined as the "sum of the squares of the proportions of total exports going to each trading partner" (Ziegenhagen, 1986:26). These scores are provided in index form.

The measurement of the variables representing governmental policies focuses on the military. Military sector allocations (MSA) are measured as defense expenditures as a proportion of total expenditures. This reflects the idea that the military competes with other sectors of society for governmental funding and represents the degree of influence the military yields within the government. The size of the military is measured as a percentage of total population. Various types of intervention reflect the policies of the governmental structure in the regulation of political conflict. Repressive measures are the most often cited and are utilized here. These measures were first used by Hibbs (1973) and include political censorship of communication (CN); political restrictions on organization, assembly, and representation (PR); political execution (PX); and a relaxation of restrictions (RR).

Finally, the economic decline of the core is equated with the decline of the United States. One indicator of such decline is the nature and magnitude of its exports. The expectation is that as the United States declines economically, as many believe it has since the early 1970s (Cox, 1987; Wallerstein, 1976), its economic profile begins to resemble that of a classic dependent nation. For example, one would expect that as a nation declines, its exports would increasingly come from one primary sector, such as agriculture. Based on the assumptions of dependency, the decline of the United States is measured with the same indicators used to express internal distortions in the Latin American nations (i.e., ESIUS, ECUS, and CERCUS).

Given the complexity of the model and the multitude of specified relationships, a series of sequential equations is specified. For direct relationships, ordinary least squares (OLS) regression analysis is utilized. For the nonrecursive linkages between government policy and political conflict, two-staged least squares (2SLS) regression analysis is used. These two sets of equations appear in Table 1.2. The first set represents the hypothesized relationship between the hegemonic decline of the United States and internal economic disorders in Latin American nations. As the United States

Table 1.2
Regression Equations

Set One: Ordinary Least Squares Regressions

```
ESI  = a + DC     (DC = ESIUS, ECUS, and CERCUS)
EC   = a + DC
CERC = a + DC
```

Set Two: Two Stage Least Squares Regressions

The 2SLS process involves the use of OLS to obtain predicted values for the variables of interest. In this case, the measure of political conflict (DV) and the measures of government policy (MSA, SM, CN, PR, PX, RR) are estimated with OLS so that the nonrecursive relationship posited between them may be examined.

These equations are estimated in the following order:

To get the predicted values of DV using OLS:
DV = a +/- MSA +/- SM +/- CN +/- PR +/- PX +/- RR + ESI + DC

```
With predicted values of DV:
MSA = a + ESI + EC + CERC + DC +/- DV
SM  = a + ESI + EC + CERC + DC +/- DV
CN  = a + ESI + EC + CERC + DC +/- DV
PR  = a + ESI + EC + CERC + DC +/- DV
PX  = a + ESI + EC + CERC + DC +/- DV
RR  = a - ESI - EC - CERC - DC +/- DV
```

Estimated for comparison & to get predicted values of Government policies using OLS:
```
MSA = a + ESI + EC + CERC + DC +/- DV
SM  = a + ESI + EC + CERC + DC +/- DV
CN  = a + ESI + EC + CERC + DC +/- DV
PR  = a + ESI + EC + CERC + DC +/- DV
PX  = a + ESI + EC + CERC + DC +/- DV
RR  = a - ESI - EC - CERC - DC +/- DV
```

Final equation:

With predicted values of government policies:
DV = a +/- MSA +/- SM +/- CN +/- PR +/- PX +/- RR + ESI + DC

These equations are based on the system illustrated in Figure 1.1. They represent the hypothesized relationships and directions among the variables of the model.

declines, these distortions are hypothesized to intensify. The second set of equations serves to evaluate the nonrecursive nature of the relationship between the government policies of the Latin American nations and the political violence in their societies. These equations also include the direct and indirect effects of ESI and DC.

REGRESSION ANALYSIS AND DISCUSSION

The results of the first set of equations are reported in Table 1.3. Each of the indicators of U.S. decline has a different impact on the economic

Table 1.3
Regression Results, Effects of Hegemonic Decline on Internal Economic Distortions

				*		
(1)	(OLS)	ESI = 16.06	-15.27ECUS		133.61CERCUS	1.39ESIUS
	2					
	R = .10		(5.94)		(326.32)	(.78)
(2)	(OLS)	EC = -.70	-.11ECUS		9.25CERCUS	.027ESIUS
	2					
	R = .04		(.13)		(6.89)	(.016)
				*		*
(3)	(OLS)	CERC = -.38	-.46ECUS		6.58CERCUS	.053ESIUS
	2					
	R = .20		(.12)		(6.49)	(.015)

* Denotes statistical significance at the .05 level. Standard errors are recorded in parentheses beneath the corresponding regression coefficients.

distortions suffered domestically by the Latin American nations. As the export concentration of the United States increases (a sign of decline), each of the Latin American distortions decreases. This impact is most significant in the areas of ESI and CERC. In the first case, it may be that a decline in the core permits sector diversification within the periphery. U.S. decline also appears to allow Latin American nations the opportunity to expand the number of their trading partners. However, a wider variety of trading partners might be caused by increased competition among the developed nations of the core over the hegemonic position. If this were the case, any benefit accruing to the periphery would be short-lived as one nation emerged from that competition in a dominant position. This scenario may also apply to economic sector inequalities.

It is interesting to note that the other two indicators of decline, CERCUS and ESIUS, have the opposite effect on the Latin American nations. Economic internal distortions increase as the United States takes on these features of dependency. Only one of these proves significant, but it offers an interesting illustration. U.S. economic sector inequality has a significant impact on the concentration of export-receiving nations in Latin America. This may indicate that as the United States becomes more active in one sector over the others, it attempts to take advantage of its trading position with Latin America. These nations might then become more dependent on the United States as a primary trading partner while providing the markets for the goods produced by the dominant sector in the United States. However, as a challenge to this finding, general trade statistics point to the decline of Latin American trade with the United States since the early 1970s. It appears that the decline of the core leads, for the most part, to a decrease in economic distortions within the periphery. Still, that these nations have taken on other trading partners during this period of U.S.

decline may only indicate a brief reprieve before another power takes the place of the hegemon or before the United States reasserts its economic position.

The results of the 2SLS analysis (reported in Table 1.4) are somewhat difficult to interpret but do offer some interesting and surprising findings. To begin with, political conflict, measured by the dominant variety indicator, is affected primarily by government policies. Allocations to the military (MSA) appear to have a substantial negative impact on political conflict. This suggests that MSA leads to a decrease in the predominance of certain types of violence and an increase in the overall variety of conflict behavior. Regulation by the government through increased allocations to the military appears to fail. The extent and type of political conflict may be spread more widely among varying opposition organizations or informal groups by increases in government repression. The wider variety of conflict activity is then harder for the government to control because it has not developed and programmed the appropriate regulatory responses. The size of the military (SM) is an even stronger influence in the same direction, and the specific types of intervention—censorship, political repression, and the relaxation of restrictions—also cause political conflict to increase. Overall, repressive government policies do not appear to work. Latin American governments do not effectively control disorder when a wide range of conflict events occur in an episode. More chaos than order results as government repression increases.

The connection of the world economic system and its manifestations to political conflict in the periphery is more difficult to discern. A good deal of this confusion results from the difference between the OLS and 2SLS analyses. In many cases the direction of the effect is opposite from one equation to the next. Because the variance explained is generally higher in the 2SLS equations, these results are the more appropriate. However, the 2SLS equation for political conflict suffers from a high degree of multicollinearity and should be examined with some caution.

The strongest impact from the system appears when the United States is in decline as indicated by its export concentration. The positive coefficient illustrates that the range of conflict events decreases—that is, the dominant variety score increases—when the United States begins to rely on fewer exports. The same is true when ESI increases in the United States.[5] These results support the notion that a decline in the core directly leads to a smaller variety of conflict phenomena within the periphery, but their impact is not as strong as that of the peripheral governments' policies. As expected, economic sector inequality in the Latin American nations produces a negative effect on political conflict. The differential treatment of economic sectors appears to increase dissatisfaction and leads to a wider variety of conflict behavior. However, this result is neither large nor significant, so

Table 1.4

Regression Results, Effects of Nonrecursive Relationship Between Government Policy and Political Violence

(2SLS = #1; OLS = #2)

(1) DV = 165.66   -201.62MSA*   -11719.08SM*   -134.44CN*   -4.59PR*
                    (55.27)   (4043.97)   (15.15)   (1.37)

                    273.89PX*   -34.83RR*   -.17ESI   13.56ECUS*
                    (32.06)   (4.49)   (.31)   (7.38)

                    1.88ESIUS   R^2 = 1.0
                    (1.34)

(2) DV = 104.63   -43.52MSA   -3369.24SM*   -9.07CN   -.94PR*
                    (37.49)   (1410.83)   (9.37)   (.47)

                    -19.04PX   -1.44RR   -27.31ESI*   .09ECUS
                    (11.64)   (2.40)   (11.24)   (1.56)

                    -.52ESIUS*   R^2 = .36
                    (.26)

(1) MSA = .35   -.003ESI*   -.05EC   .07CERC   -.10ECUS*   .005ESIUS
                    (.0009)   (.04)   (.04)   (.04)   (.004)

                    -.002DV*   R^2 = .21
                    (.0006)

(2) MSA = .22   -.002ESI*   .03EC   .05CERC   -.06ECUS   .004ESIUS
                    (.0009)   (.04)   (.04)   (.04)   (.005)

                    -.0007DV*   R^2 = .09
                    (.0003)

(1) SM = .01   -.00008ESI*   -.00007EC   .0009CERC*   -.002ECUS
                    (.00002)   (.0009)   (.001)   (.0009)

                    -.00006ESIUS   -.00007DV*   R^2 = .33
                    (.0001)   (.00002)

(2) SM = 6.12   -.00005ESI*   .0006EC   -.0008CERC   -.0008ECUS
                    (.00002)   (.001)   (.001)   (.0010)

                    -.00010ESIUS   -.00002DV*   R^2 = .19
                    (.0001)   (.000009)

Table 1.4 (continued)

```
(1)   CN = 1.22   -.002ESI   -.18EC    -.26CERC    -.30ECUS*   -.05ESIUS*
                  (-.004)    (.15)     (.17)       (.15)       (.02)
                              *
                  -.01DV                           R  = .43
                  (.002)                            2

(2)   CN = .62    .003ESI    -.07EC    -.40CERC*   -.10ECUS    -.06ESIUS*
                  (.004)     (.16)     (.18)       (.15)       (.02)
                              *
                  -.003DV                          R  = .32
                  (.001)                            2

(1)   PR = 24.85  -.04ESI    .87EC     -1.0CERC    -6.9ECUS*   .72ESIUS*
                  (.08)      (3.1)     (3.53)      (3.18)      (.37)
                              *
                  -.34DV                           R  = .46
                  (.05)                             2

(2)   PR = 4.88   .12ESI     4.37EC    -4.50CERC   -.25ECUS    .52ESIUS
                  (.09)      (3.73)    (4.24)      (3.61)      (.45)
                              *
                  -.08DV                           R  = .20
                  (.03)                             2

(1)   PX = .80    -.002ESI   .11EC     -.12CERC    -.30ECUS*   -.02ESIUS
                  (.003)     (.11)     (.13)       (.12)       (.01)
                              *
                  -.009DV                          R  = .36
                  (.002)                            2

(2)   PX = .26    .002ESI    .21EC     -.25CERC*   -.12ECUS    -.02ESIUS
                  (.003)     (.12)     (.14)       (.12)       (.02)
                              *
                  -.002DV                          R  = .19
                  (.001)                            2

(1)   RR = 3.81   -.01ESI    .73EC     .92CERC     -.63ECUS    -.08ESIUS
                  (-.02)     (.66)     (.75)       (.68)       (.08)
                              *
                  -.06DV                           R  = .37
                  (.01)                             2

(2)   RR = .47    .02ESI     1.31EC*   .19CERC     .49ECUS     .05ESIUS
                  (.02)      (.75)     (.85)       (.72)       (.09)
                              *
                  -.01DV                           R  = .18
                  (.007)                            2
```

(1) = 2SLS
(2) = OLS
* denotes statistical significance at the .05 level. Standard errors are reported in parentheses.

it remains difficult to ascertain the direct effect of this inequality on political conflict.

None of the three internal distortions of the system (ESI, EC, or CERC) has much of an impact on governmental policy. Any effect they do have is usually negative. This finding is contrary to the hypothesized positive impact for all policies except that of relaxing restrictions (RR). In accordance with *dependencia* theory, restrictions on political expression are not relaxed but are increased when economic distortions intensify. However, further analysis is required because of the lack of a significant relationship between these variables.

The decline of the core, particularly that indicated by export concentration (EC), results continuously and significantly in a decrease in military allocations, size, and intervention. The best explanation for this agrees with *dependencia* and world system theorists who believe that some of the pressure on the periphery is released during periods of hegemonic decline or increased competition among the world's economic powers. As the United States faces decline, it is less capable of providing the resources and support necessary to a repressive regime in Latin America. It is not willing to sacrifice its own resources for the domestic purposes of other nations. This provides a partial explanation for the failure of Latin American governments to effectively regulate political conflict. A lack of support from the core may cause these governments to increase their own commitments to the military and to repressive policies, creating more conflict as resources are reallocated from other government programs. In this manner, the general populations of the periphery involved in conflict activity benefit from the decline of the core in the sense that the government finds it more difficult to restrict their expressions of discontent. However, the local elite's position is then very likely in jeopardy.

Finally, political conflict, measured by the dominant variety indicator, causes all government policies, except the relaxation of restrictions, to decrease in scope. Although the coefficients are small, in each case they are significant. As the variety of conflict events narrows, repression decreases. Less repression follows what is essentially a decrease in political conflict, that is, an increase in the dominant variety of conflict. The need for more expansive government regulation diminishes. Interestingly, while the dominant variety of political conflict leads to the decrease of various repressive government policies, those policies lead to an increase in political conflict.

These findings indicate a negative feedback loop between these two sets of variables. While the results are quite understandable separately, they leave open the question of what factors lead to an increase in repression and a decrease in political conflict. One possible explanation offered by this analysis is the linkage of Latin American nations to the core, in this case the United States. The results suggest that one cause, both direct and indirect, of a decrease in the use of repressive policies by Latin American governments is the decline of the core. When the United States experiences symptoms of economic decline, Latin American nations are not only able to reverse some aspects of their own economic underdevelopment, they are also compelled to decrease their regulation of political conflict. In addition, the United States is probably no longer as willing to fund military expansion in these nations as it once was. During this period, Latin American governments are unable to limit political conflict despite their own attempts to support the military and increase repression. At the same time, the decline of the United States appears to create an increase in the dominant variety of political conflict. The decline of the core, which seems to alleviate economic dislocation, directly decreases the range of conflictual events in peripheral nations. This makes repression less necessary as it becomes simultaneously less effective. Given these results, were the core not in decline, one might expect underdevelopment to continue, repression to increase in order to maintain order, and peripheral governments to more successfully manage the political conflict that is fostered by their linkage to an economically expanding core. The relationship between peripheral governments' policies and political conflict is, therefore, affected by dynamic changes in the core nations they are most connected to economically.

IMPLICATIONS FOR DEPENDENCIA THEORY

The analysis conducted here provides a few answers to the initial questions concerning the relationship of dependency to internal political conflict. The findings do not directly support the tenets of *dependencia* theory, but neither do they offer an indictment of them. Figure 1.3 illustrates the findings in terms of their direction. The decline of the core appears to diminish the internal distortions in Latin American economies. In accordance with the theories of Frank and others, the hopes for the development of the periphery in periods of hegemonic decline seem brighter than at other times. This same decline also appears to increase the occurrence of specific types of political conflict. This direct effect is not very clear at this point, but it could be responsible for the inability to specify with confidence the effect of ESI on political conflict. ESI may only influence political conflict indirectly as it is affected through the core. Not surprisingly, a decline in the core decreases the government's repressive policy commitment. The core is unable to provide the same level of resources during periods of decline.

The internal distortions of the economic system in the Latin American nations do not produce the expected effect on government policy. This finding poses the greatest challenge to *dependencia* theorists who claim that such inequalities lead to government repression because they necessitate the need for order. It is possible, however, that these distortions

Figure 1.3
Regression Results, Cybernetic Model of Economic World System Effects on
Political Conflict in the Periphery

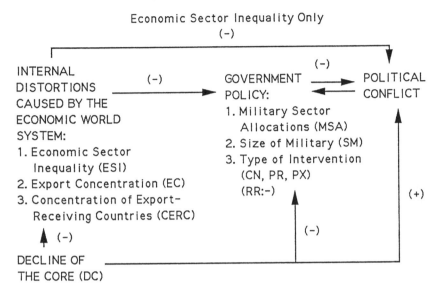

influence governmental policy through the political conflict they create. The causal loops among the various parts of the model may cause one variable to subsume the effect of another.

Finally, the interaction of government policy and political conflict remains the most difficult to explain. Changes in the structure of the world system—that is, U.S. hegemonic decline—directly and indirectly affect the relationship between government policy and political conflict. While the direct effect of decline produces a decrease in regulatory measures and in the variety of political conflict, that decline indirectly creates an increase in political conflict despite governments' attempts to regulate that conflict. These results best support those theorists who argue that the decline of the core allows for greater economic development in the periphery. This development, in turn, decreases levels of conflict, assuming economic inequalities disappear. However, the core's decline also increases the range of conflict events as peripheral elites fail to successfully regulate that conflict, probably because they are faced with fewer resources from the core. This latter scenario supports many world systems theorists who argue that new forms of conflict become manifest in periods of decline.

In short, the relationship between a peripheral state's regulation of political conflict and the nature of that conflict appears to be influenced by fluctuations in the economic prosperity of the core. While this linkage to the world system is certainly not the only, or perhaps even the most important, determinant of the relationship, it deserves to be included as a causal factor in future examinations of political conflict and its regulation by governments in both the periphery and the core. Many have recognized the relationship of national socioeconomic development to political conflict; but, as this study indicates, the connections to cycles in the international economic system must now be examined.

CONCLUSION

The purpose of the formulation and testing of this model has been to contribute an empirical analysis to the literature of *dependencia* and to establish the validity of the theoretical implications inherent in such conceptualizations of the causes and regulation of political conflict. In general, the results indicate that an international economic system exists as envisioned by most *dependencistas*, but that system is not nearly as static as they would suggest. As many *dependencistas* themselves have recognized and world systems analysts have suggested, there are possibilities for social, political, and economic development in the periphery of the capitalist world system.

Cardoso claims that there has been a poor consumption of dependency theory in North America (1977). Perhaps more examinations of the implications of these theories in areas outside of economic development will contribute to a greater appreciation of such work. Political conflict and its regulation are two such areas. Furthermore, this research represents an initial attempt to model the effects of economic fluctuations in the core of the international world system. To date, such models have not been extensively formalized and tested. A crucial factor in the examination of world system theories and *dependencia* should be the linkage between changes in the two poles of the system. Little theoretical or empirical work has been done to ascertain the effects of these linkages and their subsequent impact on phenomena of specific interest to political scientists, that is, political conflict. The development of such models may serve to unite economists, sociologists, and political scientists in a more comprehensive endeavor to understand societal behavior.

NOTES

1. The terms "core" and "periphery" were initiated by Galtung (1971) to describe the division of nations within the international capitalist system. Core nations are those advanced industrial societies that benefit from the structure of the system while simultaneously setting the rules by which that same system operates. The periphery, on the other hand, is the set of nations that is disadvantaged by the historical development of the system in general and by the core specifically.

2. Manufactured products have consistently been valued more highly than com-

modities because of their capital-intensive nature. Production of raw materials and agricultural commodities is generally labor intensive, and labor as a production cost in these areas has been relatively cheap.

3. Although the direction of the government policies' impact on political conflict is not specified, the expectation is that if repressive policies (CN, PR, PX) lead to an increase in political conflict, then the relaxation of those restrictions would have the opposite effect on political conflict. Alternatively, if repressive policies are successful in controlling political conflict, then the relaxation of restrictions would increase conflict activity.

4. The following discussion is drawn principally from the work of Eduard A. Ziegenhagen (1986:23–28) as is the discussion of the measures of the majority of independent variables.

5. The concentration of nations receiving exports from the United States is not included in the 2SLS equations because it yields no significant results in the initial OLS analysis.

2

MILITARIZATION, POLITICAL CONFLICT, AND POLITICAL DEVELOPMENT IN THE THIRD WORLD

Christian Alexander Davenport

The linkage between external and internal conflict is addressed in this chapter. Emphasis is placed on the state as an intervening variable between the two forms of behavior within a theory of domestic conflict regulation. As the regulatory process has not been considered previously, this might account for the insignificant causal relationships found within numerous studies (Rummel, 1963; Tanter, 1969; Ward and Widmaier, 1982) as well as the indeterminancy revealed within others (Simmel, 1955; Stohl, 1975). In the present literature domestic conflict is addressed without considering factors that might deter or suppress its manifestation. Since dissidents will not take part in political conflict if they understand that they will be met with severe punishment, addressing state regulation (i.e., political repression and coercive capacity) may help us to understand when, where, and in what direction the linkages between external and internal conflict will take place.

All states regulate political conflict, but only after certain behavioral deviations have been reached. How the levels or boundaries of acceptable behavior are established is at the core of this analysis. I argue that the military is the most crucial actor in determining what levels are tolerated and what levels are not. Political systems under the direct control of the military, or simply influenced by it, allow minimal levels of conflict at which time regulatory strategies are implemented. This conclusion follows from speculative and historical analysis about military control/presence and dissident behavior (Tilly, 1978; Oberschall, 1973; Gurr, 1969; Gurr, 1970; Stohl, 1975; Lichbach, 1987; Ake, 1969).

What, however, accounts for the variation in military control and presence? There are two plausible explanations: external crises (interstate conflict) and internal crises (domestic conflict). Both are explored here. This study focuses on relations between civilian government and the military across varying levels of external and domestic threats. I will test the hypothesis that within situations of domestic crisis external threats tilt the civilian-military relationship in favor of the military, who will, as a result, attempt to improve its position within society. This entails increasing its share of state expenditures, its size, and, most important for this discussion, its control over its domestic utilization (its activity in controlling political conflict). These transformations should then affect the domestic conflict that occurs within the state's jurisdiction, as those forces that can be brought against it are enhanced.

EMPHASES AND LIMITATIONS OF EMPIRICAL INQUIRY

A review of the literature yields two conclusions. First, the subject of state regulation is generally not pursued in empirical research. Second, the relationship between external and internal conflict is, as yet, inconclusive.

Addressing the first point, the attention given to the state as a regulator of political conflict is a rather limited area of systematic investigation. In fact, it has been argued that it is an altogether neglected area of inquiry (McCamant, 1984). As negative sanctions and coercive capacity have been suggested as being relevant to the outbreak of political conflict, this is problematic for empirical research concerning conflict and conflict linkages. Without considering one of the factors that might account for domestic conflict's manifestation, empirical analysis suffers from misspecification. Causal models of regulation are, therefore, much needed for the study of political conflict and, I argue, conflict linkages as well.

Generally, regulation has not been studied, for dissent has been treated as merely a systemic attribute of less developed or, in the words of Wallerstein, "peripheral" countries (Gemmell, 1982; Portes, 1976; Wallerstein, 1976). Within this perspective, the state's level of political development and its incorporation into the global economy determine its level of antisystemic behavior.

The movement to consider the state as an important factor began with a concern for governmental allocations (Deutsch, 1963; Gurr, 1969). These studies suggest that the state is accountable for appropriations of state funds, and this is related to the outbreak of political conflict. By controlling the distribution of state resources, the government can be said to regulate dissent.

More direct efforts at behavioral regulation, through negative and positive sanctions, have not yet resolved whether or not conflict can indeed be controlled by the state (Hibbs, 1973; Snyder and Tilly, 1972; Ziegenhagen, 1986). Despite the often paradoxical results obtained within these studies as well as the varied methodologies utilized in their investigations, they have moved the systematic study of conflict regulation in an important direction.

Considering the second point, this project can be seen as continuing the external-internal conflict debate. This connection is still at issue. Simmel (1955) and Coser (1956) suggest that increases in foreign conflict are related to a decrease in domestic conflict behavior. Stohl (1975), on the other hand, suggests that increases in foreign conflict are related to an increase in domestic conflict. James (1986) and Rasler (1986) suggest that increases in foreign conflict can be associated with either increases or decreases in domestic conflict, dependent upon certain governmental decisions. Finally, Rummel (1963) and Ward and Widmaier (1982) suggest that foreign conflict behavior is generally unrelated to domestic conflict.

In order to help readers understand (external/internal) conflict linkages, this study serves two purposes. The first is to utilize a model of conflict regulation. This facilitates the identification and arrangement of causal linkages involved. As a result, external factors can be assessed as to their potential internal effects.

Second, a different operationalization for external conflict is introduced. Typically, the measurement for external conflict has been interstate and global warfare (Stohl, 1975; Rasler, 1986). This is a somewhat limiting criterion, although obviously worthy of study, for war involvement is a rare phenomenon for the majority of countries in the world (Bremer, Singer, and Stuckey, 1972). Perceived external threats appear to be much more prevalent in viewing global interactions and therefore potentially more relevant in depicting linkages between external and internal conflict behavior. Perceived threats generate important domestic changes over time whereas interstate warfare is expected to generate immediate effects. This is an inaccurate as well as an unfair depiction of a very complex situation: the manifestation of internal behavior determined by external stimuli.

External threats are seen as providing observable impulses that direct and modify the internal distribution of power and authority within a given political system. These modifications determine the manner in which a state regulates conflict behavior, as the distribution of power designates what behavior is deemed acceptable as well as what actions can be used under its control. This modification, in turn, is believed to effect political conflict.

On this point, this study follows the path set by James (1986) and Rasler (1986). They introduce the state as an intervening variable, between external and internal conflict, capable of eliminating, limiting, or exacerbating conflict linkages. Furthermore, they place the state within a changing political, economic, and social environment, but with the capability to regulate that environment for its own ends. Although my conceptions of the regulatory process itself differ from those of James and Rasler, in this chapter the state is envisioned as a similar entity.

CYBERNETICS AND POLITICAL CONFLICT

The theoretical framework utilized in this chapter is taken from cybernetic theories of regulation. Cybernetics, in its most elementary formulation, involves purposive self-steering, regulation, and control (see Deutsch, 1963; Steinbruner, 1974; and Ashby, 1956). The basic tenets of the theory serve as our point of departure, and then the more direct application to the regulation of political conflict is addressed.

Cybernetic theories of regulation involve a very simple process. Initially a goal, or set of values, is established as acceptable. These values form a subset of all possible outcomes within the particular behavior of interest. If outcomes fall within this subset, then the regulator has no need to do anything and, subsequently, does not. Once, however, the set of outcomes extends beyond the values deemed acceptable, caused by whatever disturbance and filtered through whatever environment, the regulator responds. Disturbances represent those forces which are responsible for promoting unacceptable levels of the behavior to be regulated. The environment refers to various conditions that either contribute to or detract from the impact of the disturbances.

In responding to undesirable behavior, the regulator utilizes what can be considered action patterns or programs. These represent actions deemed applicable to the enterprise of behavioral modification and control. The regulator, in turn, applies and dismisses the various action patterns as it seeks to bring the outcomes within acceptable boundaries. Effectiveness in achieving desirable outcomes, as well as governmental preferences for particular strategies, determines the usage of the action patterns. The regulator is, in this sense, controlled by its historical experience as well as its internal pressure groups. The behavioral model appears in Figure 2.1.

This method of decision making and control is applied to governments' regulation of political conflict by Ziegenhagen (1986). He suggests that cybernetics is applicable to the regulation of political conflict because "the identification of a control mechanism that compares desirable to undesirable variation of the phenomena to be regulated and of control centers that initiate appropriate action to bring behavior within desired limits of variation are basic components of cybernetic theory" (Ziegenhagen, 1986:39).

Political conflict, in this case, is defined as mass protest behavior directed against the state, its policies, and its practices as well as elite behavior relevant to the removal of incumbents. As the definition intuitively suggests, conflict can come in a myriad of forms and levels of intensity directed at the state. It is assumed that the regulation of both of these dimensions, variation and intensity, is of the utmost concern to those who rule. The state, consequently, is seen as a "control mechanism," identifying undesirable conflict levels and directing regulatory efforts.

Figure 2.1
Basic Cause Control Model

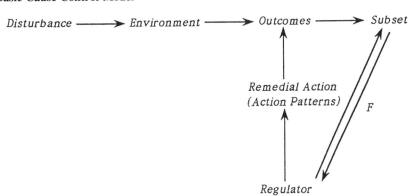

Legend:

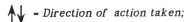

↑↓ - *Direction of action taken;*

F - *Positive and negative feedback, information in regards to unacceptable Boundaries.*

How the state can regulate conflict behavior necessitates the identification of the action patterns made available to it. Action patterns, within this conception, take a particular form. Although policy interventions (censorship, restrictions, and executions) are accepted as sources of regulation based on scholarly consensus and "conventional wisdom" (Johnson, 1966; Bwy, 1968; Hibbs, 1973; Ziegenhagen, 1986), I also suggest that indirect expressions of regulation exist as well (Hibbs, 1973; Bwy, 1968; Wayman, 1975; Ziegenhagen, 1986). These involve latent coercive capacities within a state: that is, the size of the military, military sector allocations, and military representation within the government. The effect of these factors is deterrent in nature as opposed to the more direct impact of negative sanctions. In terms of the cybernetic model outlined in the previous section, the model derived from this discussion is represented in Figure 2.2.

It should be noted that other sources of behavioral regulation exist as well. These include: levels of economic development, rates of socioeconomic change, types of structural imbalances, levels of social mobilization, and core or peripheral locations within a world system. As the present study considers only Third World nations, these strategies are not addressed. Since Third World countries do not have the resources to facilitate these forms of control, I maintain that repression serves as the only regulatory strategy applied in these countries. Primarily, this is attributed to the fact that no other alternatives are available to them. This approach appears even more reasonable when one takes into account the capacity

Figure 2.2
Modified Cause Control Model

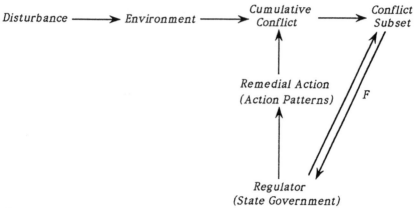

Legend:

↑↓ = Direction of action taken;

F = Positive and negative feedback, information in regards to unacceptable Boundaries.

of the regimes to implement the various strategies of behavioral control over the time period under consideration; simply, most Third World nations were in dire straits during the late 1960s and mid-1970s.

THE MILITARY AND POLITICAL CONFLICT: EXPLORING VARIATIONS IN MILITARY INFLUENCE

As stated above, the military carries a potentially significant amount of weight in the process of conflict regulation. By "weight" I mean importance, an ability to influence, if not dictate, government actions and policies. This weight is determined by the military's specialization in the application of force, that is, the action patterns identified above. What the military attempts to do with this weight is held constant over time. It attempts to institutionalize its position within society—increasing its prominence, enlarging its usage, and solidifying its role as the dominant action pattern taken in an effort to control political conflict (Perlmutter and Bennett, 1980; Janowitz, 1964; Lang, 1975; Huntington, 1957; Laswell, 1941). Most important, this suggests that the application of repressive regulatory methods will increase.

This propensity to apply repression is due primarily to four factors (Janowitz, 1964). First, political repression is the political strategy most congruent with the military organization's basic ideology, which is control through the application of force. Second, given greater access to government decision makers, the military's influence increases the likelihood that its participation in regulation will take place. Third, enhanced military involvement within society at large makes its regulatory application easier to implement. This decreases its cost. Fourth, once the military's position as the dominant action pattern is in place, given the nature of cybernetics, it is difficult to remove.

The military's ability to achieve its goals is not held constant over time. The opportunity varies with favorable conditions for its occurrence. What provides the military with an opportunity to pursue its objectives? What contributes to organizational weight?

I argue that fear of defeat in interstate conflict eliminates the objective limits on the military and enhances its power as well. External threats provide a "compelling necessity" for the military, increasing its role and its ability to direct government policy decisions, international and domestic in scope. As Lang (1975:97) states in relation to this point,

> strategy is intimately related to policy, and whenever people take seriously the possibility that war will break out, the military component in foreign policy gains in importance and along with it the weight given to the soldier expert in the counsels of government. This opens the door to the garrison state. Because the demand for their skills is great, military men begin to wield dominant power in civil-military coalitions.

It is assumed that defeat in interstate conflict is an unacceptable outcome for all states within the international system. As a result, the only option left available to the state is to be concerned with both actual and potential military threats from all feasible actors. It must be able to counter, if not surpass, these threatening activities as well as possible. This suggests an interdependency of states' military apparatuses. This also suggests that, when the situation arises, civilian government willingly defers to the expertise of the military and increases that organization's prominence by increasing resource allocations to the military, its institutional size, its status, and its role within domestic affairs—in this case the regulation of political conflict.

Subsequently, two hypotheses can be derived: (1) increases in external threats increase the prominence of the military (i.e., monetary allocations, organizational size); and (2) increases in external threats and the prominence of the military increase the military's participation in the regulation of political conflict (i.e., increased usage of repressive regulatory action).

POLITICAL CONFLICT AND REGULATION

As detailed within this study, conflict and its regulation are both dynamic enterprises. The question remains, however: How will those engaged on the dissidents' side react to attempts at regulation? The most comprehensive work to date on this question is by Lichbach (1987).

Lichbach suggests that dissidents utilize a simple decision calculus. The result of this equation determines what activities they use (if any) and at what magnitude. Since Lichbach's equation incorporates how well the dissidents are accommodated into the political system at large, this study, lacking such information, will use a more limited decision rule. The basic premise of Lichbach's work is retained, however.

First, it is believed that all those who wish to act against a particular government have a set of activities they can utilize; that is, different strategies of dissent are available. Second, it is also believed that these same individuals act in such a manner as to avoid punishment and, therefore, choose the activity which is least likely to provoke retribution. If we consider the following activities—strikes, riots, guerrilla warfare, and anti-government demonstrations—each with an equal probability of occurring, it can be stated that regulation (increased military prominence and/or repression) increases the "cost" of utilizing any one particular strategy. This is because increased fear and imposed constraints on behavior make dissent more difficult to promote. In light of these additional costs, the most rational thing to do would be to utilize a strategy of greater variation (i.e., applying different strategies of dissent). This diminishes the use, and thus the net cost, of any one particular dissident activity while enabling the remaining repertoire to continue the process of collective protest. Thus, increased prominence and political repression increase the variety of conflict confronted and decrease the dominance of any one strategy being applied.

We also examine the degree to which external conflict directly affects antisystemic behavior: that is, do dissidents take advantage of the external situation and increase dissent, or do they decrease their behavior in defense of the political system. This addresses the manifested indeterminancy currently existing within the literature.

Combining this with the previous point, the last hypothesis examined is as follows: (3) increases in external threats, the prominence of the military, and political repression increase the variety but decrease the dominance of any one particular strategy of political conflict.

It should be noted that the anticipated effect from repression on political conflict is counter to that which would be expected by the regime. Repression is generally believed to decrease antisystemic behavior. According to Lichbach (1987), however, this is not the case. As repression impedes specialization in one strategy of dissent it increases the variety of strategies employed by dissidents. This is done in order to avoid punishment and yet facilitate continual action against the state. Repression thus leads to results that are counterintuitive to the state but rational from the perspective of those acting against it. With this understood, let's now proceed to the investigation itself.

THE RESEARCH DESIGN

The theoretical framework concerning the research design is presented above; the more technical decisions concerning the unit of analysis, the variables utilized, the method of investigation, and the limitations of the empirical examination conducted are discussed below.

In order to examine behavioral regulation, the unit of analysis employed here is the conflict episode (i.e., period of domestic crisis). Conflict episodes are temporally adjacent conflict events separated by periods of relative quiescence (Ziegenhagen, 1986:3). Episodes are identified by comparing the number of conflict events occuring in any given year to a particular country's previous experience with dissent (i.e., the past mean of conflict). If conflict in any given year exceeds previous rates and the events occur in sequence, then an episode is identified. The length of the episode itself is determined by the length of sequential conflict events.

This particular strategy is utilized for two reasons. First, although state responsiveness to dissent varies, all regimes are believed to attempt regulation when confronted with historically unprecedented rates of antisystemic behavior. Second, conflict episodes solve a common problem often confronted within the conflict literature. Several studies suggest that conflict events occur in close proximity to one another, determined by certain underlying characteristics (Sorokin, 1957; Eberwein, 1987; Richardson, 1987). This renders econometrics inapplicable as the assumption of uncorrelated disturbances is violated. Research in this area, therefore, should not address individual events but series of events, grouped together within time. Simply, the grouping, not the individual events, is more useful for empirical investigation. This is exactly what conflict episodes measure. Moreover, since conflict episodes are randomly distributed throughout time and reveal significant variation within themselves as well, the assumptions of econometrics are not violated. Consequently, the use of episodes proves to be more helpful in identifying and examining the phenomena of interest and more applicable in terms of appropriately meeting the criteria for time series analysis.

In regards to the variables employed within this study, each is used as an independent and dependent variable. For purposes of clear exposition, each is defined and presented below with specific applications provided later.

The *external threat* variable is taken from Rosh (1988). Rosh operationalizes Buzan's (1983) "security complex" thesis, which maintains that the most important factor in considering what affects a nation state is its geographic neighborhood. Although conceptually useful, Buzan's conception is difficult to measure. In order to confront this problem, Rosh selects as test cases what Buzan classifies as "weak states" and "weak powers." Such a strategy is utilized to create an ideal situation. If Buzan's geographic proximity notion were to work at all, then it would work with those nations most susceptible to it: Third World nations. Justifying this action, Rosh (1988:679) suggests,

> [a]ll states, and we must assume most especially Third World states, suffer from a "loss of gradient." In other words, their military strength lessens as they are forced to engage in operations farther away from their home territory. Countries that border a given state are the most threatening to it. Therefore, Third World policymakers must concern themselves primarily with the relative military burden of their geographic neighbors.

The measurement itself entails two procedures: (1) Security complexes are identified, that is, countries within the subject state's immediate geographic proximity or regional hegemons; and (2) military expenditures as a percentage of GNP for those countries—collected from the U.S. Arms Control and Disarmament Agency—are averaged (for listing of "security webs" see Appendix 2.2). What is provided by this measurement is the degree to which all potential adversaries are "militarized." External threats consequently are derived from situations where extensive amounts of state expenditures are allocated to the military apparatuses of surrounding nations. In situations where military sector allocations are relatively low, external threats are said to be low as well.

The variables that indicate *military prominence* are taken from Banks's *Cross-National Time-Series Data Archive* (1979). These variables include the size of the military, defense expenditures, and military representation within a regime. As the first two variables are ordinal and the third nominal, I shall list the derived categorizations for the latter. The representation variable is separated into four parts: civilian, military-civilian, military, and other. "Other" refers to all regimes not falling into the other categories. For further explanation, consult Banks (1979:segments 5 and 21).

The *sanction variables*, the action patterns implemented to regulate conflict, are collected from the *World Handbook of Political and Social Indicators* (1983), assembled by Taylor and Jodice. The variables in use here are censorship, political restrictions, and political executions. Censorship, as Taylor and Jodice (1983:63) suggest,

> includes actions by the authorities to limit, curb, or intimidate the mass media, including newspapers, magazines, books, radio, and television. Typical examples of such action are the closing of a newspaper or journal, or censoring of articles in the domestic press or dispatches sent out of the country.

Political restrictions are

general[ly] restrictive measures by the authorities, such as the declaring of martial law, mobilizing troops for domestic security, and instituting a curfew. They also include actions specifically directed against an individual, a party, or other political organizations. Such specific actions include the removal of a government official reportedly because of his or her political beliefs and activities, the banning of a political party or acts of harassment against it, arrest of opposition politicians on grounds of state security, the exiling or deportation of persons reportedly involved in political protest actions, including protest demonstrations, riots, political strikes, armed attacks, and assassination attempts (63).

Finally, a political execution

is an event in which a person or a group is put to death under the orders of the national authorities while in their custody (63).

The conflict variables encompass two dimensions of antisystemic behavior. These dimensions are labeled general variety and dominant variety (Ziegenhagen, 1986). General variety constitutes a measure of the degree to which various types of conflict events are represented within episodes. Dominant variety, on the other hand, measures the degree to which a single event type occurs within an episode with respect to other types of events. In following, the derived scores for the episodes then carry with them the number of different types of events that occur as well as the most frequently utilized events.

Before proceeding to the analysis itself, three limitations of this study must be addressed. First, because of the lack of comparability between data sets, the number of countries utilized within the analysis is small, totaling twenty-two. Moreover, the countries used are all taken from the Third World: states that have per capita gross national products less than $5,000 in 1986 dollars. Both factors eliminate a great deal of variation within the objects studied, although they enable us to examine an important and often neglected issue—conflict linkages in the less developed countries. Second, the time span of nine years is limiting. Many variables perhaps take a great deal longer to produce an impact. Correspondingly, the time span investigated may not be representative of the states' general behavior. Third, the primary focus of the examination is with the connections between external threats and internal modifications that occur as a consequence of these threats. Various plausible explanatory variables are not considered— that is, attributes of the economy, societal factors, as well as involvements within military alliances. These factors could potentially have an impact on the relationship of interest. Their exclusion is necessitated by the exploratory nature of the examination. Further modifications of the model presented will address these issues, as they may attenuate or enhance state regulation and/or conflict linkages.

HYPOTHESES AND STATISTICAL RESULTS

As detailed within the discussion above, three hypotheses are investigated in situations of domestic crisis:

1. increases in external threats increase the prominence of the military;
2. increases in external threats and the prominence of the military increase repression; and
3. increases in external threats, the prominence of the military, and political repression increase the variety but decrease the dominance of any one particular strategy of political conflict.

The manner in which these have been operationalized follows. The measurements for the dependent variables accompany each equation.

1. Military prominence = f(external threats);
   measured by:
   a. size of the military;
   b. defense expenditures; and
   c. military representation.
2. Repression = f (external threats + military prominence);
   measured by:
   a. censorship;
   b. political restrictions; and
   c. political executions.
3. Conflict = f (external threats + military prominence + repression);
   measured by:
   a. dominant variety; and
   b. general variety.

With regard to the method of empirical investigation, a time series regression analysis is used to examine each equation. The statistical findings investigating each of these hypotheses appear in Tables 2.1, 2.2, and 2.3. The first three equations (Table 2.1) examine whether military representation, military sector allocations, and the size of the military (the variables denoting military prominence) are affected by external militarization. Equations 4 through 6 (Table 2.2) examine how censorship, political restrictions, and political executions (the regulatory action patterns) are affected by the prominence of the military and external militarization. Finally, equations 7 and 8 (Table 2.3) address the dominant and general variety dimensions of conflict as they are affected by external militarization, the prominence of the military, and the imposition of negative sanctions.

Table 2.1
Estimated Results for Forty-three Episodes: Military Prominence

DEPENDENT VARIABLES

EQUATION NUMBERS

EXPLANATORY VARIABLE	1 MILITARY REP.	2 MILITARY SECTOR ALL.	3 SIZE OF MILITARY[1]
EXTERNAL MILITARIZATION	.59	.8*	.72*
R SQUARED	.003	.5	.67

MILITARY REP. = Military representation
MILITARY SECTOR ALL. = Military sector allocations (defense expenditures)
[1] = logarithmic transformation performed
* = statistically significant at .05 level

EMPIRICAL FINDINGS

The first hypothesis suggests that within a domestic crisis, increases in external threats increase the prominence of the military in the threatened nation. This relationship is supported in two out of the three equations examined in Table 2.1 (equations 2 and 3). External threats, positively related to both variables, explain 50 percent of the variance in defense expenditures and 67 percent of the variance in the size of the military. Military representation, however, is not well accounted for since external threats are statistically insignificant in their effect on the dependent variable and the amount of variance explained is .003 (equation 1). This suggests that as external threats increase, the threatened nation enhances its defense expenditures as well as the size of its military in order to counter the perceived threat. The degree to which the military actually directs or controls the political system itself, however, is not directly affected by changes in external behavior.

The second hypothesis (Table 2.2) investigates whether or not, in a domestic crisis, increases in the prominence of the military increase the implementation of repressive behavior (equations 4–6). Two out of three equations support this hypothesis (equations 4 and 5). As found, external threats explain 43 percent of the variance in political restrictions and,

Table 2.2
Estimated Results for Forty-three Episodes: Regulatory Action Patterns

DEPENDENT VARIABLES

EQUATION NUMBERS

	4 CENSORSHIP	5 RESTRICTIONS[1]	6 EXECUTIONS[1]
EXPLANATORY VARIABLES			
EXTERNAL MILITARIZATION	-15.6*	.28*	.00
MILITARY REPRESENTATION	2.24	.07	.08*
MILITARY SECTOR ALLOCATIONS	.96	-.2	-.00
SIZE OF THE MILITARY[1]	134.*	-.6	-.06
R SQUARED	.34	.43	.15

[1] = logarithmic transformation performed
* = statistically significant at .05 level

collectively with the size of the military, explain 34 percent of the variance in censorship. These relationships are somewhat complex, however.

External threats lead to increases in political restrictions but decreases in censorship. External threats, thus, increase martial law, mobilization of troops, curfews, and limitations on basic rights—perhaps to counter the domestic crises. External threats also lead to decreased limitations placed upon the mass media, including newspapers, magazines, books, radio, and television. In this case, it is plausible that the state is attempting to get the population to mobilize for external conflict through the manipulation of mass communication and information. Each strategy of repression, therefore, has a different use as determined by its effects on the citizenry.

At the same time, recall that external threats also increase the size of the military apparatus. This is important because military size is found to increase censorship. What does this suggest when we consider this with the previous findings? One interpretation of the results suggests that the military is attempting to eliminate criticisms of its behavior (increasing political restrictions) as well as secure some form of propagandist mech-

Table 2.3
Estimated Results for Forty-three Episodes: Dominant and General Variety

DEPENDENT VARIABLES

EQUATION NUMBERS

	7	8
EXPLANATORY VARIABLES	DOMINANT VARIETY	GENERAL VARIETY
EXTERNAL MILITARIZATION	96.8	-9.8
MILITARY REPRESENTATION	-.82	.97*
MILITARY SECTOR ALLOCATIONS	35.1	3.1
SIZE OF THE MILITARY[1]	-165.5	-13.0
CENSORSHIP	-.59	-.00
RESTRICTIONS[1]	-9.8*	.7
EXECUTIONS[1]	-73.8*	3.6*
R SQUARED	.22	.25

[1] = logarithmic transformation performed
* = statistically significant at .05 level

anism for justifying its continued presence and activity within the nation state (Herman, 1982). Although perceived external threats decrease censorship, internal transformations that occur because of these threats increase government sanctions in order to better serve the agent of repression's own purposes.

The third hypothesis is only partly supported. Whether or not increases in applied regulatory strategies increase the variety but decrease the dominance of political conflict in a domestic crisis is still not clear. Directly, external threats exhibit no impact at all on either conflict variable. As a result, the work of Simmel (1955), Coser (1956), and Stohl (1975) is refuted. Indirectly, however, through political restrictions, external threats do exercise some effect. This supports the work of James (1986) and Rasler (1986).

Restrictions along with executions account for 21 percent of the variance exhibited in dominant variety. Both variables have negative impacts. This suggests that as negative sanctions increase in a domestic crisis, the use of any one conflict strategy decreases correspondingly, and specialization in antisystemic behavior diminishes. The modified version of Lichbach's (1987) decision calculus is thus supported.

The general variety dimension of conflict is affected significantly by political executions and military representation. Both have positive effects on the dependent variable and, collectively, explain 25 percent of the variance. Within a situation of domestic crisis, therefore, increases in executions and military representation increase the variety of manifested conflict behavior. Simply, as a result of the increased costs levied upon individual conflict events, dissidents utilize all means at their disposal to lessen the cost of any one particular strategy of conflict; that is, they increase the variety of dissident activity employed. Recall that neither variable is related to external threats, however; consequently the third hypothesis is supported, though independently of the other relationships identified. This is more easily observed in Figure 2.3.

DISCUSSION

The statistical results generally support the argument outlined within this study. In regards to the first and second hypotheses, it is found that external threats to Third World regimes do increase various aspects of the military's apparatus as well as state repressive behavior in a situation of domestic crisis. The positive impact of external threats on military sector allocations and the size of the military are by far the most well-established relationships discovered. Not as strong as these relationships, but significant nonetheless, is the effect of external threats upon the application of particular forms of negative sanctions (censorship and political restrictions). These findings lend support to the "garrison state syndrome" initially articulated by Lasswell (1941) and Huntington (1957) and more recently by Walker and Lang (1988). The garrison state syndrome is descriptive of a situation where external threats lead to increased influence of specialists on violence and greater propensity of the regimes to repress conflict.

In reference to the effects of regulatory activity, the results do not lend much support to the argument presented here. Little variance is accounted for within both dimensions of conflict behavior, and variables generally unrelated to external threats yield the most significant effects on dissident activity. If any connection between external and internal conflict does exist, then one of two possible modifications would have to take place with regards to the present model.

First, the model would need to take into account factors that explain dissident resilience in pursuing conflict in the face of increased regulatory

Figure 2.3
Model of External/Internal Linkages

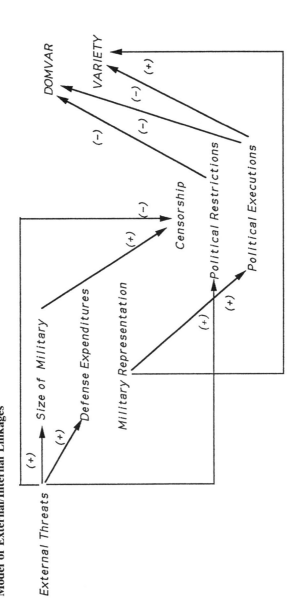

activity and capability. It may be that this study is more in line with re-source-mobilization theories (Snyder and Tilly, 1972; Tilly, 1978; Ober-schall, 1973) than relative deprivation (Gurr, 1970; Bwy, 1968; Feierabend and Feierabend, 1972). The primary difference between the two, relevant to this analysis, lies in the fact that resource-mobilization highlights or-ganizational capacity while relative deprivation highlights the motivating forces behind conflictual behavior itself. Greater emphasis on the latter perspective might account for dissident behavior in a situation of increasing regulatory activity and capability. Such an explanation would be along the lines of what Lichbach (1987) attempts to do.

The second alternative considered is that the decision-making processes of those involved in antisystemic behavior may not be as rational as others suggest. Dissidents in the Third World may not pay much, or any, attention to factors such as capacities for punishment or probabilities of punishment. This would be more in line with a cybernetic perspective of conflict be-havior. As Steinbruner (1974:87) suggests,

> The decision-maker [in this case the dissident] ... does not engage in alter-native outcome calculations or in updated probability assessments. The major theme is that the decision process is organized around the problem of con-trolling inherent uncertainty by means of highly focused attention and highly programmed response.

This model would be difficult to construct but perhaps more relevant to the manifestation of conflict behavior and conflict linkages.

Consideration of these points, in addition to the other factors identified within this study—state regulation, different dimensions of external conflict behavior, and internal militarization—should aid substantively in con-structing a comprehensive model of linkages between external and internal conflict behavior. This study cannot help but conclude, however, that as more questions have been discovered about the potential linkages between external and internal conflict behavior, continued research is necessary.

APPENDIX 2.1

Country Listing:

1. Afghanistan
2. Argentina
3. Bolivia
4. Brazil
5. Chile
6. Colombia
7. Dominican Republic
8. Ecuador
9. El Salvador
10. Guatemala
11. Haiti
12. Honduras
13. Iraq
14. Jordan
15. Liberia
16. Mexico
17. Nepal
18. Nicaragua
19. Paraguay
20. Saudi Arabia
21. Syria
22. Uruguay

APPENDIX 2.2

Security Complexes (Webs):

1. Iran, Pakistan
2. Bolivia, Brazil, Chile, Paraguay, Uruguay
3. Argentina, Bolivia, Chile, Paraguay, Uruguay, Venezuela
4. Argentina, Bolivia, Brazil, Peru
5. Brazil, Ecuador, Panama, Venezuela
6. Cuba, Haiti
7. Colombia, Peru
8. Guatemala, Honduras
9. El Salvador, Honduras, Mexico
10. Cuba, Dominican Republic
11. El Salvador, Guatemala, Nicaragua
12. Iran, Israel, Jordan, Syria, Turkey, Saudi Arabia
13. Iraq, Israel, Lebanon, Saudi Arabia, Syria
14. Guinea, Ivory Coast, Nigeria, Sierra Leone
15. Belize, Guatemala
16. None*
17. Costa Rica, Honduras
18. Argentina, Brazil, Bolivia
19. Brazil, Bolivia, Chile, Ecuador
20. Iran, Iraq, Israel, Jordan, Kuwait
21. Iraq, Israel, Jordan, Turkey, Lebanon

* Mexico's security complex is coded "none" for two reasons. First, Rosh (1988) argues that countries contiguous to superpowers (such as the United States) would not be affected by them because of the great discrepancy in power capabilities. Simply, he suggests, "they could not prevent an attack should one occur" (679). Second, just as there are countries too large to have an impact, it is also possible for a country to be too small. In the case of Mexico, it was determined that neither Belize nor Guatemala was significant enough to affect Mexico's security concerns. As a consequence, there are no countries in the security complex.

Source: R. Rosh (1988), "Third World Militarization: Security Webs and the States They Ensnare," *Journal of Conflict Resolution* 32: 671–698.

APPENDIX 2.3

Several variables reveal heteroscedasticity and thus require modification. As this implies that the variance of each disturbance term is some constant number, the easiest way to see if it is in effect is to plot all data, specifically the estimated squared residuals against the predicted values of Y. After utilizing this strategy and finding the data to be heteroscedastic, I applied a remedial measure suggested in a *Guide to Econometrics* by Gow and White (1978).

This procedure utilizes the Park test. "This test involves running the original regression and saving the residuals, and then regressing the log of these residuals squared on the log of the x variable. You can conclude that there is no heteroscedasticity if there is no relationship between the two variables" (Gow and White, 1978:90).

Running the procedure detailed in Gow and White, and examining the R^2s and significant variables, it is concluded that three of the equations are influenced by heteroscedasticity:

equation 3: $R^2 = .4334$
      1 significant variable
equation 5: $R^2 = .5239$
      2 significant variables
equation 6: $R^2 = .7080$
      3 significant variables

The remedial strategy performs a logarithmic transformation on the variables (Gow and White, 1978:103). This eliminates the heteroscedasticity problem, as the initial detection strategy is used once again on the transformed variables and yields no significant results.

3

POLITICAL CONFLICT
AND DEPENDENCY

Zehra F. Arat

Political conflict has been a subject of study, as well as a concern, for social scientists who try to explain the causes of conflict, so it can be predicted and prevented. In this study, I explore the relationship among different forms of social unrest and government response as reflections of political conflict at the mass and elite levels, respectively, and examine how they vary according to a country's status in the world system.

In a broader analysis, I treat social unrest as an intervening variable to explain the decline of democracy in developing countries (Arat, 1991). The decline of democracy is explained by government policies that create an imbalance between the two groups of human rights—civil-political rights and socioeconomic rights—by ignoring the latter group. According to this argument, the increasing gap between the two groups of rights—resembling the gap between the aspirations and actual achievement observed in the relative deprivation theory—causes frustration and social unrest. The manifest social unrest, however, is suppressed by coercive government policies that result in both quantitative and qualitative changes in the regime, making it less democratic or nondemocratic, depending on the level of coercion.

In line with the theoretical argument summarized above, in this chapter I treat social unrest as a citizens' response to government policies and socioeconomic conditions that include increasing unemployment, declining wages, and prevailing social and political injustice, and I utilize the cross-national data for the thirty-five years from 1947 to 1982 to support the following arguments:

1. Social unrest is multidimensional; the public expresses its discontent in different ways, thus there are different indicators of social unrest.

2. The adjustments and repressive measures adopted by governments to cope with social unrest vary according to the nature of the event that manifests social unrest.

3. The forms and levels of social unrest, as well as the government's response to it, vary according to the country's status in the world system.

DEFINING THE KEY TERMS: WORLD SYSTEM STATUS AND SOCIAL UNREST

World System Status

Dependency has been identified as an important structural factor that influences both economic development level and political composition of a country (Baran, 1957; Frank, 1969; Amin, 1974; Amin, 1976; Wallerstein, 1974; Cardoso, 1977; Cardoso and Faletto, 1979; Lopez and Stohl, 1989). Considering interactions between two nations and the levels of influence they exercise over each other, the level of dependency or the status in the world system is divided into three components by some dependency theorists: the core (or center) societies, peripheral societies, and semiperipheral societies. Chiro (1977:13) states the characteristics of each as follows:

> Core societies: economically diversified . . . rich, powerful societies that are *relatively* independent of outside controls.
>
> Peripheral societies: economically overspecialized, relatively poor and weak societies that are subject to manipulation or direct control by the core powers.
>
> Semi-peripheral societies: societies mid-way between the core and periphery that are trying to industrialize and diversify their economies.

Galtung (1971) defines the intermediary position of semiperipheries as a "go-between" between the "center" and "periphery" nations since they "would exchange semi-processed goods with highly processed goods upwards and semi-processed goods with raw materials downwards." Thus, "in line with its position as to the degree of processing [its export products]," as a go-between nation a semiperipheral country "would be one cycle behind the Center as to technology but one cycle ahead of the Periphery." Similarly, it would be in an intermediary position in regard to "the means of destruction and the means of communication" (Galtung, 1971:104).

For the analysis of the indicators of social unrest and government response, in line with the dependency literature, the three categories of world system status with an additional category of "centrally planned economies" are defined. This last group of countries are usually classified as semiperipheral since, despite the differences in their domestic system, they operate in a capitalist world market that is dominated by the "core" countries (e.g., Snyder and Kick, 1979). Although this explanation is valid, it overlooks the difference between these countries and the other semiperipheral ones. State intervention and control of economy are much higher in these countries, and the integration between native capitalist classes and the international capitalist elite does not apply to these cases (Wallerstein, 1976). Thus, the measure of dependency or world system status of countries is defined as a nominal variable with four categories: core countries, semiperipheries, peripheries, and centrally planned economies (Table 3.1).[1]

Social Unrest

I use the term "social unrest" as the "public" component of political conflict to refer to the collective actions by different segments of society taken against the government or other segments of the society to express their discontent and frustration with government policies and/or socioeconomic conditions. Taylor and Jodice, who compiled a comprehensive data set of social unrest events, treat them as forms of "political participation that convey discontent to the political elite" and as "overt behaviors of groups in the political system that are attempting to influence state policy" (Taylor and Jodice, 1983:17).[2] Thus, depending on the nature of the group, its goals, and its means, social unrest may appear in different forms. It may vary from peaceful protest marches to bloody rebellions. Also, the nature of violence that accompanies the event may differ not only according to the strategy of the participants, but also as a response to the reaction it receives from the government or from other groups. A protest march that is intended to be peaceful by its organizers, for example, may result in violence if the opposition to the marchers attempts to stop them by force.

Moreover, all means of protest are not available to all groups since groups face institutional constraints. For instance, while workers can protest by striking, the unemployed do not and cannot strike; thus, they riot in the streets (Piven and Cloward, 1977).

Antigovernment demonstrations, political strikes, general strikes, riots, assassinations, armed attacks, guerrilla wars, and deaths from domestic violence are different indicators of social unrest for which there is annual data available in two separate data archives compiled by Banks (1979) and by Taylor and his colleagues (1983).

Banks defines "assassinations" as "politically motivated murder or attempted murder of a high governmental official or politician." A "general strike" is defined as "any strike of 1000 or more industrial and service workers that involves more than one employer and that is aimed at national government policies or authority." "Riot" refers to "any violent demon-

Table 3.1
The World System Status of Countries, 1947–1982

Core	Centrally Planned	Semiperiphery	Periphery
Australia	Albania	Argentina	Afghanistan
Austria	Bulgaria	Bolivia	Algeria
Belgium	China	Brazil	Angola
Canada	Cuba	Burma	Bahamas
Denmark	Czechoslovakia	Chile	Bahrain
France	Germany, DR	Colombia	Bangladesh
Germany, FR	Hungary	Costa Rica	Barbados
Iceland	Korea, PR	Cyprus	Benin
Italy	Mongolia	Dominican R.	Bhutan
Japan	Poland	Ecuador	Botswana
Luxembourg	Romania	El Salvador	Burundi
Netherlands	USSR	Finland	Cameroon
New Zealand		Greece	Cape Verde
Norway		Guatemala	Central Africa
Sweden		Haiti	Chad
Switzerland		Honduras	Comoros
United Kingdom		India	Congo
USA		Iran	Egypt
		Iraq	Equatorial Guinea
		Ireland	Ethiopia
		Israel	Fiji
		Jordan	Gabon
		Kenya	Gambia
		Korea, R.	Ghana
		Lebanon	Grenada
		Malaysia	Guinea
		Mexico	Guinea-Bissau
		Nicaragua	Guyana
		Pakistan	Indonesia
		Panama	Ivory Coast
		Paraguay	Jamaica
		Peru	Kampuchea
		Philippines	Kuwait
		Portugal	Laos
		Saudi Arabia	Lesotho
		South Africa	Liberia
		Spain	Libya
		Sri Lanka	Madagascar
		Taiwan	Malawi
		Turkey	Maldives
		Uruguay	Mali
		Venezuela	Malta
		Vietnam, PR	Mauritania
		Yugoslavia	Mauritius
			Morocco
			Mozambique
			Nepal
			Niger
			Nigeria
			Oman
			Papua New Guinea
			Qatar
			Rwanda
			Sao Tome & Principe
			Senegal
			Seychelles
			Sierra Leone
			Singapore
			Somalia
			Sudan
			Suriname
			Swaziland
			Syria
			Tanzania
			Thailand
			Togo
			Trinidad & Tobago
			Tunisia
			Uganda
			U. Arab Emirates
			Upper Volta
			Western Samoa
			Yemen
			Yemen, PDR
			Zaire
			Zambia
			Zimbabwe

stration and clash or more than 100 citizens involving the use of physical force." "Antigovernment demonstrations" include "any peaceful public gathering of at least 100 people for the primary purpose of displaying or voicing their opposition to government policies or authority, excluding demonstrations of a distinctly anti-foreign nature" (Banks, 1979:14).

"Political strike" is defined by Taylor and Jodice as "a work stoppage by a body of industrial or service workers or a stoppage of normal academic life by students to protest a regime and its leaders' policies or actions" (Taylor and Jodice, 1983:21). "Armed attack" refers to "an act of violent political conflict carried out by (or on behalf of) an organized group with the object of weakening or destroying the power exercised by another organized group" (Taylor and Jodice, 1983:29, 37). Taylor and Jodice further add that armed attacks "are characterized by bloodshed, physical struggle, and the destruction of property. A wide variety of weapons may be used, including guns, explosives (conventional bombs, hand grenades, letter bombs), bricks, and other primitive hand weapons such as spears, knives, or clubs" (1983:37). "Deaths resulting from domestic violence" are considered as "an attribute of other events rather than as events themselves" and refer to the numbers of persons reportedly killed in events of domestic political conflict (Taylor and Jodice, 1983:43).

DATA ANALYSIS AND DISCUSSION

Social Unrest Indicators and the World System Status

Table 3.2 includes information on the average values of these social unrest indicators for all independent countries in the world for which data are available for the period between 1947 and 1982.[3]

When the average values of the indicators of social unrest observed in each group of countries are examined (Table 3.2), the differences in their experiences become evident. For example, peripheries tend to experience fewer political and general strikes than the other groups. Since peripheries are usually at earlier stages of the industrialization process, due to their small size and weak organizations, industrial laborers in these countries are less likely to employ strike as a protest activity.

Although core countries are not free from social unrest, the indicators in these countries tend to take less violent forms, such as antigovernment demonstrations or strikes. Despite the fact that they experience riots and armed attacks[4] more frequently than the other groups, the ultimate loss of human life in core countries is much smaller. In countries with dependent status, however, social unrest takes more violent forms with high death tolls. While the average annual number of the deaths from domestic violence is 4.41 in core countries, it is 36.46 and 42.42 in peripheries and semiperipheries, respectively.

Table 3.2
Average Values of Social Unrest Indicators by the World System Status of Countries, 1947–1982

	All	Core	Centrally Planned	Semi-periphery	Periphery
SOCIAL UNREST					
Anti-Government Demonstrations	.45	.96	.33	.59	.16
Political Strikes	1.06	1.40	1.07	1.83	.28
General Strikes	.11	.20	.03	.17	.03
Riots	.59	.97	.37	.94	.18
Assassinations	.17	.14	.04	.32	.09
Armed Attacks	16.62	30.65	10.68	14.37	14.86
Guerilla Warfare	.28	.18	.16	.43	.21
Deaths from Domestic Violence	32.34	4.41	22.99	42.42	36.46

Jackson and others (1978) expect higher levels of social unrest in dependent societies. According to their argument, the development of social distortions and inequality in the economic sphere, stemming from the failures of domestic leaders or high levels of dependency, leads to "the rise of grievances of class against class and group against group within society" (Jackson et al., 1978:631). Dependency on capital from the industrial world restricts the policy options of developing countries and often forces their governments to adopt policies—which are imposed by foreign donors, lenders, and investors—that intensify economic hardship and inequalities. As demonstrated by the cases of Jamaica and Venezuela, social unrest is often observed soon after the implementation of the austerity measures required by the International Monetary Fund (IMF). The correlation between several indicators of IMF conditionalities and the presence of protest activities is found to be consistently positive and significant (Walton and Ragin, 1990). Similarly, the analysis by Boswell and Dixon (1990) concludes that both economic dependence and military dependence promote violent social unrest through their facilitating impacts on income inequality and regime repressiveness.

Economic ineffectiveness of governments has been identified as a destabilizing factor by several authors (Cnudde and Neubauer, 1969; Gurr, 1969; Brinton, 1965; Moore, 1978; Muller, 1985; Muller and Seligson, 1987). As evident in their lower levels of national wealth but higher levels of income inequality, unemployment, and inflation rates, the economic performance in semiperipheries and peripheries has been poorer compared to core countries and centrally planned economies.[5] Consequently, the economic environment in dependent countries has been more opportune for social unrest.

The Relationship among the Social Unrest Indicators

Table 3.3 reports the correlation among the social unrest indicators. The correlation analysis indicates that although they are usually moderate, the relationships among different indicators of social unrest are positive, meaning that they tend to occur together. However, the moderate nature of the correlations suggests that the concurrence is not necessary.

The strength of the relationship between some indicators is striking. The correlation coefficient of .61 for riots and antigovernment demonstrations means that the two events tend to follow each other. Similarly, though not as frequently, riots are likely to occur with general strikes, and armed attacks result in a large number of deaths from domestic violence. However, despite these positive correlations, their moderate strength implies that social unrest is not unidimensional. Moreover, the correlation matrix challenges the commonly employed strategy of separating social unrest indicators into two groups—violent and nonviolent—and adding the num-

Table 3.3
Correlation Matrix of the Social Unrest Indicators

	Political Strikes	General Strikes	Riots	Assassina.	Armed Attacks	Guerrilla Warfare	Deaths from Dom. Violence
ALL COUNTRIES							
Anti-Government Demonstrations	.12[a]	.16[a]	.61[a]	.15[a]	.07[a]	.10[a]	.06[a]
Political Strikes		.13[a]	.17[a]	.05[a]	.04[b]	.06[a]	.03[b]
General Strikes			.28[a]	.17[a]	.12[a]	.14[a]	.17[a]
Riots				.17[a]	.12[a]	.14[a]	.17[a]
Assassinations					.07[a]	.18[a]	.10[a]
Armed Attacks						.10[a]	.22[a]
Guerilla Warfare							.19[a]
CORE COUNTRIES							
Anti-Government Demonstrations	.23[a]	.04[a]	.68[a]	.20[a]	.07[a]	.09[a]	.13[a]
Political Strikes		.34[a]	.20[a]	.10[a]	.11[b]	.29[a]	.33[a]
General Strikes			.17[a]	.06	.05	.28[a]	.16[a]
Riots				.23[a]	.15[a]	.14[a]	.15[a]
Assassinations					.11[a]	.16[a]	.09[a]
Armed Attacks						.13[a]	.32[a]
Guerilla Warfare							.26[a]
COUNTRIES WITH CENTRALLY PLANNED ECONOMIES							
Anti-Government Demonstrations	.12[a]	.30[a]	.45[a]	.02	.13[a]	.06	.10[a]
Political Strikes		.11[a]	.08	.004	.04	-.01	.03
General Strikes			.32[a]	.02	.16[a]	.08	.15[a]
Riots				.05	.41[a]	.12[b]	.28[a]
Assassinations					.24[a]	.20[a]	.17[a]
Armed Attacks						.26[a]	.64[a]
Guerilla Warfare							.18[a]
SEMI-PERIPHERIES							
Anti-Government Demonstrations	.12[a]	.24[a]	.56[a]	.19[a]	.06[b]	.08[a]	.08[a]
Political Strikes		.08[a]	.21[a]	.04	.06[b]	.06[b]	.03
General Strikes			.34[a]	.18[a]	.11[a]	.25[a]	.06
Riots				.16[a]	.30[a]	.17[a]	.29[a]
Assassinations					.14[a]	.20[a]	.08[a]
Armed Attacks						.21[a]	.49[a]
Guerilla Warfare							.22[a]
PERIPHERIES							
Anti-Government Demonstrations	.34[a]	.35[a]	.54[a]	.12[a]	.12[a]	.26[a]	.16[a]
Political Strikes		.46[a]	.36[a]	.10[a]	.10[a]	.05[b]	.15[a]
General Strikes			.28[a]	.09[a]	.03	.09[a]	.06[b]
Riots				.20[a]	.08[a]	.20[a]	.20[a]
Assassinations					.08[a]	.15[a]	.21[a]
Armed Attacks						.09[a]	.20[a]
Guerilla Warfare							.16[a]

[a]Significant at .01 level.
[b]Significant at .05 level.

ber of events in each category to develop two measures of unrest corresponding to their level of violence (Hibbs, 1973; Jackman, 1975).[6]

Parallel to the variations in the frequency of social unrest according to the world system status (Table 3.2), diverse patterns of the relationships among different indicators of social unrest are observed for each group of countries (Table 3.3). First of all, compared to the correlation coefficients reported for all countries, a polarization of relationships appears for subgroups of countries. Second, if we impose a separation among the indicators of social unrest and classify antigovernment demonstrations, political strikes, and general strikes as essentially nonviolent forms of unrest; assassinations, armed attacks, and deaths from domestic violence as essentially violent indicators of social unrest; and riots in between, we can see different clusters of events in each group of countries. There is no clear separation in core countries—both violent and nonviolent indicators tend to appear together. For example, political and general strikes are likely to take place around the same time, along with guerrilla warfare. Or, the relationship between the number of deaths from domestic violence and political strikes ($r = .33$) is as strong as it is between the deaths and armed attacks ($r = .32$). On the other hand, in centrally planned economies and semiperipheries, there appears to be a separation between the violent and nonviolent indicators. Nonviolent events tend to have strong positive relationships with others, and violent events cluster together. Finally, in the peripheries, although nonviolent forms of social unrest yield strong positive correlations among themselves, more moderate relationships are observed among the violent indicators. Moreover, the separation between the violent and nonviolent indicators is not as clear in peripheries as it is in the centrally planned economies and semiperipheries.

The Governing Elite's Response to Social Unrest

Social unrest compels government response not only when citizens raise some demands and require changes in policy or government, but also when the political activities of the discontented target some other segments of the population. Governments react to social unrest because, in either case, it threatens the institutional structures of the society. When such institutional disruptions occur, governments turn to coercive measures, especially if their economic means and/or political foundations prevent them from immediately offering a positive response (Cnudde and Neubauer, 1969; Boswell and Dixon, 1990). When financial demands are made, governments in relatively wealthy countries may be able to formulate economic and social arrangements that provide partial or relative relief without a major structural change or a significant redistribution of wealth in the society. The poor governments of developing countries, on the other hand, are less likely to have the means, freedom, or the will to pursue such a discourse.[7]

For them, repression appears not only as a means, but as the most viable option of coping with social unrest.[8] Given that one of the major obligations of government is to maintain peace and order, continuous and widespread social unrest causes the middle and upper classes to perceive the government as unresponsive and ineffective because it is not able to meet its obligation to provide security, and their status is threatened by such violent actions. "If the status of major conservative groups is threatened," Lipset says, "the legitimacy of the system will remain in question" (Lipset, 1959:89). Indeed, the last century witnessed a vast number of countries experiencing governmental coercion and authoritarian takeovers under such a threat to the status of the middle and upper classes (Stepan, 1971; Linz and Stepan, 1978; O'Donnell, 1979; Collier, 1979; Roberts, 1985). Especially if social unrest proves to be persistent and violent, then the rulers may take more permanent measures that lead to the coercive state. As stated by Gurr: "States involved in recurring episodes of violent conflict tend . . . to develop and maintain institutions specialized in the exercise of coercion" (1988:50).

It is also argued that high levels of social unrest generally result in more coercive measures in dependent countries since the regimes are engaged in "keeping conditions stable for foreign investors" (Jackson et al., 1978; Roberts, 1985; Hyter, 1971). It has been argued further that "the principal means of attaining [a] high level of coercion which are available to a relatively *poor* state must be through *some* form of *dependence*" (Jackson et al., 1978:652). Although the ultimate decision regarding the use of coercion resides with the national political elite, it is made possible and encouraged through the technology transfer, technical assistance, military aid, and other financial and advisory means provided by the industrial world.[9]

Repression, a reflection of political conflict at the elite level, may occur as an incremental policy that gradually curtails civil and political rights at different junctures or as an absolute transformation of the regime either by the incumbent or the opposition (counterelite). It should be noted that repression is not unique to authoritarian governments. It is common to witness a democratic political elite taking coercive measures. While the incrementalist policies of repression are likely to be followed by the incumbent elite and may appear in the form of constitutional amendments, changes in legal codes, proclamation of martial law, and increasing government sanctions, a complete takeover by the opposition may occur in the form of a coup d'état. Encountered by social unrest, the incumbent elite may try to ease the tension through rotations and replacement of the executives, or even through the displacement of the entire cabinet. The counterelite is likely to take over when the governing elite fails to reorganize its administration or if such changes make no major progress in curtailing social unrest. Thus, the unrest at the mass level results in instability or unrest at the elite level, which is most evident in the executive branch. The changes in the executive, however, can be through both conventional and unconventional means.

In this study, the number of major cabinet changes within a calendar year and the number of coups d'état are employed as the measures of conventional and unconventional government turnover, respectively. The number of coups d'état, as stated by Banks, who compiled the data, refers to the number of "extraconstitutional or forced changes in the top government elite and/or its executive control of the nation's power structure in a given year. The term 'coup' includes, but is not exhausted by, the term 'successful revolution'. Unsuccessful coups are not counted" (1979:17). The major cabinet changes are measured by "the number of times in a year that new premier is named and/or 50% of the cabinet posts are occupied by new ministers" (19). In addition to these two indicators, the number of government crises, defined as "any rapidly developing situation that threatens to bring the downfall of the present regime—excluding situations of revolt aimed at such overthrow," is employed as a measure of the weakness of the legitimacy of the system as felt at the executive level. Moreover, major constitutional changes, which are "the number of basic alterations in a state's constitutional structure, the extreme case being the adoption of a new constitution that significantly alters the prerogatives of the various branches of government" (18), are included as an indicator of the ruling group's effort to cope with some problems through procedural changes.[10]

Political executions and political sanctions are the measures of coercive policies that refer to the actions taken by governments that result in violation or limitation of the civil and political rights of citizens. Political sanctions comprise the actions "taken by the authorities to neutralize, suppress, or eliminate a perceived threat to the security of the government, the regime, or the state itself" (Taylor and Jodice, 1983:62).[11] Political executions refer to "the outright elimination of political dissidents" and include the events "in which a person or group is put to death under orders of national authorities while in their custody" (Taylor and Jodice, 1983:63).

Table 3.4 indicates that, similar to their experience with social unrest, dependent countries rank high also on executive unrest indicators. Although core countries are likely to experience frequent government crises and cabinet changes, such events are more commonly observed in semi-peripheries. Peripheries also experience frequent changes in governments. Moreover, compared to the core countries and centrally planned economies, the governing groups in countries with semiperiphery and periphery status seek constitutional changes more frequently. Finally, while coups d'état have been completely unknown to the core nations and have seldom occurred in centrally planned economies, dependent countries have encountered them frequently.

Table 3.4
Average Values of Government Response Variables by the World System Status of Countries, 1947–1982

	All	Core	Centrally Planned	Semi-periphery	Periphery
GOVERNMENT RESPONSE					
Government Crises	.24	.33	.10	.35	.14
Cabinet Changes	.46	.41	.25	.53	.48
Constitutional Changes	.11	.02	.05	.09	.18
Coups D'etat	.04	.00	.01	.05	.06
Political Sanctions	8.43	9.52	18.45	10.28	3.90
Political Executions	4.24	.01	16.61	2.96	3.96

The analysis of political sanctions and executions presents a more complex picture. Both of these coercive means are employed most frequently in centrally planned economies, with the average annual number of sanctions being around eighteen. Core and semiperipheral countries approach the same level, with approximately ten political sanctions per year. Peripheries, which rank comparatively low on this indicator, surpass both semiperipheries and core countries in number of political executions. On the other hand, although not completely absent, political executions are seldom exercised in core countries.

An examination of the correlations among the executive changes and coercive measures (Table 3.5) presents a strong relationship between government crisis and cabinet changes regardless of the world system status of the country. Also, except for core countries where a modest relationship is observed, cabinet changes appear to be strongly related to constitutional changes. Again, except for core countries—which are free from coups—coups d'état demonstrate a strong positive relationship with all indicators of executive instability and constitutional changes. Moreover, governments installed by coups d'état appear to employ more sanctions since the correlations between coups d'état and political sanctions are all positive and significant in all three groups of countries. Coups d'état are also accompanied by a large number of political executions both in peripheries and centrally planned economies.

The Relationship Between Social Unrest and Government Response

When we examine the relationship between the indicators of social unrest and government response (Table 3.6), we find them to be positively related. The data indicate that social unrest stimulates executive instability and leads governments to employ repressive policies, although the relationship is not necessarily strong or statistically significant for all indicators, and weak relationships are observed mostly in core countries. Political sanctions appear to have a considerably strong positive relationship with all indicators of social unrest across the board, the relationships being stronger and more consistent in core and peripheral countries.

The executive offices in core countries tend to be more sensitive to political and general strikes, as well as guerrilla warfare, as observed in their positive correlations with government crisis and cabinet changes. While political strikes and guerrilla warfare have a moderate impact on government crisis and cabinet changes, general strikes appear with a considerably strong relationship with both indicators of executive instability.

Contrary to the common belief that the executive renewals and changes in centrally planned economies are determined by the balance of power within the party, the data demonstrate that governments in these countries

Table 3.5
Correlation Matrix of the Government Response Variables

	Cabinet Changes	Constitutional Changes	Coups	Political Sanctions	Political Executions
ALL COUNTRIES					
Government Crises	.34[a]	.08[a]	.20[a]	.19[a]	.06[a]
Cabinet Changes		.24[a]	.33[a]	.10[a]	.04[a]
Constitutional Changes			.33[a]	.07[a]	.06[a]
Coups D'etat				.13[a]	.11[a]
Political Sanctions					.13[a]
CORE COUNTRIES					
Government Crises	.44[a]	.10[a]	----	.04	.04
Cabinet Changes		.09[b]	----	.03	.02
Constitutional Changes			----	.06	.19[a]
Coups D'etat				----	----
Political Sanctions					.16[a]
COUNTRIES WITH CENTRALLY PLANNED ECONOMIES					
Government Crises	.31[a]	.14[a]	.51[a]	.23[a]	.16[a]
Cabinet Changes		.34[a]	.34[a]	.15[a]	.08
Constitutional Changes			.29[a]	.09	-.01
Coups D'etat				.16[a]	.25[a]
Political Sanctions					.18[a]
SEMI-PERIPHERIES					
Government Crises	.35[a]	.06[b]	.20[a]	.26[a]	.04
Cabinet Changes		.23[a]	.36[a]	.16[a]	.06[b]
Constitutional Changes			.25[a]	.19[a]	.07[a]
Coups D'etat				.21[a]	.05[b]
Political Sanctions					.10[a]
PERIPHERIES					
Government Crises	.26[a]	.15[a]	.27[a]	.37[a]	.10[a]
Cabinet Changes		.27[a]	.34[a]	.18[a]	.06[a]
Constitutional Changes			.36[a]	.13[a]	.10[a]
Coups D'etat				.22[a]	.14[a]
Political Sanctions					.05[b]

[a]Significant at .01 level.
[b]Significant at .05 level.

Table 3.6
Correlations Between the Social Unrest Indicators and Government Response Variables

	Anti-government Demonstrations	Political Strikes	General Strikes	Riots	Assassinations	Armed Attacks	Guerrilla Warfare	Deaths from Domestic Violence
ALL COUNTRIES								
Government Crises	.14[a]	.10[a]	.29[a]	.14[a]	.15[a]	.07[a]	.24[a]	.13[a]
Cabinet Changes	.07[a]	.04[b]	.14[a]	.07[a]	.07[a]	.04[a]	.14[a]	.11[a]
Constitutional Changes	.02	.02	.002	.02	.03	.01	.003	.09[a]
Coups D'etat	.04[b]	.02	.09[a]	.04[b]	.05[a]	.02	.09[a]	.11[a]
Political Sanctions	.30[a]	.13[a]	.16[a]	.30[a]	.08[a]	.14[a]	.16[a]	.18[a]
Political Executions	.01	.01	.04[b]	.01	.04[b]	.04[b]	.04[b]	.26[a]
CORE COUNTRIES								
Government Crises	-.001	.14[a]	.38[a]	.07	.10[b]	-.03	.18[a]	.002
Cabinet Changes	-.007	.12[a]	.22[a]	.05	.06	-.03	.22[a]	.01
Constitutional Changes	-.003	.02	.01	-.01	.02	.005	.01	.03
Coups D'etat	----	----	----	----	----	----	----	----
Political Sanctions	.30[a]	.47[a]	.22[a]	.40[a]	.22[a]	.25[a]	.22[a]	.65[a]
Political Executions	.05	.05	.03	.02	.03	.04	.03	.16[a]
COUNTRIES WITH CENTRALLY PLANNED ECONOMIES								
Government Crises	.22[a]	.32[a]	.50[a]	.25[a]	.01	.08	.50[a]	.12[b]
Cabinet Changes	.23[a]	.29[a]	.35[a]	.18[a]	.06[a]	.07[a]	.35[a]	.06
Constitutional Changes	.05	.28[a]	.01	.003	.07	.10	.01	-.02
Coups D'etat	.06	.08	.58[a]	.06	.07	.25[a]	.58[a]	.10[b]
Political Sanctions	.16[a]	.07	.13[a]	.30[a]	.09	.23[a]	.13[a]	.17[a]
Political Executions	.02	.03	.23[a]	.19[a]	.07	.25[a]	.23[a]	.45[a]
SEMI-PERIPHERIES								
Government Crises	.20[a]	.07[a]	.26[a]	.23[a]	.15[a]	.08[a]	.26[a]	.05
Cabinet Changes	.13[a]	-.005	.14[a]	.11[a]	.06[a]	.07[a]	.14[a]	.05[b]
Constitutional Changes	.11[a]	.001	.03	.06[b]	.05	.04	.03	.06[b]
Coups D'etat	.05[b]	.01	.11[a]	.12[a]	.05[b]	.02	.11[a]	.11[a]
Political Sanctions	.38[a]	.12[a]	.19[a]	.39[a]	.07[b]	.18[a]	.19[a]	.18[a]
Political Executions	.08[a]	.01	.03	-.0001	.07[a]	.09[a]	.03	.13[a]
PERIPHERIES								
Government Crises	.31[a]	.24[a]	.17[a]	.36[a]	.13[a]	.17[a]	.28[a]	.31[a]
Cabinet Changes	.08[a]	.15[a]	.06[b]	.10[a]	.06[b]	.06[a]	.04	.16[a]
Constitutional Changes	.04	.11[a]	.03	.10[a]	.04	.003	.06[b]	.11[a]
Coups D'etat	.18[a]	.12[a]	.13[a]	.13[a]	.08[a]	.03	.11[a]	.11[a]
Political Sanctions	.39[a]	.37[a]	.22[a]	.44[a]	.19[a]	.17[a]	.15[a]	.32[a]
Political Executions	.01	.02	.06[b]	.05	.09[a]	.02	.10[a]	.32[a]

[a]Significant at .01 level.
[b]Significant at .05 level.

have also been affected by the scope and nature of the citizens' unrest. Both government crisis and cabinet changes yield strong or moderate positive correlations with most of the indicators of social unrest. Social unrest seems to be irrelevant only to the number of constitutional changes instituted in these countries. Coups d'état, political sanctions, and executions tend to appear with violent indicators of social unrest. These three forms of coercive government responses also tend to take place in the presence of general strikes. Knowing that general strikes do not occur frequently in these countries—with an average annual value of .03 (Table 3.2)—it can be deduced that governments have been particularly sensitive to comprehensive labor protests. Riots, which are also not common in these countries, are positively correlated with political sanctions and executions.

Antigovernment demonstrations, general strikes, riots, and guerrilla wars appear to have a strong relationship with government crisis and a moderate one with cabinet changes in semiperipheries. While constitutional changes in these countries have a moderate relationship only with antigovernment demonstration, moderate correlations are observed between coups d'état and the numbers of general strikes, riots, guerrilla wars, and deaths from domestic violence. The violent response by the government, in the form of political executions, seems to appear with a large number of deaths from domestic violence.

Peripheries respond to social unrest both with political sanctions and executive instability. Government crises in these countries concur with all indicators of social unrest, the strongest relationship being with riots, antigovernment demonstrations, guerrilla wars, and political strikes. The changes in the cabinet and the constitution mostly correspond to the number of political strikes, riots, and deaths from domestic violence. Coups d'état have moderate positive relationships with all indicators of social unrest, except armed attacks. Finally, while political sanctions are employed in the presence of all forms of social unrest, political executions are correlated with the violent indicators of unrest.

SUMMARY AND CONCLUSION

The findings from the data analysis employed for this research confirm that social unrest is not unidimensional. Different methods of political expression and protest are employed by different groups in different kinds of societies. Although the data analysis is limited to correlation analysis that cannot establish causal orders, on the basis of some theoretical insight, government instability and sanctions are treated as a response to social unrest. Again, the analysis demonstrates that the response of governments varies in countries that hold different positions in the global power structure. Social unrest may cause government crisis and result in changes in executive level in all countries, but the extent of government susceptibility to change and the procedure of change are not uniform. Also, while governments in all countries employ coercion, their tolerance level and the scope of political sanctions and executions are quite different.

The data indicate that while both core countries and centrally planned economies experience government instability and impose political sanctions in considerable amount, citizens of semiperipheries and peripheries encounter these at a higher rate. Moreover, they are subject to further suppression due to frequent occurrence of coups d'état. Coups d'état mean an increase in government coerciveness not only because coup governments tend to impose more political sanctions and carry out numerous executions, but as extraconstitutional takeovers that violate political rights of citizens, they *are* coercive measures themselves.

Coercive policies, however, directed to suppressing public demands serve only as temporary solutions. As "cyclical policies," they aim at coping with the problem rather than eliminating its causes;[12] thus, their effect is limited to the temporary control of social unrest.

The Afghan coup of 1973, four coups in Argentina (1955, 1962, 1966, and 1976), the 1960 Bolivian coup, the 1964 military takeover in Brazil, the 1972 coups in Chile and Ghana, the 1963 coup in Honduras, the 1966 coups in Indonesia and Nigeria, the 1962 and 1968 coups in Peru, and the 1960, 1971, and 1980 military takeovers in Turkey are some of the cases that display the cyclical character of coercive policies. Social unrest, which was high before the coups in these countries, was reduced or completely eliminated soon after the military coups, although economic and structural factors were left relatively constant. Consequently, despite the military governments' success in suppressing unrest once the coercive measures were removed (e.g., upon the return of the civilian rule), since they did not treat the socioeconomic causes of unrest, the cycle of social unrest and suppression started again.[13]

Coups are usually undertaken by military groups. However, it would be misleading to see the military as the only coercive group. Civilian governments, even those which are elected, also employ coercive sanctions under the conditions of persistent social unrest. Sanctions employed by civilian governments not only violate the social and political rights of citizenry but also pave the way for military intervention, which leads to further coercion. In many countries that experience high levels of social unrest, we see martial law put into effect by civilian governments. Martial law that mobilizes military or paramilitary forces to suppress social unrest legitimizes future military interventions by admitting the incompetence of the civilian law enforcement institutions in handling social unrest, by consolidating the image of the military as an effective force in maintaining social order, by politicizing the military, and by updating and boosting the coercive capacity of the military.[14] In fact, generals who take over, after several months or years of civilian rule that sought the assistance of the military and fed its coercive apparatus, justify the coup as a necessary move directed to end the civilian incompetence and corruption and to restore "law and order."

NOTES

1. Due to the relatively short time period covered by the study, the world system status of each country in the study is treated as a constant through time. Reclassification for some countries—especially for their position in the 1980s (e.g., those that are commonly referred to as newly industrialized countries [NICs] such as Thailand, and the countries that are originally classified as centrally planned economies—may be necessary. The major changes in the sociopolitical structures of these countries also make them curious cases for future study of the impact of changes in the world system status on the nature and frequency of political conflict.

2. Employing the system analysis approach, they state that "demonstrations, riots, armed attacks, and the like are means by which 'input demands' are communicated to the ruling regime" (Taylor and Jodice, 1983:17).

3. The countries that gained independence after 1947 are included in the data set starting with their year of independence or with the year for which data were available.

4. The high number of armed attacks in core countries can be attributed, in addition to their domestic political conflicts, to the fact that these countries have been subject to such attacks by foreign parties due to their involvement and dominant role in various international conflicts.

5. For the time period between 1947 and 1982, unemployment rates in semi-peripheries and peripheries was higher, 6.1 percent and 7.3 percent on the average, while core countries and centrally planned economies had much lower rates, 3.6 percent and 2.9 percent, respectively. Similarly, inflation rates were less than 2 percent for the centrally planned economies and around 6.5 percent in core countries, but jumped to 11.8 percent for peripheries and 14.3 percent for semiperipheries (Arat, 1991:99). Furthermore, income inequality in dependent countries was higher. The average Gini coefficient of income inequality was found to be .22, .36, .44, and .46 for the centrally planned economies, core countries, peripheries, and semiperipheries, respectively (Arat, 1991:98, Table 5.4).

6. The factor analyses of the social unrest indicators for each year do not necessarily provide a two-factor solution, and even for those years when the analyses yield two distinct factors, the variables do not cluster according to the expected violent/nonviolent dichotomy (e.g., the number of assassinations clusters with the numbers of strikes, riots, and antigovernmental demonstrations for many years).

7. Henderson's study (1991) of political repression (defined to include disappearance, detention, torture, and political killings) finds income inequality and rate of economic growth as two of the three most significant explanatory factors. The former is positively and the latter is negatively related to repression.

8. It should be noted that the impact of social unrest does not always have to be negative, even in poor countries. A study by Dixon and Moon (1989) discusses and supports the theory that domestic political conflict may result in the improvement and expansion of welfare benefits.

9. There is a good number of case studies and comparative research that doc-

uments the impact of dependency on government coerciveness. See Lopez and Stohl (1989), Abinales (1986), Chilcote (1984), Dominguez et al. (1979), and Ullman (1978).

10. It should be noted that the focus of the attempted control in such efforts may not be social unrest. Moreover, constitutional changes do not have to be repressive in nature and may entail expansion of rights and freedoms rather than political restrictions.

11. Taylor and Jodice specify:

> Sanctions include "censorship of individuals or institutions, general restrictions on political activity, and other restrictions on social and political behavior. . . ."
>
> Censorship includes actions by the authorities to limit, curb, or intimidate the mass media, including newspapers, magazines, books, radio, and television. . . .
>
> Restrictions on political behavior include general restrictive measures by the authorities, such as the declaring of martial law, mobilizing troops for domestic security, and instituting a curfew. They also include actions specifically directed against an individual, a party, or other political organizations. Such specific actions include the removal of a government official reportedly because of his of her political beliefs and activities, the banning of a political party or acts of harassment against it, the arrest of opposition politicians on grounds of state security, the exiling or deportation of persons for engaging in political actions or for expressing opposition regarded as detrimental to the national interest, and the arrest or deportation of persons reportedly involved in political protest actions, including protest demonstrations, riots, political strikes, armed attacks, and assassination attempts. Finally, restrictions on political behavior also encompass actions by the authorities against foreign espionage. In these instances, one or more foreigners are arrested or detained on charges of spying, sabotage, or unlawful interference in the domestic politics of the state, constituting a perceived threat to internal security (Taylor and Jodice, 1983:62–63).

12. On cyclical policies see Rose (1976).

13. Ziegenhagen, at the conclusion of his research, which employs the conflict episode as the unit of analysis, states that the coercive strategy may fail to provide even a temporary relief from social unrest because regime coerciveness may "exacerbate political conflict rather than regulate it effectively" (1986:195). Mason (1989) further argues that "state-sanction terror" is not only a reaction to social unrest, but it is "proactive in character." The empirical analyses by Muller (1985; Muller and Weede, 1990) find that regime repressiveness stimulates political violence. For a discussion of the dual effect of repression, see Opp and Roehl (1990).

14. The latter one has considerable support in the research that has found strong positive relationships between state repression and the strength of the military measured by the military budget, size, or coercive capacity (Ziegenhagen, 1986).

4

CONFLICT AND DEVELOPMENT IN TURKEY: THE PROBLEM OF THE COUP TRAP

Ali Çarkoğlu

The remarkable rise of new democracies in the Third World since World War II has been overshadowed by frequent military coups d'état. Analysis of the structural determinants of military regimes has induced a large body of literature. Three interrelated explanatory models of coup occurrence can be distinguished from the literature: first, political and economic development, social mobilization, or "modernization" explanations (e.g., Deutsch, 1961; Huntington, 1968; Olson, 1963; Needler, 1966; Germani and Silvert, 1967); second, habituation explanations (e.g., Alexander, 1958; Zolberg, 1968b; Londregan and Poole, 1990; O'Kane, 1983); and third, political conflict explanations (e.g., Eckstein, 1964–1965; Gurr, 1967–1968; Lieuwen, 1962; Needler, 1963; Pye, 1962). A persistent theme in the literature is the predictability of the coup d'état. Many empirical analyses of coup behavior include findings that the coup occurrences have common underlying factors that undermine a healthy democratic process increasing the likelihood of coups. These studies typically make a cross-sectional analysis of coup-stricken countries.[1] Although predictability of coups has been convincingly established in the literature, dissenters and their claims that idiosyncratic elements dominate the Third World coup experience remain.[2]

One weakness of previous analyses is their inability to account for single-country experiences due to their focus on cross-sectional research designs. The main objective of this chapter is to devise an empirical framework of analysis that will allow us to test the validity of these competing explanatory frameworks for the military regime experience of Turkey over the multi-party democracy period of 1950–1986. I attempt to show that with proper methodological specifications, theoretical expectations gathered in military coup literature form a powerful body of hypotheses that could be tested within the context of specific country experiences. This new framework of analysis could then be used to predict country-specific military interventions.

Since the establishment of multiparty democracy in 1950, Turkish democracy has been interrupted by the Turkish military three times, in nearly regular intervals of ten years: first on May 27, 1960; second, on March 12, 1971; and last, on September 12, 1980. Combinations of the three broad explanations mentioned above have also been asserted in analyzing the Turkish military coup experience.[3] My analyses show that military intervention in Turkey conforms to such theoretical expectations, especially to those within the framework of conflict and habituation explanations, exhibiting a considerable degree of predictability.

THEORETICAL BACKGROUND[4]

Politico-Economic Development and Social Mobilization Explanation of Coups

It is a common observation that economic development and coups are inversely related (Lutwak, 1979:33–38; O'Kane, 1987:41–62; Londregan and Poole, 1990). Coups are virtually nonexistent in the developed countries, and they are twenty-one times more likely to occur among the poorest countries than among the wealthiest (Londregan and Poole, 1990:151). Although the *level* of modernity reflected by the degree of economic development is regarded as stabilizing, the *process* of modernization is seen as undermining political stability (Huntington, 1968:41). Military rule is accordingly seen as a result of the conflict that arises due to an imbalance between the degree of social mobilization and the degree of political institutionalization. As social mobilization increases, unless political institutions that counterbalance the destabilizing effects of modernization are strengthened, disorder is bound to occur (Deutsch, 1961). Germani and Silvert (1967) hypothesize that military intervention is inhibited by the rise of the middle class, which has inherent incentives to maintain a stable civilian political system. However, they also claim that the likelihood of military intervention is greater as social cleavages grow and social consensus disappears in a society.[5] Finer (1988:99–126) argues that the propensity for military intervention is likely to decrease with increased social mobilization.[6] Economic development and industrialization as well as the availability of education opportunities are given a special importance among those factors increasing social mobilization, thus decreasing the propensity for military intervention.

Accordingly, the first hypothesis of the socioeconomic development model of coups takes the following form:

HYPOTHESIS 1: *The higher the level of modernization and social mobilization, the lower the likelihood of military intervention.*

Olson (1963), similar to Huntington (1968), argues that contrary to expectations, *economic growth* is destabilizing. Needler (1966: 617) also asserts that a successful coup or revolt is less likely when economic conditions are improving. A more focused version of the first hypothesis can thus be specified as follows:

HYPOTHESIS 1A: *The higher the level of economic well-being and social mobilization, the lower the likelihood of military intervention. However, the higher the change in the development rate, the higher the likelihood of a military regime.*

Karpat (1970) gives special importance to the effects of social mobility that changed the selection criteria of the elites disrupting the social hierarchy in post-1950 Turkey. Rapid economic development coupled with radical changes brought by the multiparty democratic regime resulted in increasing tension between civilian power circles and the military.[7] During the 1950s, the army increasingly found itself in search of a new identity in a rapidly changing society and, more important, no longer directly represented in political power structure: "[A]fter the victory of the [Democratic Party] in 1950 and during its administrations, the percentage of deputies of military origin fell sharply. Moreover, five of the six ministers of national defence during this period were civilians—as compared to their eleven predecessors, all of whom had military backgrounds" (Vaner, 1987:237).[8] Most analyses of Turkish coups also stress that economic decay and erosion of the officers' standard of living during 1950s, due primarily to high inflation, decisively shaped the determination of the officer corps in undertaking the 1960 coup.[9]

Difficulties on the economic scene also preceded the 1971 intervention. In August 1970, an austerity program, which invoked unprecedented protests by the labor movement, was adopted, which resulted in the devaluation of the Turkish lira by more than 50 percent (Pevsner, 1984:47–48). Although after 1960 there had been considerable improvements in the economic standards of the officer corps, the demonstration of noncommissioned officers' wives protesting the decline in their standard of living in 1970, just prior to the second coup in 1971, shows that deteriorating economic conditions and related decay in social status of the armed forces remained on the military's agenda (Vaner, 1987:252).[10]

Similarly, the late 1970s were also characterized by a stagnant economy and rampant inflation. As early as 1978–1979 even the left-wing government of Prime Minister Ecevit was attempting to undertake measures of radical change in economic policy away from autarchic, public sector–driven economic policies toward stabilization policies advocated by the International Monetary Fund (IMF) that primarily required a politically unacceptable devaluation of the currency (Harris, 1985:84; Karpat, 1988:142).[11] The Ecevit government could not survive its new economic program. It was the minority government of Suleyman Demirel that undertook the most radical economic reform program in the history of the Turkish Republic in January 1980. The reform program adopted the basic tenets of the IMF stabilization package and oriented the economy toward an export-led growth strategy, which relied primarily on devaluations, dismantling of public subsidies, and reduction of budget deficits. From January 1980 until the military intervention in September 1980, left-wing unions took the lead in opposing the austerity program, which resulted in a general strike in the summer of 1980.

In short, there are recurrent economic crises prior to military interventions in Turkey. As Hypothesis 1a suggests, before military interventions, economic conditions deteriorate, and there are indications that military officers might be especially vulnerable to deteriorating conditions. Devaluations and austerity programs that mark periods of sharp economic changes precede the military interventions.[12]

Habituation Explanation of Coups

Alexander (1958) stresses the internal habituation of coups, claiming that the propensity for military intervention increases with repeated military intervention. Zolberg (1968b:80) also suggests that having had a previous coup makes another coup more likely. On the other hand, the effect on the ability of the military to run a government is emphasized by Janowitz (1964), who hypothesizes that the size and sophistication of the military establishment are positively related to the propensity for military intervention in politics. We can relate this argument to that of Alexander's by assuming that coups are "exercises" in raising the sophistication of the military. Coups increase the likelihood of future coups by increasing the military's ability to run the government.[13] The habituation effect is reflected by the following hypothesis:

HYPOTHESIS 2: *Historical tradition of military rule increases the likelihood of a military regime.*

Past coups may create mechanisms to oppress social groups more effectively than before, as well as eliminate opposition groups and lessen conflict in the short to medium run. Failure to perform these tasks may further induce conflict in the society. Yet military rule may only provide temporary stability through oppression, and old cleavages may resurface as a civilian regime is established, therefore shifting to a higher level the degree of conflict and the likelihood of a new military regime. Moreover, inner dynamics of the military may be affected by recurring military regime experiences. It is a matter of the ability to control on the part of the dominant group and to meet potential challenges from different factions within the military. Thus, past coups may either increase the likelihood of conflict, resulting in higher likelihood of coups, or eliminate conflict possibilities, thus decreasing the likelihood of having a coup in the future.

There are at least five interpretations of the habituation hypothesis that are discussed at some length in the Turkish military coup literature. The first one is concerned with the internal mechanisms of the military that prepare a coup-prone milieu for aspiring officer groups to engage in secret intervention activities.[14] Even before the first coup of the democratic era, there apparently was a nucleus of a secret organization within the military. As early as November 1954, nine officers were arrested, and a two-year sentence for a major was imposed in 1957 (Harris, 1965:171; Karpat, 1970:1665; Brown, 1988:143). The failed coup attempts of Colonel Aydemir in 1962 and 1963 also show the potential for repeated coups due to military fractionalization. A common diagnosis of the 1971 intervention is that the major motivation of the officers was to finish the reforms started during the first intervention period (Vaner, 1987:254–255). However, another motive is also asserted to be that commanders acted "from their fear that, if they failed to do so, then they might well be faced with a revolt by their subordinates or dangerous divisions within the high command itself" (Hale, 1990:70; Harris, 1985:163). Similar factional problems apparently existed during the preparation phase of the 1980 coup and afterwards.[15] In short, there was a historical orientation toward political activism among the officer corps, who were ready to intervene as the situation warranted.

The second interpretation of the habituation effect in the Turkish military lies in the attitudes of civilians toward military reactions. It is clearly documented that there had been an increasing expectation that the military would intervene as crises developed (Birand, 1987). This attitude especially provided popular support for the military when it intervened.

The third interpretation is actually a claim by civilian politicians about particularly the last intervention, that the military acts in an opportunistic way. This view presumes that the military waits for the right moment to intervene, even tolerating the rise of terrorism in order to maximize popular support for the military regime by instilling a lack of confidence among the people toward a civilian government (Karpat, 1988:149). All three potential reasons or reflections of habituation effects are self-reinforcing, and as time passes we would expect that their effect on the probability of another coup would increase.

The ability of the military to deal with civilian administrative issues is expected to have increased over the last forty years and three military regime periods of an approximate total of nine years. The modernization of the military's inner administration after Turkey's membership in the North Atlantic Treaty Organization (NATO) and the increase in technical sophistication and modern educational facilities for the military officers have made the officers less reliant on the military as their only career option. However, it is not possible for us to measure this newly added career mobility and its effect on military regime experience. Nevertheless, it is not plausible to assume that all ranks in all different forces have been equally affected by this development.

An alternative, fifth interpretation is concerned with the ability of the military to control political conflict in society as a whole, mainly through coercion, and to establish a persistent order. As we shall see below, the Turkish experience before the third intervention is that conflict in society tended to increase to new heights after each intervention. Although it is not possible to claim that military interventions alone caused conflict events to rise, it seems that military regimes played the role of ultimate conflict management tools in the Turkish democracy by suspending democracy regularly as violent conflict ran out of control and by restoring a normal state of affairs within several years. From this point of view the Turkish political system was "habituated" or "addicted" to military regimes.

Political Conflict Explanation of Coups

Besides the interaction of the effects of politico-economic development and the occurrence of coups, students of military regimes have also given some attention to violent political conflict. Lieuwen (1962:132–133) and Needler (1963:76–85), for example, claim that the tendency toward military intervention increases with increasing political violence. Similarly, Pye (1962:84), Gurr (1967–1968:245), and Eckstein (1964–1965:133–134) all observe that coups occur in societies experiencing violent disorder. Combining these views with those of Huntington (1968) and Germani and Silvert (1967), we have:

HYPOTHESIS 3: *Conflicts during the transition to modernity increase the tendency for a military coup.*[16]

The rise of political tension, coupled with violent conflict events, is the most striking common characteristic of all three military interventions in Turkey. Weiker (1981:1–24), Karpat (1970: 1673), and Harris (1965:169–176) all give vivid accounts of increasing political tension. Prior to the first intervention, demonstrations and riots in universities and big cities were handled with brutality by the government. This seriously undermined the government's authority in the precoup months of 1959 and 1960. Before the second intervention, student demonstrations turned into urban, guerrilla warfare. Left-wing revolutionaries on the one hand and ultranationalist groups on the other routinely clashed with each other. The rise of youth violence was further aggravated by the increasing activism of the labor movement. Labor activism reached an apex in June 1970 with demonstrations in Istanbul against a legislation that threatened to limit union organization. The protest turned violent and could be controlled only by the use of paratroopers and tanks.[17] Following the purges of the military regime of 1971, violence started to rise gradually again after the 1973 elections. Compared to early periods of violence, the pre-1980 incidents were unprecedented. Both the number of deaths and the complexity of participating groups were remarkably high. Coupled with youth violence this time were clashes between ethnic (Kurds and non-Kurds) and religious (Turkish Shiite Alevis and Sunnis) groups. Clashes in the southeastern city of Kahramanmaras in December 1978 took more than 100 lives.[18] Despite martial law imposed following these events, the death toll continued to rise. Dodd (1990:32) reports that deaths from political violence rose from 35 in 1975 to about 3,500 in 1980. It is a common diagnosis in the literature that the military was very sensitive to increasing violence in the late 1970s. After the intervention, the regime stressed that the main reason for intervention was to restore order and security in the nation.

MODELLING THE COUP EXPERIENCE

Actual military coup experiences are shaped not by only one factor but by a combination of the factors considered above. Nevertheless, I first test the validity of alternative explanations in isolation within a direct effects model and later combine different factors to test for improvements in prediction. The logic of these models is to isolate factors that are considered important in determining coup behavior and asserting a direct effect from them to coup occurrence. Any interaction among the determining factors or feedback from coup to the determining factors is not considered.[19] In the following sections I also estimate a joint additive effect model of the coup experience.

Before developing empirically testable models within the framework of these two broad interaction forms, conceptualization of the dependent variable and the methodology of empirical analysis are addressed.

Coup Behavior and the Nature of the Empirical Analysis

The measurement of coup experience determines the basic statistical methodology of the analysis.[20] In the following analysis of Turkish coups, I use a dichotomous dependent variable (M_t), which represents either the existence (1) or nonexistence (0) of total control of government by the military at each observation year for at least six months or more. This

dichotomous specification of the dependent variable necessitates the use
of probit estimation. Under this specification we are not only concerned
with the occurrence of coups, but our focus is also on the period that a
military regime stays in power.

In this model the nature of the estimation process entails the following
conceptualization.[21] We assume there is an underlying propensity to have
a military regime during year t. Let that propensity be denoted by an index
m_t. If m_t is positive, it shows the probability that a military regime will be
in power. If it is negative or zero then there is no chance that a military
regime can prevail. Assume further that the index m_t is a random and
normally distributed variable and that it is determined by a set of factors
X_t. We could analyze this relationship with the usual linear specification
only if we could observe the values of both X_t and m_t:

$$m_t = a + b X_t + u_t \qquad (4.1)$$

where u_t is the error term. However different from the ordinary least square
estimation problem, our measurements can only grasp the certainty cases;
that is, we only observe a successful coup and successfully prevailing military regime. Even when we observe an unsuccessful coup we do not observe the level of propensity that actually causes the unsuccessful attempt.
Assuming that the index of the propensity to have a military regime at a
given year is a linear function of variable set X_t, the probit model provides
a suitable way to estimate the coefficients in equation 4.1.

The theoretical index m_t and the observed values M_t—that is, 1 for the
existence of military regime and 0 for a civilian one—are related in the
following manner. For every year, assume that m_t^* represents the critical
threshold value of the underlying propensity to have a military regime that
translates into a successful occurrence of military government. Thus, we
have:

$$\text{Military government } (M_t) \begin{cases} \text{exists} & \text{(1) if } m_t > m_t^* \\ \text{does not exist (0) if } m_t \leq m_t^* \end{cases} \qquad (4.2)$$

Accordingly, if a military government exists, then it has to be true that

$$(a - a^*) + (b - b^*) X_t > u_t^* - u_t \qquad (4.3)$$

The probability that a military government exists, then, can be expressed
in the following way:

$$P_t (M_t = 1) = P_t (m_t > m_t^*)$$
$$= P_t [(a - a^*) + (b - b^*) X_t > u_t^* - u_t] \quad (4.4)$$
$$= P_t (Z_t > v_t) \quad (4.5)$$

where $Z_t = (a - a^*) + (b - b^*) X_t$ and $v_t = u_t^* - u_t$.

Using the cumulative distribution function F(.) and the probability density function f(.), we obtain

$$P_t (M_t = 1) = P(Z_t > v_t) = F(Z_t) = \int_{-\infty}^{Z_t} f(v_t) dv \quad (4.6)$$

Assuming that v_t is normally distributed with mean zero and unit variance, we have the normal cumulative distribution function:

$$P_t (M_t = 1) = F(Z_t) = \frac{1}{\sqrt{2\pi}} \int_{-\infty}^{Z_t} \exp \left(\frac{-v_2}{2} \right) dv \quad (4.7)$$

P_t, which represents the probability that a military regime is in power at time t, lies in the unit interval [0,1].

Applying the inverse of the cumulative normal function to equation 4.7, we obtain an estimate of the index m_t (Pindyck and Rubinfeld, 1991:255):

$$M_t = F^{-1}(P_t) = a + bX_t \quad (4.8)$$

Our predicted M_t values can be interpreted to be the unobserved conditional probability to have a successful coup given that X_t is realized (Pindyck and Rubinfeld, 1991:254–256). Due to the nonlinearity of the cumulative normal function, ordinary least squares cannot be applied to estimate the probit model. Instead, maximum-likelihood estimation (MLE), which provides consistent and asymptotically efficient estimates of the coefficients, is used.[22]

MLE has a different objective than the usual least squares estimation. The objective of MLE can be explained as follows. Since the conditional probability of having a military regime at time t is given by $P_t = P_t(M_t = 1 \mid X_t)$ or simply by equation 4.7, then $P_t = P_t (M_t = 0 \mid X_t) = 1 - P_t$, Zand the probability of observing outcome M_t, whether it be 0 or 1, is given by $P(M_t \mid X_t) = P^{M_t}(1 - P)^{1 - M_t}$. If we assume that each individual observation in a sample of N observations is independent of every other observation, the probability of observing a particular sample of N values of M, say h, given the observations of independent variable X, is given by the product of N probability expressions (Aldrich and Nelson, 1984:50). We have

$$P(h \mid X) = \prod_{t=1}^{N} P^{M_t} (1 - P)^{1 - M_t} \quad (4.9)$$

Equation 4.9 is the so called likelihood function. The value of this function, using the sample observations and particular values of the parameters, gives a number within the interval [0,1] that corresponds to the probability, or likelihood, of observing that particular sample of M if the employed value of the parameters was the "true" value. With MLE we choose an estimate of the parameters of M that makes the likelihood of having observed this particular y as large as possible (Aldrich and Nelson, 1984:50).

Maximization of the likelihood function requires solving of nonlinear first-order conditions from the likelihood function, which in turn requires the use of iterative numerical estimation methods. The following estimation includes values of the log of the likelihood function, which represents a likelihood measure of the goodness of fit in various specifications of the Turkish military regime experience.[23] The higher the likelihood the better the estimations are.

A goodness-of-fit measure analogous to R^2 is the likelihood ratio index (LRI),

$$LRI = 1 - \left(\frac{\ln L1}{\ln L0}\right)$$

where $L1$ is the value of the likelihood function for the estimated model and $L0$ is the value of the restricted likelihood function with all coefficients except the intercept set equal to zero (Greene, 1990:682).[24] I also report the root mean square error of the forecasts as a more common sense measure of the goodness of fit.[25]

An alternative measure of the success of explanation can be obtained by adopting a well-known criterion used in judging the success of time series models in predicting the turning points. Assuming in the following analysis that any prediction greater than or equal to 0.5 is a prediction of the existence of a military regime, we can obtain indicators of predictive success.

Following Theil (1961:28–31), we can divide our predictions into four categories. The first group of predictions ($P1$) is comprised of those that are correctly predicted; that is, a military regime is predicted, and a military regime actually existed for that year. The second group of predictions ($P2$) includes those that incorrectly predict a military regime; that is, no military regime existed that year, but the prediction indicated that there was one. The third group ($P3$) consists of incorrect predictions of no military regime. In other words, even though a military regime actually existed in that year, the prediction falsely predicted no military regime. The fourth group of predictions ($P4$) includes those years the prediction correctly indicated that no military regime existed.

P1 through P4 cover all possible cases of predictions. P2 and P3 represent prediction failures, whereas P1 and P4 represent successful predictions. The following indicators can be used to judge the success of predictions:

$$I1 = P1 / (P1 + P3)$$
$$I2 = (P1 + P4) / (P1 + P2 + P3 + P4)$$
$$I3 = P1 / (P1 + P2)$$

The first indicator, $I1$, represents the proportion of correctly predicted military regimes in total military regime years. $I2$ represents the proportion of correctly predicted military regime years in the sample period. $I3$ represents the proportion of correct military regime predictions in total military regime predictions.

A chi-square statistic, similar to an F statistic in ordinary least squares, will also be provided to test the joint hypothesis that all coefficients except the intercept are zero (Aldrich and Nelson, 1984:54–56).

ANALYSIS

The Social and Economic Development Explanation of Coups

To test Hypothesis 1a, I use the following explanatory variables.[26] As a direct reflection of Hypothesis 1a, both the *level (GNP) and growth rate (GROWTH) of per capita Turkish gross national product (GNP)* are used as explanatory variables.[27] The *ratio of the growth in GNP per capita to inflation rate (GRGNIN)* also provides a proxy for economic hardship that may be due to slow growth in per capita GNP and/or faster growing price level, that is, impoverishment in real terms. The *yearly percentage change in this ratio* is given by *CGRGN*. As indices of economic development, I also use the *ratio of the gross domestic product (GDP) in agricultural and industrial sectors (AGIND)* along with the *change in the ratio of GDP in agricultural and industrial sectors (CAGIN)*. A decrease in *AGIND* reflects economic modernization indicated by a higher contribution to GDP by the industrial sector relative to the contribution of the agricultural sector. A growing increase in this ratio from year to year represents the pace of economic modernization that, according to Huntington (1968), may bring about political instability.

The result of the probit estimation is as follows:

Sample range : 1950 – 1986

Absolute values of t-ratios are given in parentheses.

$$COUP_t = 2.96 - 3.55 \times 10^{-6} GNP_t - 1.04\ GRGNIN_t - 1.40\ AGIND_t$$
$$(1.68)\quad (1.40)\qquad\qquad (1.34)\qquad\qquad (2.16)$$

$$+\ 0.02\ CAGIN_t + 0.002\ CGRGN_t \qquad\qquad\qquad (4.10)$$
$$(0.59)\qquad\quad (0.49)$$

Log-likelihood = − 15.89 $\qquad\qquad$ LRI = 0.22

Root mean square error = 0.383 $\qquad\qquad$ Chi-square = 9.26

$P1 = 3$ (1980, 1981, 1983)[28] $P2 = 3$ (1974, 1978, 1979) $P3 = 6$ $P4 = 25$

$I1 = 3/9$ $I2 = 28/37$ $I3 = 3/6$

The result of the estimation in equation 4.10 shows that the coefficient of the *level* of per capita GNP is negative. That is, an increased level of economic development, as hypothesized by Huntington (1968), decreases the likelihood of military regime. The coefficient for the ratio of growth in per capita GNP to inflation rate is negative; as the real GNP per capita rises, the likelihood of military regime falls. The positive coefficient of the percentage change in real growth rate suggests that percentage changes in real growth rate of per capita GDP are the real destabilizing factor. In other words, since political instability may be a consequence of modernization, the evidence suggests a tradeoff between modernity and the modernization process. If the politico-economic system can deliver policies of modernization, which are represented in the above equation by both the level and rate of change in per capita GNP, the system is likely, according to these results, to stay stable. A positive coefficient for the change in the rate of real growth rate (*CGRGN*) represents the real tradeoff in modernization. What breeds political instability, depicted here by military regimes, are the positive changes in real growth rate in GNP per capita. Such an outcome is consistent with the arguments of Huntington (1968), Needler (1966), and Olson (1963).

Similarly, the coefficient of the ratio of GDP in agriculture to GDP in industry, representing the economic modernization as the ratio gets closer to zero, is negative and statistically significant. That is, as the relative size of the industrial sector grows in relation to the agricultural sector, the likelihood of military regime decreases. However, as the positive coefficient of the change in the ratio of GDP in agriculture to GDP in industry indicates the negative rate of change in economic modernization increases the likelihood of military regime. This result is consistent with Deutsch (1961), Huntington (1968), and Olson (1963).[29]

It should, however, be noted that statistical significance of the estimated coefficients is quite poor. Only the negative effect of the level of modernity represented by the ratio of GDP in agriculture to GDP in industry is statistically significant at a 95 percent confidence level. However, overall significance of the equation tested by the chi-square statistic indicates that the estimated equation is significant at the 90 percent significance level. Nevertheless, the LRI also indicates a low predictive success ratio. We only predict three out of nine military regime years, all in the 1980s. Our model also wrongly predicts a military regime for three years: one year after the second military regime period, and two years prior to the last one. Accordingly, despite the theoretically plausible direction of estimated relationships, it is not possible to claim that economic development and modernization hypothesis holds satisfactorily in Turkey.

Deutsch's (1961) and Finer's (1988) claims about the effects of *social mobilization* on the likelihood of military intervention are operationalized and tested with the following variables. Following Deutsch's (1961) own operationalization, I use the *size (URBAN) and the change (CHGURB) in the size of the nonagricultural population*. These indicators jointly account for the state of internal immigration in the country from villages to cities, the exposure to "modernity" with changes in nuclear family structure and the related value systems that come with urban life, and the relative importance of a modern market economy versus an agrarian subsistence economy (Jackman, 1978:1265).[30]

Moreover, *literacy rates (LITTOT)* and the *size of the university student body as the percentage of young people between fifteen and twenty-four years of age (UNVPRC)* are used as indicators of mobilization.[31] The relation of youth violence to the establishment of military regimes has been a common observation in Turkey (Weiker, 1981:16–17; Karpat, 1970:1673; Karpat, 1981:11–12: Harris, 1965:174–175; Mardin, 1978). The index I adopted tries simply to capture the capacity of the education system to accommodate the potential demand of university age youth. I expect that as the percentage of youth in the university system rises, the likelihood of military regime should decrease. The *difference between male and female literacy rates (LITDIF)* is also used as a proxy of the social mobilization of women. This variable captures the differential growth rate in male and female literacy rates. Given an originally lower literacy rate among women, if literacy among women grows faster than among men, the difference between the two sexes will diminish. A widening gender gap in education indicates a stagnant social mobilization, which has an increasing effect on the likelihood of a military regime.

The result of the social mobilization model of military regimes is as follows:

Sample range : 1950–1986

Absolute values of t-ratios are given in parentheses.

$$COUP_t = 3.41 + 0.001\ URBAN_t - 0.39\ CHGURB_t - 0.40\ LITTOT_t$$
$$(0.56)\quad (2.00)\qquad\quad (0.97)\qquad\qquad (1.55)$$

$$+\ 0.38\ LITDIF_t - 2.49\ UNVPRC_t \qquad\qquad\qquad (4.11)$$
$$(1.69)\qquad\quad (1.69)$$

Log-likelihood = − 12.22   LRI = 0.40

Root mean square error = 0.334   Chi-square = 16.6

$P1 = 4$ (1980, 1981, 1982, $P2 = 1$ (1984) $P3 = 5$ $P4 = 27$
          1983)

$I1 = 4/9$ $I2 = 31/37$ $I3 = 4/5$

Contrary to our theoretical expectations, a higher level of urban population increases the likelihood of military regime. Again surprisingly, the urbanization process represented by percentage change in urban population (*CHGURB*) has a decreasing effect on the likelihood of military regime. Thus the results imply that in Turkey the level of modernity as represented by the level of urban population increases the likelihood of military regime. However, the rate of urbanization decreases the likelihood of military regimes. Both are contrary to our expectations. Since the level variables are results of a process of accumulation and the rate of change specification is similar to a flow into or out of the process of accumulation, the following interpretation may be useful in making sense of the above result. Internal immigration releases people from their traditional surroundings. It, thus, represents a first step to modernity, providing a certain social and economic mobility that decreases the likelihood of political instability. However, as the flow of newcomers to the cities accumulates in shanty towns, and their expectations and aspirations are not satisfied, the likelihood of political instability that leads to a military regime increases.

An increasing total literacy rate decreases the likelihood of a military regime, but the increasing difference in male and female literacy rates increases the likelihood of military regime. In other words, as long as the literacy rate increases in an unbalanced fashion for males and females, the stabilizing effects on the political system of increased mobility due to better education is reduced by the positive effect of the difference in literacy rates between sexes on the likelihood of military regime.

As expected, the destabilizing effects of an unresponsive education system are represented by the negative coefficient of *UNVPRC* in equation 4.11. As the percentage of university students among the youth population between the ages of fifteen and twenty-four decreases, the likelihood of a military regime increases. Considering the fact that youth played an important role in conflict events prior to all three military regimes, this result is not surprising.[32] As the opportunity of university education is expanded to include a larger percentage of the youth, the potential tension due to lack of social mobility among the youth is released and, thus, the likelihood of military regime declines.

The overall fit of the equation is better than the economic development and modernization equation above; the log likelihood improves slightly from -15.89 to -12.22. Compared to the previous model, the likelihood ratio index accordingly improves. Lower root mean square error for the social mobilization model indicates that it performs better in explaining the Turkish military regime experience than the economic development model. The chi-square statistic is significant at 99 percent significance level, indicating that the overall equation fits the data rather well.

In terms of the predictive capacity of the model we see that the improvement is not substantial; still the model cannot predict either of the first two military regime years. All years in the last military regime are correctly predicted, but the model also wrongly predicts that the military regime ends one year later in 1984.

None of the explanatory variables except the size of the urban population has a statistically significant coefficient. Consequently, it is not possible to claim strong statistical support for the social mobilization hypothesis in Turkey.

Political Conflict Model of Coups

Analysis of the effects of political conflict in Turkey on the likelihood of military regimes suffers from lack of reliable indicators of conflict collected from Turkish sources. Fortunately, Banks's *Cross-National Time-Series Data Archive* (1979) includes several indicators of political conflict derived from daily files of the *New York Times*. Assassinations (*ASSNTN*), guerrilla warfare (*GWF*), major government crises, riots (*RIOTS*), and antigovernment demonstrations (*ANTGOV*) have been coded for the case of Turkey during the entire Turkish multiparty democracy period of post-1950 to 1986.

The estimation result of the conflict model of military regime behavior is as follows:[33]

Sample range: 1950–1986

Absolute values of t-ratios are given in parentheses.

$$COUP_t = -1.52 + 0.77 \, ASSNTN_t + 0.18 \, ASSNTN_{t-1} + 1.00 \, GWF_t + 2.08 \, GWF_{t-1}$$
$$(3.24) \quad (1.16) \qquad\quad (0.55) \qquad\qquad (0.90) \qquad\quad (2.24)$$

$$- \, 0.96 \, RIOTS_t - 0.12 \, RIOTS_{t-1} + 0.96 \, ANTGOV_t + 0.30 \, ANTGOV_{t-1} \qquad (4.12)$$
$$(1.60) \qquad\quad (0.35) \qquad\qquad (1.82) \qquad\qquad (0.90)$$

Log-likelihood = -10.79 LRI = 0.47

Root mean square error = 0.302   Chi-square = 19.46

$P1$ = 6 (1960, 1971, 1972, 1973, 1980, 1981) $P2$ = 2 (1976, 1985) $P3$ = 3 $P4$ = 26

$I1$ = 6/9 $I2$ = 32/37 $I3$ = 6/8

All conflict event types in equation 4.12, except riots, have positive coefficients, supporting the claim of many analysts of Turkish coups that polarization of the society, reflected in civil disorder, is among the main factors that trigger the establishment of military regimes (Birand, 1987; Dodd, 1990:31–34; Pevsner, 1984:68–83). The only surprising result is the negative effect of riots on the likelihood of military regime. The riots variable in Banks's *Cross-National Time-Series Data Archive* (1979) shows the greatest variance among the conflict event series and persistently appears with a negative coefficient in many different specifications of the conflict model. One possible explanation may be the bias in coding of the riot data due to reliance on the *New York Times*. As Doran, Pendley, and Phillips (1973) suggest, globally oriented sources in conflict event databases may be considerably biased against peripheral countries compared to regionally oriented databases, reducing not only the number of events but also misrepresenting the characteristics of the events of specific countries.

Another possible explanation of the negative effect of riots, independent of the question of dependability of the data, may be related to the nature of conflict involved in riots. What distinguishes riots from assassinations, guerrilla warfare, and antigovernment demonstrations is their violent nature involving a considerable number of citizens. Although antigovernment demonstrations also involve the participation of large numbers of people, they are peaceful. Assassinations are directed toward the regime in power and aim at figures of authority, and they involve relatively few people. Guerrilla warfare involves larger groups of people in armed activity aimed at overthrowing the present regime, but these groups are usually isolated organizations that are easier to locate. However, neither assassinations nor guerrilla warfare involves as many people as riots in violent acts of demonstration against a regime.

Ziegenhagen and Koutsoukis (1992:59–74) differentiate between mass and elite forms of conflict. Mass political conflict in the form of antigovernment demonstrations, riots, and general strikes differs from elite forms of conflict such as assassinations and guerrilla war by both objective and capability. The primary objective of mass conflict is to communicate with a regime in an unambiguous manner in anticipation that some change will be initiated by the regime. It may be argued that military intervention to deal with relatively isolated incidents of violence against the regime, such as assassinations and guerrilla warfare, is a more plausible strategy to "manage" conflict. The military may not perceive intervention against a sizable group of insurgent citizens engaged in open riots as a plausible response to protect the regime. Controlling relatively peaceful demonstrations or dealing with isolated guerrilla groups or small groups engaged in assassinations for the sake of protecting the state may be easier for the military than to control sizable groups of citizens. Any failure in such an attempt may very well undermine the popular support that military regimes usually enjoy in Turkey.

In other words, the negative effect of riots on the likelihood of a military regime may be an indication of the fact that the military is reluctant to deal with large groups of citizens in its effort to contain violence and protect the state. This is directly in line with Ziegenhagen and Koutsoukis's (1992:60–61) suggestion that "military intervention may be more or less effective in coping with different forms of political conflict and different forms of conflict may vary in their ability to precipitate military intervention."

Equation 4.12 represents considerably better fit compared to the two previous specifications; the likelihood ratio index rises to 0.47 compared to 0.40 and 0.22 of equations 4.11 and 4.10, respectively. The chi-square statistic is significant at a 95 percent significance level, indicating a good overall fit for the whole equation. The first military regime years for all three experiences are correctly predicted. In total, six out of nine military regime years are correctly predicted. Overall, thirty-two of the thirty-seven observation years are correctly predicted. However, it is also wrongly predicted that military regimes exist in 1976 and 1985.

As an alternative specification, instead of taking the contemporaneous and one-period-lagged values of conflict event variables. I use the sum of the contemporaneous and one-period-lagged conflict variables. The results are as follows:[34]

Sample range: 1950–1986

Absolute values of t-ratios are given in parentheses.

$$COUP_t = -1.46 + 0.45\ ASSNTN2_t + 1.73\ GWF2_t - 0.49\ RIOTS2_t + 0.57\ ANTGOV2_t$$
$$(3.36)\quad(1.77)\qquad\qquad(2.86)\qquad\qquad(2.14)\qquad\qquad(2.19)\qquad(4.13)$$

Log-likelihood $= -12.14$ LRI $= 0.41$

Root mean square error $= 0.320$ Chi-square $= 16.76$

$P1 = 5$ (1971, 1972, 1973, 1980, 1981) $P2 = 2$ (1984, 1985) $P3 = 4$ $P4 = 26$

$I1 = 5/9$ $I2 = 31/37$ $I3 = 5/7$

Unlike the previous estimates, the coefficient estimates in equation 4.13 are all significant at a 90 percent confidence level. Estimates with new specification of the independent variables suggest that the effect of violent conflict on the likelihood of military regime is cumulative. The previous year's events together with contemporaneous events affect the likelihood of military regime. The effect of riots on the likelihood of a military regime still remains negative. Nevertheless, a lower likelihood ratio index indicates that the fit is weaker. Specifically, equation 4.13 misses the coup years of the early 1960s.

To test the conflict hypothesis in a more general form, I constructed two conflict indices. The simplest one is an aggregation of conflict scores for assassinations, guerrilla warfare, riots, and antigovernment demonstrations (*INDEX1*). It assigns equal weight to all types of conflict. The other conflict index (*INDEX2*) is obtained through factor analysis of all conflict event variables in the *Cross-National Time-Series Data Archive* (Banks, 1979). The factor scores obtained represent a conflict index that combines the conflict event variables by assigning different weights to each of them.

Table 4.1
Factor Loadings: Threat to Authority versus Reaction from the Center

Variable	Factor Loadings
Riots	0.84
Government Crises	0.70
Anti-Government Demonstrations	0.68
Assassinations	0.63
Guerilla Warfare	0.61
Revolutions	0.53
Purges	-0.15
Percent of Variation Explained	39.41

Table 4.2
Conflict Model of Coups in Turkey (sample range: 1950–1986)

Dependent Variable: COUP			PROBIT Estimation
Constant	-1.62	Constant	-0.96
	(3.95)		(3.31)
$INDEX1_{t-1}$	0.07	$INDEX2_{t-1}$	0.61
	(1.12)		(1.93)
$INDEX1_{t-2}$	0.04	$INDEX2_{t-2}$	0.11
	(0.60)		(0.38)
$INDEX1_{t-3}$	0.15	$INDEX2_{t-3}$	0.59
	(2.32)		(2.12)

Log Likelihood=-13.25 LRI=0.35	:	Log Likelihood=-13.05 LRI=0.36
RMSE= 0.34 Chi-square=14.54	:	RMSE=0.32 Chi-square=14.94
P1=4 (80,81,82,83) P2=0	:	P1=4 (73,80,81,82) P2=2 (78,79)
P3=5 P4=28	:	P3=5 P4=26
I1=4/9 I2=32/37 I3=4/4	:	I1=4/9 I2=30/37 I3=4/6

RMSE: Root mean squared error
Absolute values of t-ratios are given in parentheses.

Table 4.1 reveals a clear structure of political conflict and its conse-quences in Turkey. Threat to the state authority through assassinations, guerrilla warfare, riots, revolutions, and antigovernment demonstrations, as well as their possible consequences in the form of government crises, are all positively loaded. The reaction of the central authority through purges is negatively loaded. In other words, the factor revealed by the conflict event data combines regime-challenging acts and regime responses to still the violence. A positive factor score represents, in a sense, "net conflict" that could not be controlled by the central authority, whereas a negative or zero score represents the "success," in a sense, of the central authority to control the conflict events challenging its authority.

As Table 4.2 reveals, both indices perform satisfactorily in explaining military regime behavior.[35] Three-period-lagged values of indices represent the distributed lag effects of conflict in the system. All three-period lags of both conflict indices have positive effects on the likelihood of military regimes. Simple aggregate *INDEX1* performs slightly better in explaining the behavior of military regimes. Specification with *INDEX2* wrongly predicts military regimes for 1978 and 1979. However, both equations miss the first coup and the following military regime years of 1960 and 1961. Except the two-year-lagged value of the specification with *INDEX2*, all independent variables have a statistically significant estimate at a 90 percent confidence level. Both equations are significant at a 99 percent confidence level. However, compared to equation 4.12, both specifications give poorer results.

One persistent deficiency of the predictions so far is the inability of the models to predict the coup of 1960. Only equation 4.12, using contemporaneous and one-year-lagged values of conflict variables, predicts the military regime year of 1960. However, equation 4.12 misses the military regime year of 1961.

Habituation Model

To estimate the habituation models of coups, I used a variable defined as the *total number of past years under complete military rule in any given year (TOTCOU)*. To account for a nonlinear effect of time since the last coup, the variable indicating the *square of the number of years past since the last coup (A^2)* is included.

Over the turbulent four decades of democracy in Turkey, besides the three successful coops and their regimes, there were several failed attempts to establish a military regime.[36] The existence of factions within the military willing to attempt to overthrow the existing regime, either civilian or military, may be an indication of the potential danger of a new military regime. On the other hand, the very fact that an attempt failed may indicate a tendency toward stability. Three variables are devised to capture the effects of failed coup attempts. The variable *FAIL* represents the *cumulative number of failed coup attempts at any given year* during the span of this analysis. The variable *AF* represents the number of years since the last failed coup attempt. *DUMFAI* is simply a *dummy variable taking the value of 1 for the years a failed coup attempt occurred and 0 otherwise*. The result of the complete habituation model estimation is as follows:

Sample range: 1950–1986

Absolute values of t-ratios are given in parentheses.

$$COUP_t = -1.09 + 2.81\ COUP_{t-1} + 0.04\ A^2 + 0.97\ TOTCOU_t - 0.50\ DUMFAI_{t-1}$$
$$\quad\quad (1.94)\quad (2.53)\quad\quad\quad\quad (2.01)\quad\quad (1.94)\quad\quad\quad\quad (0.30)$$
$$-0.49\ AF_t - 1.15\ FAIL_t \quad\quad\quad\quad\quad\quad\quad\quad\quad\quad\quad\quad (4.14)$$
$$(1.72)\quad\quad (1.94)$$

Log-likelihood $= -10.52$ LRI $= 0.48$

Root mean square error $= 0.437$ Chi-square $= 20$

$P1 = 2$ (1971, 1980) $P2 = 0$ $P3 = 7$ $P4 = 24$

$I1 = 2/9$ $I2 = 26/37$ $I3 = 2/2$

We see that the two most important habituation effects increasing the likelihood of military regime come from one-period-lagged value of the dependent variable and the square of the years since the last coup. A positive coefficient of A^2 suggests that as the years pass under a civilian regime, the likelihood of intervention increases at an ever increasing rate.

Moreover, the impact of failed coup attempts clearly decreases the chances of a military regime. The dummy variable *DUMFAI* for the occurrence of a failed coup attempt has a negative coefficient. Similarly, as the years pass since the previous failed coup attempt, the likelihood of military regime steadily declines. The cumulative effect of failed coup attempts, represented by *FAIL*, is also negative. Thus, a failed attempt represents a power gain for the civilian forces.

Statistical fit of the overall habituation model is significant at a 99 percent confidence level. All variables except *DUMFAI* and *AF* have significant coefficient estimates at a 90 percent confidence level. Root mean square error and likelihood ratio index indicate a better fit compared to economic development and social mobilization models. However, the habituation specification only predicts the first years of the second and third military regimes of 1971 and 1980. Accordingly, although equation 4.14 provides some support to the habituation hypothesis in Turkey, its predictive power remains limited.

COMPARING ALTERNATIVE SPECIFICATIONS

Among the alternative explanations of military regime behavior, the so-called conflict model advocated by Lieuwen (1962), Needler (1963), Eckstein (1964–1965), Gurr (1967–1968), and Pye (1962) seems to explain best the behavior of military regimes in Turkey. Our results show a clear *increase in the likelihood of military regime as violent conflict events increase*. Analysts of the Turkish military agree that an important factor in the army's decision to intervene has always been their conviction to save the country from a violent collapse (Harris, 1965:174; Karakartal, 1985:52–54; Dodd, 1990:34). Supporting this "army as the protector of the state" argument in Turkey, different specifications of the conflict model result in considerably better estimates of military regime behavior.

An interesting finding is the decreasing effect of the mass riots on the likelihood of military regimes. This suggests that the military might be reluctant to deal with mass violent conflict in the society. When it comes to violent elite forms of conflict, such as assassinations and guerrilla war, the likelihood of an intervention by the army increases. In other words, the conflict regulation function of the military is primarily geared toward elite forms of conflict rather than the mass forms of conflict. However, relatively mild mass conflict also is found to have a positive effect on the likelihood of a military regime. Only the relatively more violent forms of mass conflict seem to deter military rule.[37]

Nevertheless, there is also some evidence to support alternative views of the inherent dynamics of military regimes. Especially in the aftermath of the 1980 intervention, precoup Prime Minister Süleyman Demirel, and other politicians, claimed that "the military deliberately failed to use its power to stabilize the situation in order to discredit the civilian government and bring the populace to such a point of desperation that the intervention would be welcomed and the orders of the military regime followed without dissent" (Karpat, 1988:149). Although our procedures cannot test this hypothesis, the habituation model performs well in the case of Turkish military regimes. Our findings indicate a growing likelihood of military regimes simply due to the fact that some time has elapsed since the last military regime. Moreover, the effect of the time elapsed since the last coup increases nonlinearly. The cumulative effect of past years under military regime is also found to increase the likelihood of new military regimes.[38]

The performance of the politico-economic development and social mobilization models is somewhat weaker in explaining the behavior of Turkish military regimes than that of the habituation and conflict models. However, basic tenets of the arguments represented in Hypothesis 1a hold for the Turkish case. Both the level of economic development, represented by the level of per capita GNP, and the level of real growth rate of per capita GNP decrease the likelihood of military regimes, whereas changes in the growth rate of real per capita GNP increase the likelihood of a military regime. The effect of the level of modernity on the economy, represented by the ratio of agricultural and industrial GDP, is negative, but the rate of change in this modernity index has a positive effect on the likelihood of military regime.

Contrary to our theoretical expectations, the level of urban population increases, whereas the urbanization rate decreases the likelihood of military regimes. However, I see this result as a reflection of the problems of modernization that accumulate in the formation of peripheral shanty towns around the cities. The rate of urbanization accordingly represents the modernization process that induces stability, but the accumulation of urban population induces instability. The effect of increasing literacy is found to decrease the likelihood of military regimes, whereas differential growth of literacy rates between men and women raises the likelihood of military regimes. The difficulty of higher education representing the tendency of destabilizing activism of the university youth is also found to increase the likelihood of military regimes.

Joint Additive Models

The above models indicate that all three theoretical frameworks—politico-economic development and social mobilization, conflict, and habituation models—have additive effects on the propensity of military regimes in Turkey. However, these specifications do not allow alternative explanatory variables to jointly account for the military regime behavior within the same equation.

Table 4.3 extends the basic conflict model to account jointly for additive social mobilization and habituation effects. Indicators of the goodness of fit improve substantially. The likelihood ratio index reaches 0.57 and 0.6 for equations I and II respectively. Moreover, expected signs of the variables are obtained; except for riots, all conflict event variables have positive signs. Habituation effects all increase the likelihood of a military regime in both equations I and II. The improvement of the estimates when both conflict and habituation effects are included in equation I in Table 4.3 may also be seen as supporting the arguments about the protective attitude of the military (Harris, 1965:174; Karakartal, 1985:52–54; Dodd, 1990:34). The level of urbanization switches its sign from the previous specification and obtains the originally expected negative sign. The rate of urbanization has an increasing effect on the propensity of military regime. Once a larger number of theoretically important factors is included in our specification, not only does the fit improve, but we also obtain theoretically more consistent results.[39] However, the weakness of these results is that they do not yield statistically significant results for almost any of the coefficients. Only a period-lagged dependent variable is significant at a 90 percent confidence level in equation I. However, as the chi-square statistic indicates, the overall fit of both equations is statistically significant.

Nevertheless, the predictive power of the joint additive specification is quite impressive. Figure 4.1 shows the estimated behavior of Turkish military regimes according to equation II in Table 4.3. The timing of the military regimes is estimated with a considerable degree of success. In the first two military coups, the estimated likelihood of military regime suddenly jumps from nearly zero to a high level exactly at the years when actual coups occur. As the civilian regimes take over the executive office, the predicted values of the likelihood of military regime sharply fall. It is also noticeable that our predicted likelihood values are positive during the years when the failed coup attempts occur.

The last coup occurs after a continuously rising likelihood of military regime. By 1979 it reaches about the same likelihood at which the first coup occurs in 1960. Our prediction of the 1980 coup is perfect. This, in

Table 4.3
Joint Additive Models of Military Regime Behavior

	I	II
Constant	-3.02	-2.95
	(2.24)	(1.17)
Assassinations	0.32	0.53
	(0.76)	(1.06)
Guerrilla Warfare	1.36	1.21
	(1.57)	(1.33)
Riots	-0.40	-0.57
	(1.00)	(1.21)
Anti-government Demonstrations	0.66	0.85
	(1.59)	(1.57)
Urban Population		-8.39×10^{-5}
		(0.83)
Percentage Change in Urban Population		0.10
		(0.41)
$COUP_{t-1}$	2.46	3.32
	(1.88)	(1.62)
A^2	0.01	0.03
	(0.43)	(0.78)
(Dummy for Failed Coup Attempts)$_{t-1}$	0.32	0.09
	(0.26)	(0.06)
Log Likelihood	-8.63	-8.12
LRI	0.57	0.60
Root Mean Square Error	0.334	0.309
Chi-square	23.78	24.8

	I	II
P1	6 (61,71,72,73,80,81)	6 (61,71,72,73,80,81)
P2	3 (77,78,79)	2 (78,79)
P3	3	3
P4	25	26
I1	6/9	6/9
I2	31/37	32/37
I3	6/9	6/8

Conflict variables are the sum of contemporaneous and one period lagged observations.

Figure 4.1
Social Mobilization, Conflict, and Habituation Model of Military Regimes in Turkey, Joint Additive Specification

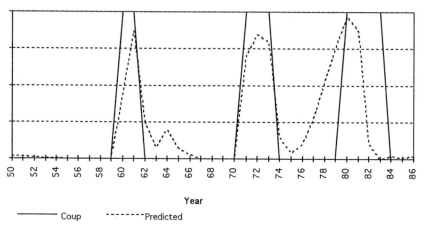

                                            Year

―――――――― Coup   --------Predicted

a sense, shows the inevitable developments that lead to the third military regime. Birand (1987:39) and many other analysts agree that the military had planned the intervention for quite some time. However, the model wrongly predicts an early end of the military regime, showing a clear tendency toward a civilian regime as early as 1981–1982, whereas the actual transfer occurs in 1984 after the election of November 1983.

CONCLUSION

My analysis indicates that the three major theoretical perspectives on the occurrence of military regimes are quite powerful in explaining the behavior of Turkish military regimes during the multiparty democracy period of 1950–1986. The likelihood of a military regime in Turkey is primarily affected by political conflict factors and the so-called habituation factor. As political conflict events, such as antigovernment demonstrations, assassinations, and guerrilla warfare, increase, the likelihood of a military regime rises. However, mass political conflict is persistently found to decrease the likelihood of a military regime. This suggests that the military is reluctant to intervene against mass political conflict.

The habituation factor represents the inner mechanisms, aspirations, and, to some degree, the protective attitude of the military in the case of perceived danger to the state. Similar to Londregan and Poole's (1990) and O'Kane's (1983:34) conclusion, I find that previous military regimes increase the likelihood of future military regimes.

Economic development and social mobilization explanations are comparatively weaker. Nevertheless, there is some evidence that modernity is stabilizing although the process of modernization is destabilizing, leading to military regimes.

These three factors jointly constitute the "coup trap" that locks the Turkish democracy into a vicious circle of periodic military regimes. Modernization efforts within a growing economy breed political instability that periodically explodes into increasingly uncontrollable violence, which in turn triggers the move of the military to protect the state. However, this very move by the military has so far not been effective in restoring a harmonious order compatible with the modernization dynamics of the country. Every new military regime brings with it the seeds of new instability and contributes to the inability of civilian regimes to develop mechanisms to cope with recurrent crises of modernization.

Probit specification of military regime behavior performs satisfactorily in predicting the behavior of military regime occurrence and the transition to civilian regimes. These results imply that for countries of comparably frequent military regime experience, similar time series models can be formed to analyze the underlying causes of military regimes.

NOTES

1. Cross-sectional analyses include Jackman (1976; 1978); O'Kane (1981; 1983; 1987); McGowan and Johnson (1984); and Johnson, Slater, and McGowan (1984). Pooled cross-sectional analyses of coup experiences include Zuk and Thompson (1982), and Londregan and Poole (1990).

2. See Zolberg (1968a) and Decalo (1976) on the random nature of coups.

3. Literature on Turkish military regimes is quite extensive. The following is a selection of analyses on the causes of Turkish military regimes: Birand (1987), Brown (1987; 1988), Dodd (1990), Fidel (1970–1971), Harris (1965), Heper and Evin (1988), Karakartal (1985), Karpat (1970; 1981), Pevsner (1984), Sunar and Sayari (1986), Vaner (1987), and Weiker (1980).

4. Although the hypotheses discussed in this section are asserted mostly within the context of a specific geographic area, such as Latin America or Africa, for the purposes of this study I treat them as purely theoretical arguments. Putnam's (1967) introductory survey is the starting point of this theoretical background. An outdated, yet still useful, introduction to the literature on coups d'état in developing countries is Lissak (1964). Also refer to Finer (1982), Janowitz (1964), Lutwak (1979), and O'Kane (1987) on military regimes and political development.

5. Disappearance of social consensus and increasing likelihood of a military regime may be a violent process. In this sense Germani and Silvert (1967) relate to political conflict arguments discussed later.

6. Putnam (1967:92–97) finds supporting evidence for this assertion from the context of Latin American countries.

7. Karpat (1970:1655–1656) states:

The rise of the new elites, on the basis of economic power and through party channels, from the agrarian, entrepreneurial, and professional groups, changed not only the hierarchical order of the elites, but also the system of political values. . . . [T]he rise of civilian elite groups and their clash with the statist-bureaucratic elites, including the military, was a crucial landmark in the history of Turkey, not only in precipitating the Revolution of 1960, but also bringing about a new political structure.

8. Perhaps nothing reflects the deterioration of military power within the administration better than Prime Minister Adnan Menderes's "uncourteous criticism" of the military for its failure to control the anti-Greek demonstrations on September 1955 in Istanbul. Menderes was widely quoted as asserting that he would run the military with reserve officers if necessary. See Karpat (1970:1662) and Harris (1965: 170).

9. Karpat (1970:1662–1663) notes that "the cost of living in 1960 was about eleven times what it had been in 1950–53, while salaries had barely doubled, causing hardship for those in the military and assigning to them, as individuals, the responsibility for all the shortcomings of Turkey. . . . The social standing of the military deteriorated, while the values cherished in the past disintegrated under the assault of the materialism supposedly promoted by the new power groups." Harris (1965:170) also notes that the ruling Democratic Party's slogan of "a millionaire in every quarter" "outraged the officer corps who were struggling to make ends meet on salaries vulnerable to the galloping inflation of the 1950's." Fidel (1970–1971:23) also points to economic hardship as the triggering factor of the 1960 coup.

10. The economic conditions of military officers were carefully planned during the post-1960 coup years primarily through the establishment of the Army Mutual Assistance Association, which acted as a social security organization aimed to improve the material conditions of the officer corps through compulsory savings levied at the source (Vaner, 1987:251).

11. See Harris (1985:84–88) and especially Keyder (1987:303–305) on the economic crisis of the late 1970s.

12. On the theoretical linkage between political development and coups, Finer (1988:18) argues that where public attachment to civilian institutions is strong, likelihood of military intervention in politics is weak. Similarly, the propensity for military intervention in politics is expected to decrease with increasing popular attention to and participation in politics (Johnson, 1962:127). The likelihood of military intervention decreases with increasing strength and effectiveness of political parties, of political interest groups, and of civilian governmental institutions (Finer, 1988:18, 99–126; Alexander, 1958:157). Clearly, there are severe measurement problems associated with operationalizing the concepts such as "effectiveness of political parties," "attachment to civilian institutions," or "alienation from democratic institutions." Some also claim that expression of different interests in a multiparty system breeds instability in the political system; that is, multiparty democracy increases as democratic participation increases (Huntington, 1968:425–426; Weiner and La Palombara, 1966:416). In contrast, Deutsch (1961) and Hayward (1973) claim that multiparty systems stabilize the political system by enlarging the power base in the society. Accordingly we have:

"Strong" civilian institutions—that is, multiparty democracy and high participation—reduce the likelihood of military regime.

The authors on Turkish military regimes commonly agree that polarization of the political system contributed significantly to the collapse of the democratic regimes. Refer to Harris (1965), Karpat (1970), Ozbudun (1981), Pevsner (1984), Eroglu (1987), Sunar and Sayari (1986), and Dodd (1990:34–49) on the polarization of politics during the multiparty democracy period.

This hypothesis, however, is not subject to test in this chapter. The main difficulty in a time series analysis of military regimes addressing political development issues is that by definition the independent variables such as political participation, Rae's (1968) fractionalization index, or any other that depends on democratic processes cease to make any sense as the military intervention occurs and as long as the military regime continues to exist. Accordingly, any such series representing political development behaves as if it is a dummy variable for the military regime years and, thus, provides a false good fit. Such a problem, however, does not exist in a cross-sectional analysis of coups.

13. O'Kane (1983:34) as well as Londregan and Poole's (1990:161–163) pooled cross-section analyses show that there is support for various versions of habituation hypothesis. Londregan and Poole's effort is primarily concentrated in operationalization of the habituation concept within an empirically testable form. They find that "the probability of a coup is increased markedly when previous governments have been overthrown" (Londregan and Poole, 1990:178).

14. Harris (1965), Fidel (1971), Karpat (1970), and Vaner (1987) provide a survey of motives and inner dynamics of various conspiratorial groups before the coups and during the military regimes. Also refer to Rustow (1959) and Karakartal (1985) for a survey of the historical structure of the military that the new republic inherited from the Ottoman Empire and on the shaping of the predisposition of the military for coups during the premultiparty democracy period.

15. See especially Birand (1987) and Karpat (1988:150–151) on the efforts to keep the control within the chain of command during the 1980 coup. Also refer to Fidel (1971) and Vaner (1987) for detailed analyses of the inner structure of the command groups during three military regimes.

16. The qualification that conflicts during the transition to modernity are associated with higher likelihood of military regime is important. It asserts that the modernization process coupled with conflict elements is the driving force behind the hypothesis. Clearly, conflict of various forms in a developed and modern context may be considerably less dangerous in inflicting military rule.

17. Pevsner (1984:45–50), Samim (1987), and Agaogullari (1987) provide a survey of violence on the right and on the left during the early 1970s.

18. Refer to Birand (1987:59–61) and Pevsner (1984:73–75) on Kahramanmaras incidents.

19. A slight modification of the direct effect model is made by incorporating a feedback from the past coup experience to the future likelihood of military regime, which in this case is specifically the habituation hypothesis.

20. Coup participants typically establish their own government under the precept of making way for a civilian democratic system. That has been the common promise in all Turkish military interventions. However, during the process of preparing the country for a civil rule, the military government may last several years. Direct and indirect control of the executive office by the military makes it difficult to easily label a regime as a military regime. See Finer (1982) and O'Kane (1987:chapter

2) for good surveys of the issues involved in the definitions of coup d'état and military regime. In the case of Turkey, even the occurrence of the second coup could be questionable. The military in 1971 did not directly assume power but rather orchestrated the establishment of a nonpartisan cabinet to impose martial law, which carried out a tight oppression of extremist movements, censoring of the media, and banning the labor movement, along with extensive arrests. However, there seems to be a consensus on the fact that the act of intervention through a communiqué and the regime that followed during the early 1970s were incidents of a coup and military regime (Pevsner, 1984; Karpat, 1981; Karpat, 1988; Harris, 1985:161–165).

21. The following discussion of the probit model is after Londregan and Poole (1990), Aldrich and Nelson (1984), and Pindyck and Rubinfeld (1991:248–257).

22. Usual interpretations and tests of significance of the estimated coefficients apply to probit estimation. For differences and details refer to Pindyck and Rubinfeld (1991), Aldrich and Nelson (1984), and Cramer (1991).

23. All logarithms in the text are natural logarithms.

24. Note here that LRI takes values between 0 and 1, but the values in this interval have no natural interpretation as that of R^2 in ordinary least squares. However, LRI increases as the fit improves (Greene, 1990:682).

25. Root mean square error is the square root of the average of the squared values of the forecast error (Kennedy, 1989:206). On the problems of using pseudo R^2 values in maximum likelihood estimation, see Pindyck and Rubinfeld (1991:268–269) and Aldrich and Nelson (1984:55–59).

26. Refer to Appendix 4.1 for detailed description of the variables and sources of data.

27. Although it is by now commonly agreed that GNP is not an adequate measure of economic development, for our purposes per capita GNP represents a good approximate index of development. Using income distribution measures is desirable, too, but such measures over the entire period are not available. See Meier (1984:5–33) for a discussion of misconceptions and measurement problems in assessing and comparing economic development.

28. The years of prediction under P1 and P2 categories are provided in parentheses.

29. I also estimated the same equation with lagged independent variables and found similar results with slightly worsened fit.

30. Karpat (1981:18) and many others see the source of socioeconomic and cultural change in Turkey as migration from villages to rural areas.

31. See Harris (1985:24) and Weiker (1981:151–163) on education and social mobility in Turkey.

32. See Weiker (1981:151–163) for a short survey of the problems in Turkish education. Also refer to Weiker (1963:16–17), Karpat (1965:1673; 1981:11–12), Harris (1965:174–175), and Mardin (1978) on student activities that played an important role in triggering the military interventions.

33. In the specification below, both contemporaneous and one-period-lagged values of conflict variables are used due to the fact that contemporaneous variables may show a decline in conflict events due basically to the control of the military during part of that particular year. One-period-lagged values capture the effect of events under civilian regimes on the likelihood of military regime.

34. The new specification of the independent variables can be specified in the following general form: $X2 = X_t + X_{t-1}$.

35. The correlation between the two indices is 0.92.

36. The following events are coded as failed coup attempts: The 1957 disclosure of a secret organization within the army, arrest of nine officers, and imprisonment of one major (Brown, 1988:143); in February 1962 and May 1963, Colonel Talat Aydemir's failed coup attempts that finally resulted in his execution (Brown, 1988:143; Lutwak, 1979:206; Karpat, 1970:1680; Karakartal, 1985:50); the May 1970 arrest of two colonels, charged with conspiring for a coup (Brown, 1988:113); and the March 1975 army faction's coup attempt (Lutwak, 1979:206).

37. See Ziegenhagen and Koutsoukis (1992) for a discussion of the different effects of various forms of conflict.

38. It is commonly argued that Turkish military regimes do not seem to be willing to establish a permanent military rule (Dodd, 1990:27; Karpat, 1988:149). Although this is an argument primarily about the intent of the military that we cannot empirically determine, our finding that only one-period-lagged value of the dependent variable is significant in explaining the military regime behavior may be considered as suggestive of this argument.

39. I also estimated interactive effects of conflict and social mobilization, as well as conflict and economic development models. Similar to Jackman (1978), multiplicative explanatory variables are constructed for economic (E) and conflict (C) variables. The interactive explanatory variables take the form of $E \times C$. Estimation results are substantially poorer, and the theoretical consistency of the results disappears.

APPENDIX 4.1

Dependent Variable:

COUP: Dichotomous variable taking the value of 1 at the year when there is a complete control of the government by the military for at least six months

Independent Variables:

GNP: Per capita gross national product

GROWTH = [GNP − GNP (−1)]/GNP (−1); percentage change in per capita GNP

INF: Inflation rate

GRGNIN = GROWTH/INF

GDPAGR: Gross domestic product in agriculture

GDPIND: Gross domestic product in industry

AGIND = GDPAGR/GDPIND

CAGIN: Yearly percentage change in AGIND

CGRGN: Yearly percentage change in GRGNIN

TOTLIT: Aggregate literacy rate

LITDIF: Male literacy rate − female literacy rate

URBAN: Size of the urban population

CHGURB: Percentage change in the urban population

UNIPOP: Size of the university student population

YNGPOP: Size of the population between ages fifteen and twenty-four

UNVPRC = UNIPOP/YNGPOP: university students as a percentage of population of people between fifteen and twenty-four years old.

ASSNTN: Assassinations; "Any politically motivated murder or attempted murder of a high government official or politician" (Banks, 1979:14)

GWF: Guerrilla warfare; "Any armed activity, sabotage, or bombings carried on by independent bands of citizens or irregular forces and aimed at the overthrow of the present regime" (Banks, 1979:14)

RIOTS: Riots; "Any violent demonstration or clash of more than 100 citizens involving the use of physical force" (Banks, 1979:14)

ANTGOV: Antigovernment demonstrations; "Any peaceful public gathering of at least 100 people for the primary purpose of displaying or voicing their opposition to government policies or authority, excluding demonstrations of a distinctly anti-foreign nature" (Banks, 1979:14)

PURGES: "Any systematic elimination by jailing or execution of political opposition within the ranks of the regime or the opposition." (Banks, 1979:14)

DUMFAI: Dummy variable for failed coup attempts; 1 for the year if a failed attempt exists, 0 otherwise.

TOTCOU: Countervariable showing the total number of coups in the past during any given year.

A: Countervariable showing the number of years past since the last coup.

Sources: All conflict event data are from *Cross-National Time-Series Data Archive* (Banks, 1979). Size of the population between the ages of fifteen and twenty-four is from United Nations, *World Population Prospects* (1990). Data about military regime experience are coded according to the definitions above, and the remaining data are from various issues of the *Statistical Yearbook of Turkey* (State Institute of Statistics, 1950–1990).

5

POLITICAL CONFLICT AND POLITICAL DEVELOPMENT IN GREECE: 1946–1986

Kleomenis S. Koutsoukis

The main concerns of this chapter are: (1) to review theories of political conflict and development as they pertain to Greece in the postwar era; (2) to provide a short, descriptive account of issues that have divided Greek society; and (3) to explore relationships among indicators of political development, political conflict, and economic development for Greece during the period of 1919–1981. Greece has been a conflict society due to its delayed process of modernization and the slow accommodation of change through protracted conflict.

THEORETICAL CONSIDERATIONS

Political Conflict and Political Development

Erikson (1962) argues that human nature can best be studied in a state of conflict. If this proposition is correct, then the state of conflict is particularly appropriate in the study of the nature and evolution of a society. All societies experience diverse opinions, discords, and dissensions, which at times may take the form of open confrontation. Conflict as a social phenomenon constitutes the epicenter and also the instrument for interpreting history and the overall evolution of society.

Societies, in their course of development and modernization, tend to experience more or less intense social, class, and political conflicts. Most developmental theorists attribute these conflicts to the struggle for modernization basically marked by a clash between tradition and modernity, old and new values (Huntington, 1968; Wiener and Huntington, 1987; Apter, 1987). One way or another, societies attempt to manage such conflicts in a manner to preserve social order and maintain social functions (Ziegenhagen, 1986; Pirages, 1976). Society moves from a state of conflict to a state of accommodation, or, more accurately, it oscillates between conflict and accommodation as conflicts are continuously generated and resolved.

Conflicts persist for varying time periods. Accommodation may require the passing of a generation, as is particularly the case of conflict over social and political transformation in the course of modernization (Black, 1966). Even if overt conflicts end through the defeat of one party by the other through military means, the symbols of conflict persist and become incorporated into the political process (Lasswell and Kaplan, 1950; Duncan, 1968; Nieburg, 1969).

Viewing a society from this conflict-accommodation continuum, one can judge whether it is more or less integrated depending on whether a society approaches accommodation for all or part of its conflictual issues and if such issues occupy more or less time in its evolution. Furthermore conflict and accommodation can take place at either the mass or the elite level or both. If conflict is intense at the elite level, society and politics are highly unstable until elite accommodation is achieved. This phase is often followed by mass conflict directed against the elite, followed by repression and the onset of authoritarian regimes. The extension of accommodation beyond the elite to the masses becomes possible as society becomes pluralistic and the political system becomes democratic in nature. (See Figure 5.1.) As stability and democracy are achieved as a result of accommodation both at the elite and mass level, the society can advance toward the goal of development and, eventually, its overall transformation. Accommodation does not mean by itself development, but constitutes a necessary precondition whereby development as a social goal can be facilitated. One must observe conflict behavior for the purpose of understanding the process of political development and that of the development of the society as well. These phenomena accompany the process over time regardless of whether conflict occurs at the elite or the mass level.

Most of the empirically based studies of political development include the thesis that political conflict is associated with political development, and the greater the level of political development, the greater the ability of a government to avoid political conflict, particularly that which could assume a violent and disastrous form (Seidman, 1978). This proposition is based on the notion that the more developed countries and the more democratic governments are better able to cope with the demands made of their political systems. They are capable of directing these demands to provide satisfaction or accommodation through the process of interest aggregation and articulation by political institutions such as political parties and representative bodies. So long as demands are satisfied or accommodated, it is not necessary or wise to employ political violence to achieve

Figure 5.1
Political Conflict and Accommodation

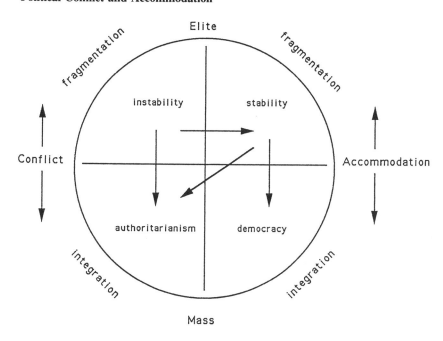

these goals. Efforts to focus attention on policy issues and to generate support through the use of nonviolent mass demonstrations, however, are likely to persist.

Flanigan and Fogelman (1970), among others, examine the relationship between political development and political violence as well as the influence of economic development. While economic development does not seem to play an important role in eliminating political violence, countries that achieve a high level of political development tend to experience low levels of political violence. Cutright (1963) also finds a negative relationship between political development and internal political strife, particularly manifestations of political violence such as deaths, armed attacks, and assassinations. But he finds no relationship between political development and mass protest such as general strikes and demonstrations. However, Hibbs (1973) concludes that no causal link exists between political development and any indicator of political violence. Although the preponderance of results support linkages between political development and at least some forms of political conflict, the exact nature of this association is not clear.

Economic Development, Political Development, and Political Conflict

From a completely different perspective, political conflict and political development are viewed by dependency theorists as a function of the structure of the world economic system (see, for example, Wallerstein, 1976; Portes, 1976; Geller, 1982; Duvall et al., 1981). According to this outlook, nations at the periphery of the system experience high levels of political conflict due to the overall dependent character of their societies. Their economies develop in response to demands put forward by the capitalist metropolis. Domestic needs for local economic development are ignored or at least marginalized, producing capital accumulation and class differentiation. Social inequality then becomes a source of political conflict. Concurrently political development is retarded in order to prevent mass participation in representative bodies, which could threaten the economic interests of core nations. Therefore, governments of the nations at the periphery tend to be authoritarian, antidemocratic, and highly centralized in the form of civilian or military dictatorships.

External trade is a major component of the mechanism that serves the interests of the core nations. Commodities exported by peripheral states tend to be products of mining and agriculture, and imports tend to be finished products manufactured by the core states. Additionally, a single core nation often dominates as the trading partner of particular nations at the periphery. In both instances, trade practices favor the interests of the core states at the expense of the periphery and tend to perpetuate economic dependence, low levels of political development, and high levels of political conflict.[1]

Social Mobilization, Political Conflict, and Political Development

All of the explanations offered above are based on some notion of developmental imbalance that is the source of the problems experienced by less developed nations. Social mobilization also shares this attribute to some extent. The concept is based on the observation that developing nations often share particular attributes, among them rapid advances in urbanization, communication, and education, often accompanied by political conflict (Deutsch, 1961; Coleman, 1968; Feierabend, Feierabend, and Nesvold, 1969). Major changes in the economic and social structure of society are not balanced by the growth of governments' abilities to accommodate vastly increased demands for restructuring both society and the economy. For example, rapid urbanization occurs without provisions for adequate transportation, water, and waste disposal systems. Persons educated for positions in administration and the physical sciences have no prospects for employment.

Most governments respond unsuccessfully to performance demands without attempting to restructure themselves or change their basis for support in society. The failure of conciliatory efforts often gives way to repressive measures and periods of severe and protracted conflict.

DEVELOPMENT AND CONFLICT IN THE GREEK POLITICAL SYSTEM

Greece can be considered a transitional society in that it partakes of two worlds: a developed and an undeveloped one. The theory outlined above is useful for considering salient issues in Greek society but must be qualified to accommodate developmental aspects peculiar to Greece.

Modern Greece began its transformation through a nationalist revolution in the beginning of the nineteenth century, a pattern often followed by various nationalist revolutions in Third World nations later, mostly in the second half of the twentieth century. Yet, the overthrow of a colonial power; the transfer of foreign political, administrative, and legal institutions to the newly emerging society; and the renewed foreign intrusion in the form of economic dependence are shared with these other nations. Although basic elements are similar, the political and economic world context in which they occur is not. This difference has major implications for the transformation of Greece.[2]

Greece, since the end of World War I, has suffered from various intense conflicts that have contributed to severe social and political divisions. A graphic representation of issues and participants is shown in Figure 5.2. These events took different forms until the last national crisis of 1974, which accommodated previous change and resolved accumulated issues. These issues included: (1) legitimacy, resolved by a referendum in favor of abolishing the monarchy; (2) political participation, resolved by the legalization of the Communist Party and the end of anticommunist ideology; (3) language, settled by recognition of the popular idiom *demotiki*, often associated with leftist political orientations; and (4) education, resolved by implementing technical curricula in all levels of schooling, although the discussion about the way classics ought to be taught continues. All these issues were accompanied by concurrent changes in social rights and democratic political procedures eventually guaranteed by the new constitution. In a more general sense, political development proceeded from a police state to a state of law to a version of the welfare state.[3]

Accommodation was accompanied by periods of intense political conflict in Greece, dominated by continuous strife among military and civilian leaders from the War of Independence in 1821 until the restoration of democracy in 1974 (Koutsoukis, 1978; 1982). Unstable governments, fre-

Figure 5.2
Elites and Conflict in Greek Society, 1821–1974

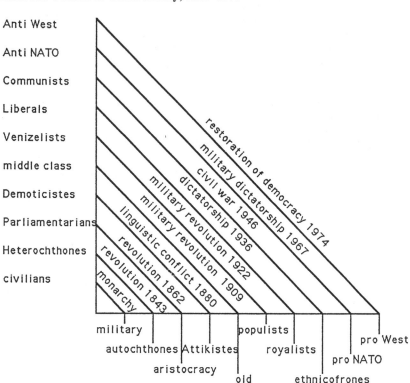

quent cabinet changes and government crises, and frequent military inter-vention were accompanied by political violence and civil war.[4]

PROCEDURES

The operationalization of complex concepts always presents epistemo-logical, conceptual, and methodological challenges. In this analysis, two indices of political development are used in order to capture two basic dimensions: the effectiveness of political institutions and the degree to which they can be considered democratic. The effectiveness aspect is mea-sured by the degree to which institutional differentiation has occurred (e.g., the existence of a substantially autonomous legislative body with the au-thority to levy taxes, disburse funds, and override executive vetoes of legislation). The democratic aspect of development is measured by the degree to which members of political institutions are selected by participation in the electoral process (e.g., legislative and executive bodies are selected by direct or indirect popular elections rather than by heredity or other ascriptive procedures). Both measures are adapted from Banks's *Cross-National Time-Series Data Archive* (1979).

Political conflict is measured by eight event types, including general strikes, riots, guerrilla war, coups, and revolution to represent mass and elite action against a regime, but also cabinet changes, governmental crises, and constitutional changes to represent government instability.

Social mobilization is represented by indicators regarding communications: newspaper and radio, urbanization, and education at the elementary and university level. Finally, dependency is represented by a measure of world trade.

Data are collected for a period of fifty-seven years from 1919 to 1981 but excluding 1940–1945 for which no reliable information exists. Correlation analysis is chosen as an appropriate means to identify linkages but not to assign causal relationships in this exploratory effort.

RESULTS

A correlation matrix of indicators can be found in Table 5.1.

Political development and political conflict are linked in much of the literature. Political conflict can advance development by promoting the growth of democratic institutions, but it also can contribute to the demise of a democratic regime as a result of coups. As one can expect, guerrilla war and coups are negatively associated with both forms of political development in Greece. However, some mass forms of conflict such as antigovernment demonstrations and riots are associated with government instability in the form of cabinet changes, government crises, and coups but not with democratization or effectiveness. Other forms of mass conflict, such as general strikes, are closely and positively associated with advances in political development. For Greece, highly organized forms of mass conflict such as general strikes may be a form of political expression that stimulates political and administrative institutions functioning in the absence of political parties. Such results represent a departure from previous studies that fail to find these specific linkages (Cutright, 1963; Hibbs, 1973) but are consistent with studies that identify such behavior as a symptom of nation building (Cohen, Brown, and Organski, 1981).

Social mobilization hypotheses are at least as strongly supported by the results, although some exceptions also appear. Both forms of political development are strongly and positively associated with some measures of communication but not with others. For example, newspaper circulation is highly correlated with democratization and effectiveness, but radios and book production are not. Similarly, the extension of both elementary and university education is associated with political development. Although

Table 5.1

Correlation Matrix of Political Development, Political Conflict, Social Mobilization, and Dependency Indicators

Indicator	1	2	3	4	5	6	7	8	9	10	11	12	13	14	15	16	17
1. PDev 1	1.0																
2. PDev 2	.9	1.0															
3. Const	-.3	-.4	1.0														
4. Cabinet	-.07	-.08	.4	1.0													
5. Crises	.05	.1	.1	.7	1.0												
6. G War	-.4	-.4	-.1	-.2	-.2	1.0											
7. Strikes	.2	.2	.3	.01	.01	.4	1.0										
8. Coups	-.4	-.4	.5	.5	.1	-.05	-.06	1.0									
9. Riots	.04	.2	.07	.01	.8	-.1	.1	.3	1.0								
10. Revol	-.4	-.3	.6	.3	.1	-.1	-.1	.8	.1	1.0							
11. Radio	.05	-.04	.2	.1	-.1	-.1	.6	-.09	.2	.2	1.0						
12. News	.7	.8	-.1	-.07	.2	-.3	.07	-.1	-.08	-.1	-.2	1.0					
13. Book	.2	.2	-.06	-.2	-.3	-.07	.6	-.2	-.1	.4	.8	-.1	1.0				
14. U edu	.5	.4	.4	.06	-.01	.2	-.4	.1	.3	.3	.9	-.6	.5	1.0			
15. E edu	.4	.3	.3	.01	.01	.09	-.4	-.01	.08	.2	.8	-.5	.6	.9	1.0		
16. Urban	-.4	-.5	.4	.01	-.09	.2	.4	.03	.01	.3	.8	-.6	.6	.9	.9	1.0	
17. Trade	-.5	-.6	.7	.2	.2	.2	-.01	.1	.1	.3	.5	-.4	.3	.8	.7	.7	1.0

education is associated with both forms of political development, it is related differently to each. University-level education is most closely associated with advances in measures of political effectiveness rather than democracy, possibly indicating the need for specialized skills in the advance of political institutions capable of meaningful responses to political demands, particularly in the administration of policy. By contrast, increases in elementary education are more closely associated with democratic political development, possibly reflecting the advance of meaningful participation with an electorate capable of informing itself of the full latitude of participation as well as the nature of the issues that require policy responses.

The relationships of dependency indicators to political development are the most perplexing. One would expect that advances in world trade position would represent movement from the periphery to the semiperiphery and correspondingly greater political development. Such is not the case, as world trade position is correlated negatively with both democratization and effectiveness. One possible interpretation is that increases in trade position within the confines of the periphery represent greater integration within the world economy and correspondingly less ability to develop politically. Given this interpretation, advances in world trade position confined to a particular range of dependency could be expected to be negatively related to political development.

CONCLUSIONS

For Greece, some results are in conformity with the theory and findings reported above, but some nonconforming patterns also are apparent. Most studies of political development, political conflict, and policy have not only been done for each of these concepts separately but also have included aggregates of states and have been for different time periods. One would expect findings for a single political system to vary somewhat from those secured by drawing on the experience of many. Additionally, findings may differ because the states included in the analysis are in different stages of development. The prominence of elite conflict in Greece, high levels of instability, and the significance of social mobilization measures may be characteristic of early to middle-range stages of development. One would expect to see the emergence of other salient aspects of development and changes of relationships as Greece enters a new stage.

NOTES

1. Social resources are also disproportionately distributed to sectors of society for the purpose of protecting the capital investments of the core states. Armed forces most often perform this function, as they have in Latin America. See, for example, Duvall et al. (1981), Portes (1976), and Geller (1982).

2. It is not my intention to attempt the analysis of the evolution of modern Greek society. I am limiting myself to a schematic reference of particular points of interest that should shed some light on the analysis to follow.

3. Such crises can be considered as a way of reaffirming national goals in a changing international environment. Regimes stay in power until a crisis becomes intense and management requires new leadership. These crises correspond to changes in development although the process of development is not necessarily linear.

4. For a conflict profile of Greece from 1945 to 1986, see Ziegenhagen and Koutsoukis (1992).

PART TWO

GENERAL PROCESS MODELS OF POLITICAL CONFLICT AND POLITICAL DEVELOPMENT

6

POLITICAL CONFLICT, REGULATION, AND POLITICAL DEVELOPMENT

Han-Jyun Hou

To maintain order in society, governments regulate conflicts of an anti-system character (Hibbs, 1973:10). Nevertheless, a government could be a party to the conflict (Nardin, 1971:32–34). Tilly and Tilly's (1981) collective action theory of conflict claims that conflict might be triggered by any historical incident, and the life cycle of a political conflict is a function of the interactions between challenge and governing. Nordlinger (1972:17) argues that the outcome of the interactions is that political conflict will "result in violence or repression unless certain conditions prevail which prevent these outcomes." His statement points out some other elements critical to the relationship between political conflict and repression. Among those elements, political development has been significantly recognized (Gurr, 1972; Huntington, 1968). Therefore, it is reasonable to assume that repression and political conflict could be the consequence and the cause of each other, contingent on the degree of political development.

Gurr (1972:27–47) speculates about the causal relationships between repression and the occurrence of conflict. In regard to repression as a cause of conflict, Gurr suggests that a high level of repression can deter escalation of conflict effectively, while a moderate level encourages challengers to exercise more opposition. Figure 6.1 shows the nonlinear relationship.

In his discussion of the determinants of state terrorism—a particular form of repression—Gurr (1986b:51–67) identifies repression as a consequence of conflict, arguing that political threats by challengers stimulate repression. Gurr's speculations can be summarized as a conflict-repression loop, shown in Figure 6.2. Accordingly, this loop should generate an equilibrium relationship between conflict and repression. That is, the increase of conflict will elevate the level of repression, by which conflict will be

Figure 6.1
Conflict and Repression

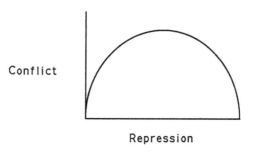

Figure 6.2
The Conflict Repression Loop

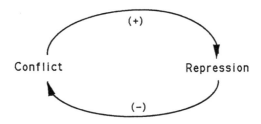

later reduced. By the same token, the decrease of repression will increase the level of conflict, by which repression will be later elevated. However, this is not all true in the real world. In many underdeveloped and developing countries the loop functions like a vicious circle. Revolution and extreme political tranquility are examples. As to the former, increase of conflict elevates repression that provokes a total rebellion. As to the latter, the increase of repression reduces conflict that encourages further increase of repression. Aware of the insufficiency of the repression-conflict loop in explaining those phenomena, Gurr identifies a number of variables parallel to Nordlinger's assumed to be able to prevent repression. The variables are classified into four categories: the challengers, the state and political ideology, social heterogeneity and inequality, and the global environment. Figure 6.3 depicts those variable categories and their relationships with repression, demonstrating that political development leads to different levels of repression.

Moreover, Gurr's elaboration of relationships between the categories makes it clear that political development also impacts on conflict (i.e., in

Figure 6.3
Factors Contributing to State Repression

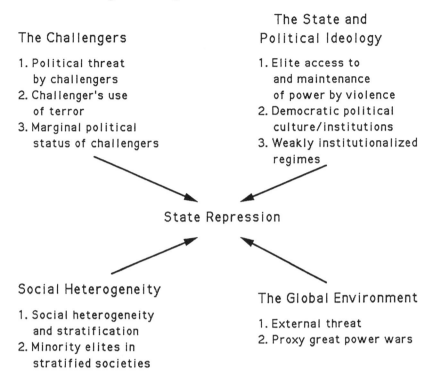

Figure 6.4, the relationship between A1 and B5). Figure 6.4 duplicates Gurr's (1986b:64) model.

Based on the discussion above, a simplification of Gurr's model can be written as in Figure 6.5.

Hibbs (1973) designs a similar model that systematically investigates the causes of political conflict. In his model political development is also treated as an exogenous factor. Nevertheless, repression and conflict can have impacts on political development. For example, Coser (1967:19) argues that "conflict prevents the ossification of the social system by exerting pressure for innovation and creativity." In this sense, one might consider political conflict as a determinant of political development. Meanwhile, repression as a convenient instrument for political control and coercion of power will usually uproot any effort to develop a democratic polity. As a result, relationships among political conflict, repression, and political development should look like Figure 6.6.

Figure 6.4
Conflict Model Linkages

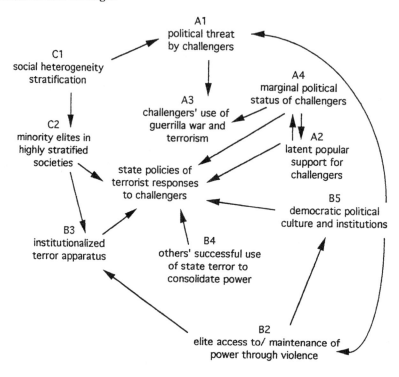

Figure 6.5
Gurr's Model of Repression, Conflict, and Political Development

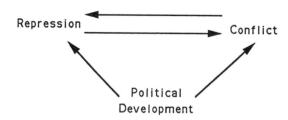

METHODOLOGY: CONCEPTUAL AND
OPERATIONAL ISSUES

For all scientific study, the conceptualization of observed phenomena determines the direction of inquiries, strategy of approach, methodology

Figure 6.6
A Composite Model of Repression, Conflict, and Political Development

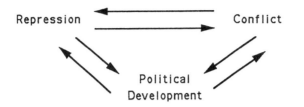

of investigation, and interpretation. A specific study method is demanded by the study of policy issues such as conflict regulation. Strauch (1983:31) raises an important point for anyone attempting to analyze a phenomenon as the outcome of a government's policies. "Policy analysis, however, must deal with questions as they occur, and must provide understanding on the basis of existing information. Its criteria cannot be problem-independent since it does not have the choice of rejecting problems for which the criteria cannot be met."

The necessity of using problem-dependent criteria creates some difficulties when it comes to comparative study. Przeworski and Teune (1985:92–93) elaborate on this point. They list certain requirements that must be met in order to make a comparative study meaningful. "Whether two or more phenomena are "comparable" depends on whether their properties have been expressed in a standard language. A language of measurement defines classes of phenomena by providing specific criteria for deciding whether an observation can be assigned to a particular class." However, "The argument against the use of general inferential rules in comparative measurement is that the only appropriate framework for assessing characteristics of social phenomena must be derived from the systems in which observations are made."

Indeed, the meaning of political conflicts is historically determined because they are conceived and developed in a historic bloc. Cox (1987:409), in clarifying and supplementing Gramsci's original thought, interprets the block as "the particular configuration of social classes and ideology that gives content to a historical state." A historic bloc sets the foundation for both "the machinery of coercion or the monopoly of the legitimate use of physical force within a given territory" and "the machinery of organizing consent." Thus, the existing conflict event data, which are observed and recorded in a specific temporal and spatial location, provide information that is organized in a who-does-what-to-whom and where-in-what-time format. This sort of format makes the comparison of the magnitude of the various conflict behaviors less meaningful, for the political and social meaning of each conflict event is subjected to the logic of participants. For example, in terms of the impacts a conflict generates, there are no plausible theories or empirical evidence to justify whether or not one type of conflict is more revolutionary than another. Similarly, the commensuration of the meaning of the conflicts having the same name can be invalid or unreliable. For instance, *demonstrations* in Tiananmen Square appeared to be much more threatening to the Chinese authorities than anti-Vietnam-War *demonstrations* in Washington, D.C., appeared to the White House. As a result, a proper comparative analysis of political conflict requires the identification of criteria that entail the maximum amount of common dimensions among the conflicts observed in different spatial-temporal surroundings. To be specific, the units of analysis should function as a linkage between conceptualization of the phenomena and the operationalization of empirical tests. What kind of units of analysis can provide comparable and generalizable dimensions of conflict events? In terms of the preceding discussion, proper units of analysis have to include information on what is being observed, when it occurred, and where it occurred—that is, the dimensions of behavior typology, time, and behavior space.

Ziegenhagen (1986) conducts an episodic analysis endeavoring to meet the difficulties. Based on territorial jurisdictions, that is, nations, conflict episodes record a series of adjacent conflict events bounded by periods of political quiescence. Its rationality assumes the following (Ziegenhagen, 1986:58):

> the phenomena of conflict can be more readily understood through consideration of the association of conflicts to each other for periods delimited by temporal proximity. Temporal and spatial dimensions of conflict episodes can then be related to political, social, economic and policy attributes of the environment in which they occur.

Accordingly, the design of episode resembles a historic bloc or a phase of the bloc so that information contained in the episode recognizes the historical and territorial characteristics of conflict events. This alleviates the uneasiness entailed in the problem-dependent criteria. Moreover, Ziegenhagen (1986:58) argues that "[i]t would seem to be particularly appropriate to investigate a series of occurrences that can be distinguished from a more comprehensive pattern, but yet exist as part of it."

Recognizing that a conflict event seldom occurs as a sporadic and independent incident, the episodic analysis becomes an appropriate method for the comparative study of political conflict that "interpretations are made not in terms of the meaning of particular indicators but rather of the overall patterns of relationships" (Mlinar and Teune, 1978:51). As a result, comparing a number of episodes in a sequence of time can be considered an operationalization of Wallerstein's (1974) system analysis that the part-whole relationships direct the interpretation of the phenomenon under examination. Hopkins (1978:204) describes the logic of Wallerstein's analysis: "I have in mind the figure-ground movement where if one refocuses, what was ground becomes figure. . . . I think the methodological directive with which we work is that our acting units or agencies can only be thought of as formed, and continually reformed, by the relations between them."

Another advantage of the episodic analysis as a tool for comparative study is illustrated by Ziegenhagen, who adopts the concept of variety as the measurement of conflict. Two kinds of variety are identified in an episode. General variety constitutes a measure of the degree to which various types of conflict events are represented within episodes. Dominant variety is a measure of the degree to which a single event type occurs in an episode with respect to other event types. Ziegenhagen (1986:64) states the theoretic significance of variety as the following:

> According to theories of regulation, especially requisite variety, a system must contain sufficient variety to be able to cope or regulate the variety of the phenomena in question. Some regimes may be able to cope with large numbers of intermittent antigovernment demonstrations or riots, but the appearance of greater degrees of conflict variety—e.g., riots, demonstrations, general strikes, etc.—requires a greater range of coping ability from a regime.

Variety is a dimension more capable of elaborating a philosophy of political conflict than the event frequency. Meanwhile, variety differentiates the impact of various types of events on society without making subjective judgments as to which event is more politically significant than another. In this respect, variety better grasps the gist of information in a who-does-what-to-whom format.

A justification has to be made to reassure the advantage of episodic analysis. While some scholars recognize that conflict is "primarily cyclical in its development and moves through a predictable sequence of stages" (Wehr, 1979:9), the conflict episode does not utilize the information of the sequential array of conflict events. Nor does it investigate the developmental process of individual events. In other words, the potential significance of temporal relationships between adjacent events is neutralized in the analysis. For example, other things being equal, an episode with a demonstration-riot-assassination event structure generates the same degree of threat to the regime as does an episode with an assassination-demonstration-riot one. Also, the distribution of conflict events in an episode is not taken into consideration. For instance, assuming that two episodes have the same duration and event structure, 80 percent of events in an episode might be observed in the first two years, while in another, events are distributed evenly throughout the whole duration. Again, these two episodes are treated in the same way. The major reason for not incorporating these considerations into the analysis is that one might quickly find oneself back at the starting point, dealing with the conventional issues of conflict frequency and the idiosyncrasy of individual conflict events. Nevertheless, these competing hypotheses deserve serious treatment in future research.

In summary, the validity of making generalizations from the conflict events data is secured in a cross-episodic analysis. The comparison of various episodes is, thus, theoretically and operationally superior to the comparison of individual events with respect to the heterogeneity that individual events entail.

Two technical issues are worth mentioning. First, while general variety and dominant variety are tested separately, total variety, which is the combination of the two, is also tested. The fact that dominant variety and general variety are highly negatively correlated with each other suggests that in some occasions these two variables might vary independently. For example, two conflict episodes might hold the same level of general variety, but one may have a higher dominant variety than another, or vice versa. In such cases, the total variety is more accurate than individual variety in measuring the pattern of conflict behavior; that is, the total variety can differentiate an episode ranked 10 percent in general variety and 80 percent in dominant variety from an episode that is also ranked 10 percent in general variety but 40 percent in dominant variety.

Second, a system dynamic approach is needed to explore the formation of the conflict, of which conflict regulation is an essential force, making for breakdown or adaptation. Thus, the method of simultaneous equations is employed. Consequently, the two-stage least squares calculation is applied to regression analysis because the ordinal least squares is unable to accommodate the existence of dynamic conflict–political development–regulation relationships.

DATA

The conflict episode is constructed by exploiting two archival data. They are Banks's *Cross-National Time-Series Archive* (1979) and the *World Handbook of Political and Social Indicators* organized by Taylor and Jodice (1983). Two data sets together provide information of political conflict, government's policies, and social, economic, and political characteristics of a system in which political conflict and regulation policies interact. Covering 65 nations in continuous existence from 1946 to 1982, 434 conflict episodes are identified by Ziegenhagen (1986:72).

The annual data recorded in the two archives are aggregated in an episode. Since measuring of an episode begins when a conflict event can be observed continuously for at least a year, the minimum amount of conflict variety—dominant and general—in any episode is greater than zero. The aggregated episodic data include measures of general pattern, change amplitude, and change direction (Ziegenhagen, 1986:74–76). The general pattern is obtained by calculating the mean value of aggregated data. In this case, the conflict duration serves as a denominator. The amplitude is a measure of the range between the highest and lowest value of a variable—except for conflict variety—in a conflict episode. The formula is:

$$\frac{V(max) - V(min)}{duration}$$

The direction is indicated for each episode lasting for more than two years. The distinction between the direction and the amplitude is that the former takes the sequential order of maximum and minimum values into consideration. If the maximum value of the variable precedes the minimum value, a negative value is imposed on the measure. Each of the three measures has its own theoretical significance. Hence, they can be used independently. This chapter employs the measure of general pattern for all variables.

HYPOTHESES

As previously mentioned, the main interest of this chapter is to discover the dynamics contributing to different behaviors of the conflict–political development–repression loop. The major concerns center on the explanation of the presence or absence of repressive policy outcomes. Analysis primarily examines the relationships among the occurrence of conflicts, political development, and regulative activities. Three questions are to be answered:

1. Other things being equal, what impact does the occurrence of various types of conflict have upon the regulative behavior of government, especially repressive behavior?
2. What role does political development play in the process of conflict-repression interactions?
3. Other things being equal, what impact do different repressive behaviors have upon the occurrence of various types of conflict?

In response to the first question, conflict variety (general and dominant) reflects the pattern of conflict behavior. It basically asks two questions: (1) How many types of conflict events occur in an episode? and (2) does any type of conflict occur most frequently, and how frequent it is? This is a cybernetic way to perceive conflict. According to Aulin (1982:102–105), increasing variety of disturbance raises the risk of a system perishing. Thus, in association with Ashby's (1956) Law of Requisite Variety, Aulin claims that creation of order in the process of regulation necessitates a reduction of variety in a system. However, repression could decline as conflict continues to increase. For example, compromise and negotiation are often made when a government finds its repressive measures do not work. Accordingly, the first hypothesis is made:

HYPOTHESIS 1: *A higher level of conflict variety tends to generate greater threat, which increases the likelihood of repressive actions. However, repression might decrease when conflict is extremely high.*

Further, "effective regulatory ability" of a regulator depends more on "how to use the available regulatory acts in an optimal way in each case" than on "how to react to each disturbance" (Aulin, 1982:107). Thus, it is assumed that conditions for avoiding an escalation of repression and conflict depend on rulers' considerations and mobilization of: (1) resources able to generate effective and efficient conflict resolution; and (2) the quantity of each type of resource, such as the size of military or public support. Since judicious actions are not possible without the establishment of social and political institutions that secure the utilization of various resources in the society, political development, which is operationally defined as the establishment of various political institutions, can logically serve as an explanatory variable in relation to the concept of conflict variety and repression.

This definition of political development is based on general systems theory. As a society develops, according to Huntington (1968:8–9), the existing political institutions might become inadequate and insufficient to deal with a newly emerging clash of social forces. Since a political institution is "an arrangement for maintaining order, resolving disputes, . . . and thus promoting community among two or more social forces," a regime failing to develop sufficient political institutions might result in escalation of conflict as well as in repressive actions to opposition. Teune (1978:150–156) has a similar view. He defines development as "the integrated diversity of system," and diversity is determined by the variety of a set of properties possessed by components of a system. Integration refers to a process in which the components acquire the properties contributing to their variety rather than their similarity. When the velocity of integration does not match that of the emergence of diversity, developmental change leads to an increase in conflicts. In addition, the establishment of various political institutions can been viewed as political pluralism from which a monopoly power is unlikely to emerge. When different opinions are carefully considered to respond to antagonists, repressive measures are not likely to be the first or only treatment of conflict.

On the other hand, the protracted crush-down and chaos in many autocratic countries lead to speculation that when political development is not possible, either repression or conflict is high. Thus, the hypotheses are:

HYPOTHESIS 2: *The higher political development a regime is able to achieve and maintain, the less likely a variety of conflict will emerge.*

HYPOTHESIS 3: *The higher political development a regime is able to achieve and maintain, the less likely it will employ repressive policy.*

HYPOTHESIS 4: *An increase of conflict variety tends to decrease political development.*

HYPOTHESIS 5: *An increase of repression tends to decrease political development.*

Third, repression may change the cost-benefit ratio of a challenging measure from positive to negative. Hence, the conflicting groups are likely to increase the variety of their strategies when previous strategies are repressed to ineffectiveness. A better explanation is given by the theory of evolution. When the environment becomes harsher, something new must be tried. This is exactly the argument of adaptation by ultrastability which Ben-Eli (1979:292) elaborates:

> On a higher "metalevel," however, [it] operates not just by selecting particular organizations at random, but by systematically encouraging variability in general. The outcome, as manifest by organic evolution on earth, is a local increase in the range and variety of adaptive possibilities and a consistent general trend characterized by a succession of progressively more complex organizations.

Nevertheless, as Gurr speculated, extreme repression is able to limit challengers to few options or nothing at all. Thus, the hypothesis is:

HYPOTHESIS 6: *An increase of repression tends to encourage challengers to try various types of actions. However, extreme repression reduces conflict variety.*

MODEL

A model is constructed based on the proposed hypotheses. Figure 6.7 features the diagram of the model expressed as the following functional forms:

Conflict variety = f (negative sanctions, political development, conflict duration, urbanization)

Figure 6.7
A Model of Repression

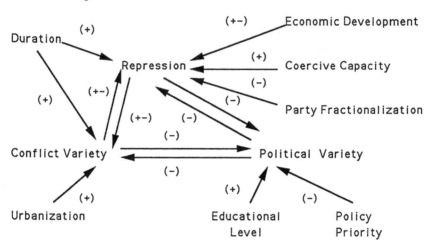

Negative sanctions = f (conflict variety, political development, conflict duration, coercive capacity, economic development, party fractionalization)

Political development = f (conflict variety, negative sanctions, educational level, policy priority)

Two types of variables are identified in response to the model. The first contains variables endogenous to the model. Endogenous refers to a variable that is allowed to be explained by the other variables in the model—either endogenous or exogenous. Three endogenous variables are identified. They are conflict variety (general and dominant), negative sanctions, and political development.

Based on the functional expressions, a set of simultaneous equations is written describing these three endogenous variables, where:

e = error term

+ = a positive relation is expected

− = a negative relation is expected

* = an expression of curvilinearity

Conflict variety = a + b1 negative sanctions − b2 political development + b3 duration − b4 (negative sanctions)^{2*} + b5 urbanization

As hypothesized earlier, repression has a curvilinear impact on conflict variety, and political development provides challengers with incentives to exercise or abandon certain kinds of activities.

Duration influences the opportunity of the emergence of various types of conflict. A protracted conflict can lead to the emergence of new patterns of conflict behavior. A study by Cohen, Brown, and Organski (1981:902) suggests that conflict might be largely morphogenic or evolutionary in nature. Urbanization can cause conflict simply because it increases the chance of personal interactions. Also, urbanization provides a foundation for collective action.

Negative sanctions = a + b1 conflict variety − b2 political development + b3 duration + b4 coercive capacity + b5 economic development + b6 party fractionalization − b7 (economic development)$^{2^*}$ − b8 (conflict variety)$^{2^*}$ + e

Both conflict variety and political development can impact on repression. Besides, this equation states that it is possible that the longer the conflict lasts (duration), the less tolerable the opposition becomes, thereby incurring deterrent policies.

Coercive capacity can also increase the magnitude of repression. This might be done in two ways. First, the organizational structure is a mechanism determining rulers' capability of implementing repressive policies. Second, while a certain amount of coercion is maintained by all rulers, a strong coercive capacity usually incorporates cruel means that can magnify the fear of conflicting groups and the general population.

Several empirical studies report that nations with a higher income and living standard tend to be less repressive (Wolpin, 1986:98–106). Nevertheless, moderate economic development might not bring about a reduction of repressiveness. The phenomenon of liberty tradeoff can be found in almost all developing countries in which governmental repression is popularly adapted to cope with conflicts that are viewed as detrimental to the promotion of economic performance. Huntington (1987:14) states the following:

> O'Donnell's theory of bureaucratic authoritarianism challenged the proposition set forth . . . that higher levels of economic development were associated with the prevalence of democratic political systems. In a more general sense the conflict between growth and democracy is seen in terms of what Jack Donnelly calls "the liberty tradeoff."

Finally, a regime that has strong support or a dominant political status (party fractionalization) tends to employ repressive measures against its challengers.

Political development = a + b1 conflict variety − b2 negative sanctions + b3 education level − b4 policy priority + e

According to Hypotheses 4 and 5, this equation states that conflict variety and repression are associated with political variety in a negative manner. Since repression implies the dismissal of the functions of legitimate political agents, the impact of repression on political development is assumed to be linear.

When a state allocates a high percentage of its societal resources to the military, political development is likely to be deterred. Empirical evidence has shown that in several developing countries military agents from time to time dominate or even replace the existing political institutions in dealing with civilian issues. Nevertheless, greater financial allocations to military rather than civil purposes are not necessarily linked to brutal regulation (Wolpin, 1986:105). As a result, the government's policy priority relates more directly to political development than to repression.

Education is treated as a vital socioeconomic factor fostering political development. The level of individuals' education is essential to build up a psychological modernity upon which "the successful functioning of a modern society and its political institutions depends" (Banuazizi, 1987:287).

IDENTIFICATION OF THE MODEL

These equations are linear in parameters but nonlinear in the endogenous variables. A nonlinear model consists of two kinds of endogenous variables. The basic endogenous variables are those appearing on the left-hand side of the equations, and all the other endogenous variables—i.e., negative sanctions[2]—are the additional endogenous variables that are a function of basic endogenous variables. In passing, note that in a nonlinear model additional endogenous variables can be expressed as the sum of two components—a nonlinear function of predetermined variables and a disturbance term (Kelejian, Oates, and Wallace, 1981:293).

When an additional variable is regressed on the first K powers of predetermined variables, the estimated value of the additional endogenous variable approximates the polynomial form of the predetermined variables. If this assumption holds, proved by Kelejian and Oates, the observations on the additional variable could be determined once predetermined variables are observed (Kelejian et al., 1981:294–295). Consequently, for reducing a nonlinear model to a linear one, the additional variable can be replaced by its "mean function" in the predetermined variables. In other words, the additional endogenous variables should be grouped with the predetermined variables for the purpose of identification.

Thus, in a fully identified nonlinear model, the number of basic endogenous variables appearing on the right-hand side of the ith equation must be less than that of predetermined variables and additional endogenous variables appearing in the model but not appearing in the ith equation

(Kelejian et al., 1981:294–295). According to this rule, all equations above are identified.

VARIABLES

The variable conflict variety is discussed in detail in the preceding sections. This section discusses the measurement issues of other variables.

The degree of repressiveness imposed by a government indicates not only the extent a system of governance will tolerate its political challengers, but, from an organizational behaviorist's point of view, the plan of a coercive compliance structure. Etzioni (1961:74) states, "political organizations whose goal is control over the legitimate means of violence are more likely than other political organizations to apply coercion in the control of their members."

Accordingly, repressiveness can be measured by looking at government's regulations which deprive basic human and political rights. From this perspective, government's negative sanctions can serve as a measure of degrees of repressiveness. They are observed in the forms of political censorship of communication (CN); political restrictions on organization, assembly, and representation (PR); and political executions (PX).

It is theoretically sound to use the extent to which an action aims to restrict the latitude of expression as an indicator of repressiveness. Freedom of expression is broadly conceived as a major component of democracy. People cannot express their opinions and thoughts without communicating with each other either on a face-to-face or on a mass media basis. By manipulating the character and scope of communication media, the government can repress challengers because the chance for them to succeed is principally determined by the timing, group consensus, and organizational properties (Halebsky, 1976:122–123). The government can also repress the appearance of conflicting interests by imposing restrictions on regular channels of political expression. For instance, prohibition of an independent political party prevents people from possessing expressive and representative instruments, since a political party not only transfers the "contrasts in the social and the cultural structure into demands and pressures for action or inaction," but forces "the spokesmen for the many contrasting interests and outlooks to strike bargains, to stagger demands, and to aggregate pressure" (Lipset, 1985:117–118). Thus, political restrictions can indicate another dimension of repressiveness. Finally, political executions measure a psychological dimension of repressiveness. Killings, both situational and institutionalized, are the most manifest expression of repressiveness as they contribute to a general pattern of life-threatening behavior. It will frustrate sturdy opponents who might find their supporters are giving way to the messages of intimidation (Gurr, 1986b:47–51). Furthermore, the severity of penalty can weaken a system's commitment to protect certain forms of expression (Zashin, 1972:272).

Repressive actions might be checked as a political system develops. While the concept of political development is rather multifarious (Weiner, 1987:vii), it is broadly accepted that development is a process in which a closed system moves toward an open one associated with Western democratic government. Nordlinger (1972:17) outlines some characteristics of an open regime: "We may also be confident that there are channels which allow for the expression of significant political demands of a substantive and procedural variety. Governmental decisions are significantly influenced by conflict, competition, and compromise among the various politically relevant associations."

Consequently, the indicators of substantive and procedural variety should include the presence or absence of particular institutions and relationships among them. The identification of "the particularities" follows a basic political thought: the principles of separation of power and checks and balance. As Montesquieu (1989) argues, there can be no liberty when legislative and executive powers are united in the same person or in the same body of magistrates. As a result, the existence of an independent legislative body and the selection of legislators can be viewed as important indicators of political development. The equal opportunity to access the decision-making process is another important principle of democracy. In the contemporary world, a political party that survives and grows through winning elections of decision makers plays a crucial role in securing democracy. For this reason, the characteristics of party system must be taken into consideration.

Political development is a process of "institutionalization," also. Huntington (1968:12) defines the level of institutionalization of a political establishment in terms of "the adaptability, complexity, autonomy, and coherence of its organizations and procedures." Thus, the indicators must be able to measure these characteristics.

Banks (1979) develops a number of indicators measuring various elements of democracy. Five indicators are combined to a composite index of political development. They are: (1) effectiveness of legislature; (2) nominating process; (3) legislative coalitions; (4) party legitimacy; and (5) legislative selection. Table 6.1 exhibits the measuring technique of the composite index.

There are seven exogenous variables: policy priority, coercive capacity, duration, economic development, urbanization, educational level, and party fractionalization. The proportion of military expenditure over total expenditure measures the government's *policy priority*. An intensification of military control over civilian life implies the expansion and reinforcement of the *coercive structure* (Zwick, 1984:128). Thus, the size of military (military expenditure per capita) can be used as a measurement of organiza-

Table 6.1
Components of the Composite Index of Democracy

```
Effectiveness of Legislature:          Nominating Process:

   (3) Effective                          (3) Competitive
   (2) Partly effective                   (2) Partly Competitive
   (1) Largely ineffective                (1) Essentially non-
   (0) No legislature                         Competitive
                                          (0) No legislature


Legislative Coalitions:

   (3) More than 1 party, no coalitions
   (2) More than 1 party, government coalition, opposition
   (1) More than 1 party, government coalition, no opposition
   (0) No coalition, no opposition


Party Legitimacy:                      Legislative Selection:

   (3) No parties excluded                (2) Elective
   (2) One or more minor or               (1) Nonelective
       extremist parties excluded         (0) No legislature
   (1) Significant exclusion of
       parties (or groups)
   (0) No parties, or all but
       dominant party and satellites excluded



Maximum value = 14
Minimum value =  0
```

These variables are discussed in detail in Banks (1979).

tional structure of coercive forces. *Duration* is the time length of a conflict episode, measuring an ecological dynamic that steers both the policy response and behaviors of challengers. As Ziegenhagen (1986:62–63) explains, duration is "related directly to the distribution of effort and resources by the regime in coping with challenges to it." *Economic development* is measured by GNP per capita. The level of *urbanization* indicates the frequency of interpersonal contacts. Secondary school enrollment per capita indicates the *educational level* of a nation. According to Rae (1968:414), *party fractionalization* gives a probabilistic estimate for the rate of partisan disagreement among the members of a system. This measurement includes the indicators of the party system structure and of the cohesiveness of a party. For example, it is unlikely to see fractionalization either in a single party system or in a multiple party system in which each party is cohesive. Thus, party fractionalization measures the marginal political support for ruling elites in terms of decision making.

FINDINGS

Tables 6.2 to 6.10 list major findings about endogenous variables. These tables are sorted in terms of different measurements of conflict variety and repression. For example, each of the negative sanctions—censorship, restrictions, and execution—is arrayed with general variety, dominant variety, and total variety, respectively.

The impact of general variety on each of the negative sanctions (censorship, restrictions, and execution) is shown in Tables 6.2 to 6.4. The findings support the hypothesis that the increase of general variety leads to a higher level of repression, whereas a profound increase of general variety tends to encourage a regime to reduce repressiveness. While the t-test is insignificant in the case of political execution (in Table 6.4), slope coefficients follow the expected direction—a curvilinear relationship. This could be interpreted as a regime's constant attempts to prevent and eliminate the emergence of new conflict, for if this is not so a regime might lose control of the situation. Similar results are obtained by testing total variety (shown in Tables 6.8 to 6.10). However, the curvilinear pattern does not hold consistently when dominant variety is tested (shown in Tables 6.5 and 6.6).

The harmful impact of conflict variety—general, dominant, and total—on political development is statistically significant across the board. That the increase of various conflict types is negatively related to political development implies that political development progresses only as certain types of conflicts are employed routinely by the challengers. This result can often be observed in most developed countries in which a few opposition activities are recognized as appropriate by the government and general population and protected by law.

The expectation of a curvilinear impact of government repression on conflict variety is largely supported. In eight cases (Tables 6.2, 6.3, 6.4, 6.6, 6.7, 6.8, 6.9, and 6.10), the slope coefficients support the hypothesis; five of them are statistically significant (in Tables 6.2, 6.3, 6.4, 6.6, and 6.10). Only in one case the slope coefficient goes the opposite direction with an insignificant t value (in Table 6.5). Thus, it is not careless to accept that repression will complicate a conflict situation in which challengers might exhaust all possible tactics to achieve goals. But there is less room for challengers to maneuver their options as repression becomes great.

The negative impact of repression—censorship, restrictions, and execution—on political development is confirmed across the board (all ts are significant). Obviously, once repressive policies are implemented, there is little opportunity for a regime to develop a democratic system.

The increase of political development tends to reduce the level of conflict significantly in most cases. Only in two cases do the slope coefficients not go in the expected direction (in Tables 6.4 and 6.10). Also, in Table 6.7,

Table 6.2
General Variety, Censorship, and Political Development

	Endogenous Variables		
	General Variety	Negative Sanctions (Censorship)	Political Development
Conflict Variety	-------	6.47 (2.14)	-0.54 (-4.51)
Conflict^2 Variety	-------	-0.76 (-2.18)	-------
Negative Sanctions (Censorship)	1.09 (2.80)	-------	-0.50 (-2.86)
Negative^2 Sanctions	-0.06 (-2.53)	-------	-------
Political Development	-0.13 (-3.94)	-1.98 (-2.14)	-------

Table 6.3
General Variety, Political Restrictions, and Political Development

	Endogenous Variables		
	General Variety	Negative Sanctions (Restrictions)	Political Development
Conflict Variety (General)	-------	71.86 (2.29)	-8.37 (-2.32)
Conflict^2 Variety	-------	-10.25 (-2.08)	-------
Negative Sanctions (Restrictions)	0.14 (3.67)	-------	-0.06 (-3.49)
Negative^2 Sanctions	-0.0008 (-3.44)	-------	-------
Political Development	-0.10 (-2.67)	-19.78 (-2.06)	-------

Table 6.4
General Variety, Executions, and Political Development

	Endogenous Variables		
	General Variety	Negative Sanctions (Execution)	Political Development
Conflict Variety (General)	-------	0.71 (0.89)	-0.48 (-4.06)
Conflict^2 Variety	-------	-0.09 (-0.94)	-------
Negative Sanctions (Execution)	10.47 (4.06)	-------	-1.89 (-4.17)
Negative^2 Sanctions	-2.90 (-3.93)	-------	-------
Political Development	0.06 (0.84)	-0.54 (-2.42)	-------

Table 6.5
Dominant Variety, Censorship, and Political Development

	Endogenous Variables		
	Dominant Variety	Negative Sanctions (Censorship)	Political Development
Conflict Variety (Dominant)	-------	0.27 (1.06)	0.05 (4.52)
Conflict^2 Variety	-------	-0.002 (-1.00)	-------
Negative Sanctions (Censorship)	0.20 (0.03)	-------	-0.55 (-3.14)
Negative^2 Sanctions	-0.03 (-0.08)	-------	-------
Political Development	2.12 (4.70)	-1.24 (-3.32)	-------

Table 6.6
Dominant Variety, Political Restrictions, and Political Development

	Endogenous Variables		
	Dominant Variety	Negative Sanctions (Restrictions)	Political Development
Conflict Variety (Dominant)	-------	5.68 (1.87)	0.04 (4.11)
Conflict^2 Variety	---------	-0.04 (-1.83)	-------
Negative Sanctions (Restrictions)	-1.21 (-2.13)	-------	-0.07 (-3.87)
Negative^2 Sanctions	0.007 (2.09)	-------	-------
Political Development	1.65 (3.22)	-11.6 (-2.64)	-------

Table 6.7
Dominant Variety, Executions, and Political Development

	Endogenous Variables		
	Dominant variety	Negative Sanctions (Execution)	Political Development
Conflict variety (Dominant)	-------	-0.38 (-3.39)	0.04 (3.89)
Conflict^2 variety	-------	0.003 (3.43)	-------
Negative Sanctions (Execution)	-33.42 (-1.31)	-------	-1.89 (-4.16)
Negative^2 Sanctions	8.31 (1.13)	-------	-------
Political Development	1.32 (1.96)	-0.08 (-0.31)	-------

Table 6.8
Total Variety, Censorship, and Political Development

| | Endogenous Variables | | |
	Total Variety	Negative Sanctions (Censorship)	Political Development
Conflict Variety (Total)	-------	0.076 (2.02)	-0.07 (-4.96)
Conflict^2 Variety	-------	-0.0001 (-2.10)	-------
Negative Sanctions (Censorship)	30.60 (0.94)	-------	-0.51 (-2.92)
Negative^2 Sanctions	-1.44 (0.90)	-------	-------
Political Development	-13.74 (4.16)	-1.87 (-2.01)	-------

Table 6.9
Total Variety, Political Restrictions, and Political Development

| | Endogenous Variables | | |
	Total Variety	Negative Sanctions (Restrictions)	Political Development
Conflict Variety (Total)	-------	0.85 (2.08)	-0.007 (-4.53)
Conflict^2 Variety	-------	-0.001 (-2.17)	-------
Negative Sanctions (Restrictions)	1.24 (0.4)	-------	-0.06 (-3.56)
Negative^2 Sanctions	-0.007 (-0.34)	-------	-------
Political Development	-14.18 (-5.09)	-18.66 (-1.79)	-------

Table 6.10
Total Variety, Executions, and Political Development

	Endogenous Variables		
	Total Variety	Negative Sanctions (Execution)	Political Development
Conflict Variety (Total)	-------	0.003 (0.34)	-0.007 (-4.22)
Conflict^2 Variety	-------	-0.00005 (-0.36)	-------
Negative Sanctions (Execution)	754.19 (3.72)	-------	-1.79 (-3.90)
Negative^2 Sanctions	-204.1 (-3.52)	-------	-------
Political Development	2.00 (0.36)	-0.39 (-1.95)	-------

the t-test is marginally significant. Hence, it is fair to claim that the establishment of various political institutions encourages parties in conflict to employ certain types of challenges acceptable to the society. More important, it supports the cybernetic argument that "only variety in regulation can destroy variety in the original disturbance" (Aulin, 1982:104).

The hypothesis that the more political development a regime achieves and maintains, the less likely a regime will implement repressive policies is to a great extent verified, although the t-tests are not significant in Tables 6.7, 6.9, and 6.10.

Tables 6.11 to 6.13 summarize relationships among individual exogenous variables and endogenous variables.

Duration has a significant impact on escalating the level of conflict. However, its impact on repression is not obvious (the *t* ratio is not significant and the signs of parameters are not identical). Similarly, coercive capacity is not clearly related to repressive behaviors.

Although it is not statistically significant, across-the-board policy priority is associated with political development in a negative manner. In other words, the more resources a regime invests in noncivilian buildup, the less likely a regime will develop its political system.

Education level is crucial to the establishment of various political institutions. In all the cases, findings support that a higher education level contributes to a higher degree of political development.

Table 6.11

General Variety, Negative Sanctions, Political Development, and Exogenous Variables

	Conflict Variety 1. (General) 2. (General) 3. (General)	Negative Sanctions (Censorship) (Restrictions) (Execution)	Political Development
	Endogenous Variables		
Duration	0.43 (11.96) 0.35 (7.48) 0.34 (5.45)	0.17 (0.88) 2.50 (1.20) 0.03 (0.69)	------- ------- -------
Coercive Capacity	------- ------- -------	-5.10 (-0.08) 92.13 (0.29) -0.71 (-0.05)	------- ------- -------
Policy Priority	------- ------- -------	------- ------- -------	-2.36 (-1.03) -1.63 (-0.71) -0.02 (-0.01)
Education Level	------- ------- -------	------- ------- -------	138.33 (3.92) 154.30 (4.29) 112.13 (3.27)
Party Fractionaliza- tion	------- ------- -------	20.94 (2.09) 208.2 (2.01) 5.24 (2.15)	------- ------- -------
Economic Development	------- ------- -------	0.001 (1.73) 0.012 (1.40) 0.0003 (1.95)	------- ------- -------
Economic^2 Development	------- ------- -------	-1.5 E-7 (-1.53) -1.1 E-6 (-1.11) -3.1 E-8 (-1.48)	------- ------- -------
Urbanization	-0.63 (-0.56) -1.44 (-1.18) -3.56 (-1.85)	-------- -------- --------	------- ------- -------

Table 6.12
Dominant Variety, Negative Sanctions, Political Development, and Exogenous Variables

	Endogenous Variables		
	Conflict Variety 1. (Dominant) 2. (Dominant) 3. (Dominant)	Negative Sanctions (Censorship) (Restrictions) (Execution)	Political Development
Duration	-2.77 (-5.55)	0.06 (0.64)	-------
	-1.86 (-2.80)	2.31 (1.87)	-------
	-2.39 (-4.16)	-0.13 (-2.43)	-------
Coercive Capacity	-------	-19.05 (-0.62)	-------
	-------	7.65 (0.02)	-------
	-------	16.20 (0.82)	-------
Policy Priority	-------	-------	-0.83 (-0.37)
	-------	-------	-2.29 (-1.02)
	-------	-------	-0.84 (-0.37)
Education Level	-------	-------	138.23 (3.93)
	-------	-------	155.40 (4.35)
	-------	-------	111.10 (3.23)
Party Fractionaliza-tion	-------	11.51 (2.98)	-------
	-------	101.16 (2.21)	-------
	-------	0.80 (0.31)	-------
Economic Development	-------	0.001 (2.93)	-------
	-------	0.008 (1.53)	-------
	-------	0.0004 (1.71)	-------
Economic^2 Development	-------	-1.4 E-7 (-2.60)	-------
	-------	-6.7 E-6 (-1.17)	-------
	-------	-3.8 E-8 (-1.31)	-------
Urbanization	-15.8 (-1.02)	-------	-------
	-2.98 (-0.17)	-------	-------
	-1.79 (-0.1)	-------	-------

Table 6.13
Total Variety, Negative Sanctions, Political Development, and Exogenous Variables

	Conflict Variety 1. (Total) 2. (Total) 3. (Total)	Negative Sanctions (Censorship) (Restrictions) (Execution)	Political Development
	Endogenous Variables		
Duration	34.19 (11.81) 33.93 (9.38) 26.40 (5.57)	-0.09 (-0.42) -0.30 (-0.14) -0.004 (-0.14)	------- ------- -------
Coercive Capacity	------- ------- -------	-18.03 (-0.26) 48.13 (0.06) 0.65 (0.06)	------- ------- -------
Policy Priority	------- ------- -------	------- ------- -------	-2.28 (-1.01) -1.48 (-0.66) -0.17 (-0.08)
Education Level	------- ------- -------	------- ------- -------	127.84 (3.64) 144.36 (4.03) 103.83 (3.03)
Party Fractionaliza-tion	------- ------- -------	19.98 (1.89) 199.35 (1.78) 3.63 (1.63)	------- ------- -------
Economic Development	------- ------- -------	0.002 (1.69) 0.014 (1.38) 0.0003 (2.08)	------- ------- -------
Economic^2 Development	------- ------- -------	-1.4 E-7 (-1.34) -1.1 E-6 (-0.94) -2.7 E-8 (-1.65)	------- ------- -------
Urbanization	-18.51 (-0.21) -12.25 (-0.13) -27.27 (-1.85)	------- ------- -------	------- ------- -------

While it is not significant in all the cases, party fractionalization is positively related to repression. If a political system starts to be monopolized by a single political party or single opinion, the rulers tend to act more aggressively.

In terms of the sign of parameter, across-the-board economic development relates to repression in a curvilinear way. This finding confirms the liberty tradeoff argument, that is, that achieving economic promotion is an excuse for repression until an absolute high level of economic well-being is reached.

Finally, urbanization goes in a direction opposite to what is expected, although the t-tests are insignificant. This implies that change itself is not a necessary condition to cause conflict. In other words, an unbalanced development—that is, the lack of variety to adapt and regulate—might be the intrinsic cause of conflict.

CONCLUSIONS

In conclusion, the findings basically verify the hypotheses. Other things being equal, the argument that conflict variety can stimulate a regime's repressive behavior is largely supported. In two out of three cases, when general and total variety are tested, the emergence of new types of conflict is encountered by repression. However, when all rival strategies are employed, a regime might be forced to compromise with challengers, or collapse for losing control. A number of implications can be perceived. First, as certain types of challenges develop through a gradual process bounded and controlled by rationality and goals, they become legitimate and productive to the conflicting groups as well as socially acceptable to the society (Himes, 1980). Eventually, the government tends to be less repressive. Second, if new types of challenges are beyond the government's capability to predict as well as to resolve in a due manner, repression is inevitable. However, repression cannot be sustained in the long run. It seems that the exhaustion of different strategies by the challengers is the ultimate way to act against repressive policies. Third, the impact of political executions on conflict follows the expected direction in all three cases. This might suggest that the enhancement of punishment seems to be the most popular measure employed by the regulators when they confront a great array of different conflict events. This could be explained by the following (Stohl and Lopez, 1986:8–9): "the audience to the act or the threatened act may be more important than the immediate victim. . . . Kill one, frighten ten thousand. . . . the victim serves as a persuasive advertisement of the power of the state, and the message reaches more people than the government might elect to coerce through physical acts."

That political development leads to the decrease of conflict and repression is also supported to a great extent. To allow a wider spectrum of dissenters to express their opinions and complaints could lower the chance of political conflict. The findings remind one that political development is an antonym of repression. However, the two insignificant t-tests obtained in the case of political execution (Tables 6.7 and 6.10) suggest that regimes tend to retain certain means of control in order to prevent any fundamental change that occurs in society, even when they are willing to respond positively to dissent by permitting some social and political changes (Zashin, 1972:270–271). It is observed that in several newly industrialized countries a certain amount of freedom is given to the general population while punishment for intolerable actions remains intact. For example, regardless that great efforts have been made on democratization in the last ten years, in 1984 the Taiwanese government assassinated a political dissident who immigrated to the United States decades ago.

The curvilinear impact of repression on conflict is confirmed. However, the point is that while challengers might be pacified by intensive repression, a negative impact of repression is generated for political development. Consequently, the ultimate outcome is a new wave of conflict that might be higher than before. That is, until the policy-making process is open to various groups in the society, there is little chance that conflict can be dismissed without the loss of political well-being.

7

CONFLICT AND REPRESSION: FRUSTRATION-AGGRESSION AND RATIONAL-CHOICE MODELS

Michael Dillon

The purpose of this investigation is to help explain the observed variation in mass political conflict, paying particular attention to the relationship between such conflict and government-sponsored acts of repression. Mass political conflict, such as demonstrations, strikes, or riots, is often considered an expression of popular dissatisfaction with a political system. It has even been argued that the potential for conflict is necessary to promote progressive political change (Nieburg, 1963). In contrast, regimes justify the use of repression as a necessary evil to control against anarchy, which can accompany political conflict, and to promote the normal functioning of the political economy. One might predict conflict to have a positive effect on repression and for repression to have both a positive and a negative effect on future conflict.

Figure 7.1 predicts that if the government responds to conflict with repression, this will increase popular dissatisfaction and hence the propensity for more conflict. If this positive feedback loop between government repression and mass political conflict continues unchecked, it will create a spiraling crisis pitting government against the insurgent population, culminating in revolution. Therefore, knowing how repression deters conflict (the negative loop) is critical to understanding the dynamics between conflict and repression.

FRUSTRATION-AGGRESSION THEORY

To explain how something works, one must begin with a model of the process under investigation. To explain mass political conflict, this investigation begins with a fairly sophisticated psychological model for why

Figure 7.1
Positive and Negative Feedback Loops Between Repression and Conflict

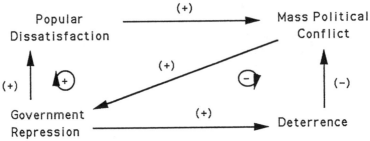

+ arrow = "causes increases in"
− arrow = "causes decreases in"

individuals act aggressively: frustration-aggression theory.[1] Explaining group behavior using theories of individual behavior must not be over-extended. However, in the case of participants in mass protest, each individual can be thought of as acting out of frustration with his or her political system. Indeed, in setting out their theory, Dollard and others (1939:151–156) explicitly make the link between psychological and group behavior.

Frustration-aggression theory begins with the assumption that all behavior is goal-directed and that aggression occurs as a result of individuals being inhibited from obtaining those goals (frustration). The degree to which the individual will direct aggression against the perceived inhibitor of his or her goal is explained by four additional assumptions to the basic postulate:

1. Aggression is positively correlated with the number and intensity of frustrated actions. That is, the level of frustration is accumulative; a sequence of small frustrations can have the same effect as one intense, frustrated act (28–31).

2. Aggression is negatively associated with the punishment an individual expects to receive from acting aggressively. In short, aggression can be deterred through inhibition (27–37).

3. Aggression inhibited against the main agent of an individual's frustration will be displaced onto another source of frustration. Frustration always promotes aggression, so the question is where that aggression will be directed. If an individual finds it difficult to act against the main source of frustration, he or she will find another avenue to release anger. If all avenues to express aggression externally are blocked, individuals will release frustration by acting aggressively toward themselves (39–50).

4. Aggression reduces the overall level of frustration an individual feels toward the environment (catharsis). This implies that aggression in one

Figure 7.2
Frustration-Aggression Model: Mass Political Conflict and Government
Repression

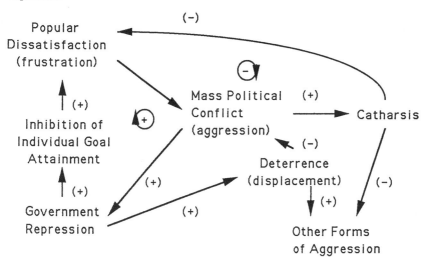

form will decrease other forms of aggression. Moreover, catharsis implies that aggression will reduce the propensity to instigate further aggression of the same type, though this reduction will only be temporary if the source of the frustration is not removed (Dollard et al., 1939:50–53; Berkowitz, 1962:189).

Figure 7.2 incorporates the assumptions of frustration-aggression theory into our model for mass political conflict and repression (Figure 7.1). Repression increases the probability of conflict by inhibiting individual goal attainment, increasing the likelihood individuals will band together to take out their frustration in popular displays of dissent against the regime. At the same time, repression increases the anticipated costs of such protest (e.g., the possibility of arrest), leading individuals to displace the anger they feel toward their government onto other objects in their environment (or onto themselves). The existence of catharsis means participants in mass political conflict should experience a decrease in their overall frustration level. This will lower both their propensity for other forms of aggression and, it is argued here, their propensity to participate in future acts of conflict (at least in the short run).

While conflict lowers future conflict through catharsis, conflict promotes future conflict by lowering the propensity of participants to displace their displeasure with the regime onto other objects of frustration. Essentially, mass protests focus the attention of those frustrated with the regime so they are able to do something about it.[2] In Figure 7.2, this relationship is depicted by the two negative-signed arrows between mass political conflict and displacement, indicating an overall positive relationship. Conflict increases the probability of future conflict only if the effect of overcoming displacement is stronger than the cathartic effect of lowering the overall level of frustration.

Figure 7.2, while it fills in some details on how conflict may occur, does not predict the cumulative effect of repression on conflict. To determine this, one would need to know the strength of the association between each variable in our model. As well, to determine the dynamics of the relationship, one would need to know the time it takes for repression to affect both the level of frustration and the level of displacement in the system.

To illustrate the importance of time, consider Hibbs's (1973:185) evidence of a short-term positive, long-term negative effect of government coercion on elite conflict. Assuming the adequacy of the frustration-aggression theory to explain such behavior, the results point to a short-run effect of coercion on the level of frustration, spurring increased conflict, along with a stronger but delayed displacement effect of that coercion.

Gurr (1970:240) hypothesizes a curvilinear (inverted U) relationship between the negative sanctions a government imposes on its population and the propensity for that population to produce political conflict. It seems that at low to moderate levels of sanctions, the level of frustration will increase while the effect of displacement will be minimal. However, as the level of repression intensifies, the effect of displacement will overshadow the rise in frustration, leading to a decrease in conflict.

The reason high levels of governmental repression have a negative effect on conflict may be somewhat more complicated than simply the effect of displacement. Berkowitz (1962:67–70), suggests two reasons why the level of frustration experienced by potential participants of aggression may actually decrease if inhibition persists at high levels. First, individuals' goals tend to diminish as they come to realize that such goals are unattainable. Second, as individuals become accustomed to not achieving their goals, they tend to become immunized from the frustration experienced by such disappointment. This is pointed out to suggest that there may be a time element involved in producing a curvilinear relationship between conflict and repression. In the long run, high levels of repression may lower the probability of conflict by lowering expectations, thereby decreasing the frustration individuals feel toward repression.

CRITIQUE OF FRUSTRATION-AGGRESSION THEORY

Frustration-aggression theory can be criticized for containing both too few and too many assumptions. As for omitted variables, the model does not depict other reasons for aggression—namely, that it may be instru-

Figure 7.3
Rational-Choice Model: Mass Political Conflict and Government Repression

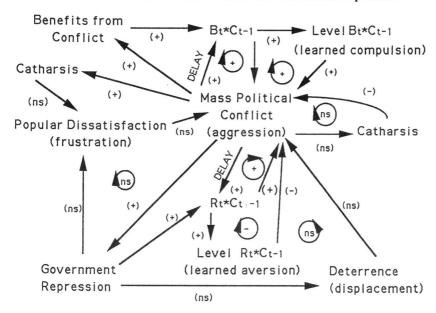

mental for getting what one wants. Even advocates of using frustration-aggression theory to explain conflict readily admit that aggression may be positively reinforced, just as it may be negatively deterred (Gurr, 1970:211–215; Berkowitz, 1962:29–36). However, if the relationship under investigation can be adequately modeled as simply a cost-benefit calculation between anticipated cost and gain, there is little reason to add assumptions concerning the psychological makeup of the participants (e.g., frustration, displacement, catharsis). In short, if frustration-aggression theory provides no better explanation for the relationship between conflict and repression than does a much simpler rational-choice model, the latter approach should be used since it is more parsimonious.

Since the rational-choice model does not directly contradict the frustration-aggression model, both approaches may be incorporated into a single model to show how they are related. In Figure 7.3, the interactive variable combining repression and conflict is intended to capture each time a participant perceives repression as a response to conflict. If repression becomes the anticipated outcome of conflict (the level of conflict × repression is high), this should decrease the probability of conflict. Alternatively, if conflict is associated with some benefit, the reverse process will occur and the individual will learn to anticipate benefit from conflict. If these relationships dominate the model, the variables relating to frustration, displacement, and catharsis are insignificant, indicating they are not necessary in an explanation of why conflict occurs.

To illustrate the difference between the rational-choice and frustration-aggression models, consider the 1992 outbreak of mass conflict in Los Angeles. The phenomenon precipitating the riots was a not-guilty verdict in a court case involving a black man beaten by white police officers. While the verdict sparked the rioting, many see a long-standing policy of police brutality and governmental neglect, along with socioeconomic conditions of decaying neighborhoods and extraordinary high youth unemployment, as underlying causes for the disturbances. In the aftermath of the riots, speculation arose whether there would be spill-over effects in other U.S. cities experiencing similar decay and neglect in their urban neighborhoods (Ayres, 1992).

An explanation of this phenomenon using the frustration-aggression model emphasizes the accumulative effect of the underlying causes for the riots, such as the long-term frustration many in East Los Angeles may feel given their environment. The rational-choice model would concentrate on the potential benefit participants may have received from rioting. Anticipated benefits extend not just to looted goods but to publicity of their plight, noting that turbulence is sometimes necessary to gain the necessary assistance (Piven and Cloward, 1971:338).

The fact that, once the rioting began, potential participants could anticipate benefits from looting abandoned shops brings up another possible explanation for the variation in the rate of conflict. While the general breakdown of the status quo in a society may be due to pent-up frustration, the behavior of participants once the crisis begins may depend on the anticipated consequences of that behavior.[3] Referring to Figure 7.3, this means the interactive variables (conflict × repression, conflict × benefit) directly affect conflict, in contrast to the level variables that are derived from them (learned aversion, learned compulsion). The level variables represent the accumulative effect of the interactive variables in the long run, while the interactive variables represent only the immediate impact.

HYPOTHESES

To investigate the usefulness of either frustration-aggression theory or rational-choice theory in explaining mass political conflict, a list of behavior predicted from those models are drawn as hypotheses. Special emphasis is placed on testing whether frustration-aggression or rational-choice better explains mass political conflict. Tests are then conducted using data on political conflict and several possible explanatory variables to see what empirical evidence there is to support or reject either model of behavior.

The first hypothesis derived from frustration-aggression theory is that occurrences of mass political conflict are not normally distributed over time. Aggression resulting from thwarted goal-directed behavior presumes that as long as goals are reasonably met, individuals will not alter the status quo by acting aggressively. If, however, a large gap is created between an individual's goals and their attainment, aggression will occur until either catharsis, displacement, or change in regime behavior curtails the impetus toward political conflict (Davies, 1969). In short, mass political conflict is characteristically a lumpy good. It is assumed that there is a threshold of frustration that, once passed, produces the critical mass necessary to organize mass protest.

Hypothesis 2, also consistent with frustration-aggression theory, is that one should be able to observe the event or events that promote individuals to respond to frustration with mass political conflict. Indeed, it is the existence of such trigger event(s), combined with high levels of frustration, that is sufficient cause for political conflict. As illustrated in Figure 7.2, these trigger event(s) can either increase the gap between goals and their attainment or negatively affect prospects for displacement. Both increase the level of frustration toward the regime, increasing the probability of conflict.

Hypothesis 3, our most direct test of the frustration-aggression model, is that the probability of conflict should be affected by the level of repression present in a society. A positive relationship between conflict and repression supports the proposition of a positive effect of repression on the level of societal frustration. A negative relationship supports theories for the deterrent value of repression. A curvilinear relationship indicates that there is both a positive and a negative effect of repression on conflict but that the effect is dependent on the intensity of the repression applied.[4]

Hypothesis 4, directly testing the rational-choice model, is to decide what consequences participants in political conflict are likely to think of as beneficial or adverse and then to see if they follow a strategy predicted to bring beneficial results. In this investigation we explore the possibility that participants in mass political conflict perceive government instability, defined as changes in the makeup of the executive branch (e.g., cabinet change), as a potential benefit of conflict. To compare the relevance of either model, assumptions from both models are run in a single equation (see Figure 7.3) to see which approach better explains political conflict.

METHODOLOGY

The example of the Los Angeles riots points to some of the practical difficulties involved in investigating mass political conflict using quantitative analysis. The exact event or sequence of events that instigates conflict may differ from case to case. Likewise, what causes the feelings of dissatisfaction may differ from person to person as well as from group to group. Still, statistical inference necessitates a move from the rich historical evidence

Table 7.1

Relative Frequency of the Distance Between Conflict Events in Sixteen European Countries, 1948–1981

```
Total Number of Events: 2595
Total Number of Observations: 178192
Mean Number of Days Between Events: 64.1 days
```

Days between Events	Number of events	Relative Frequency	Accumulated Frequency
1	446	17.2	17.2
2 to 5	586	22.7	39.9
6 to 10	281	10.8	50.7
11 to 25	410	15.8	66.5
25 to 50	295	11.4	79.9
50 to 100	205	7.9	87.8
101 to 1000	300	11.5	98.5

available in case studies to the more structured sources of data collected and coded from a sample of cases. Since the focus of this investigation is to explicate the relationship between government repression and conflict, we have tried to find data appropriate for this task.

The data source used for this experiment is the Taylor and Jodice (1983) daily event database. Using mostly newspaper accounts, the dataset records forty-three catagories of events occurring over the years 1948 to 1982. The events are catalogued by date and country, and can be broadly summarized as evidence of mass political conflict, political repression, and political instability occurring in different countries over that time period. Three types of behavior are operationalized using information from the data set. Mass political conflict is evidenced by the occurrence of political demonstrations, riots, or political strikes (by both students and workers). Political repression is evidenced by governmental acts of political restrictions, censorship, or political execution. Political instability is assumed to occur whenever there is an unscheduled change in the membership of the executive branch of government.

To test Hypothesis 1, the nonnormal distribution of political conflict over time, we calculate the distance, in days, between instances of conflict using a sample of 16 different European countries.[5] The number of days between events can range from 1, if some form of conflict occurs on successive days, up to 12,000 or so, the number of days from 1948 to 1982.[6] Table 7.1 shows the frequency distribution for several different distance intervals.

Table 7.1 provides strong evidence that mass political conflict is not a normally distributed event. While the average length of time between conflict events is sixty-four days, there is over a 50 percent probability that if conflict occurs on any one day, conflict will occur again within the next ten days. Clearly, the existence of conflict on one day increases the prob-

Table 7.2
Correlation Between Mass Political Conflict and Governmental Repression

Unit of Analysis	Correlation Coefficient
Country-Day	.1856
Country-Week	.3912
Country-Month	.5664

ability that conflict will occur in the near future, and the nonoccurrence of conflict reverses this probability.

Table 7.1 also gives some clue as to what time dimension to use as the appropriate unit of analysis in statistical tests of the other three hypotheses. The short distances between many instances of political conflict, including many occurring on successive days, indicate the need to either make the time dimension of the dependent variable a single day or justify the decision to aggregate the data over a larger time period. While aggregation over time is a useful technique to smooth out noisy data, Table 7.2 suggests the cost of aggregation in this instance.

Given political repression's theoretical importance in our models of political conflict, it is important to try to disentangle the time sequence between the two events. But even using daily data,[7] the probability that conflict and repression occur on the same day is 0.18. Increase the time dimension to a week and the correlation between the number of days during which some form of conflict is experienced and the number of days in which the government initiates repression increases to 0.39. Using a month as the unit of analysis, the correlation coefficient jumps to 0.56. The choice is clear. Unless instrumental variables are found to construct a system of equations comprising these two events, the best one can do is to push the data set to be as finely grained as possible, in this case, using observations of a single day. The noise in the data set will be a hindrance, though it should work against finding a significant relationship where it may in reality exist. If the noise is random, it should wreak equal havoc against tests for either theoretical perspective. If this is the case, the damage the noise produces should be minimal, similar to placing too small an alpha in tests of statistical inference to protect against type 1 errors (Goldstein and Freeman, 1990:39–41).

Given the unit of analysis, it was decided not to differentiate between the intensity of events occurring within a single observation. That is, the variables for conflict, repression, and instability are dichotomous, taking on the value of one or zero depending on whether or not they happened in a particular country on a particular day. There are several reasons for this decision. First, given that the variables are summations of different types of events, there is no *a priori* reason to weight one type of event, such as instituting political restrictions, differently from another type of event, such as political executions. Second, since there is more than one country in our sample, and countries have different sized populations and governmental apparatuses, it would be difficult to determine, without adjusting for these differences, what multiple occurrences of an event on a single day might mean in terms of their intensity level measured across countries.

A third reason for dichotomizing variables has to do with the characteristic of the dependent variable, mass political conflict. Conflict occurs in less than 2 percent of the observations. Given its skewed distribution, this means there are long periods during which no conflict occurs. In such instances, the use of linear regression techniques is problematic and should be dropped in favor of maximum likelihood estimation (King, 1989). In our experiment, this is most easily accomplished by applying probit or logit techniques to estimate the probability of the dependent variable occurring given the explanatory variables. While these procedures do not restrict the dependent variable from taking on more than two values, concerns mentioned above about the use of different sized countries and weighing between different types of events suggest simplifying to "yes" or "no" the answer to whether there is political conflict in a particular country on a particular day.

The decision to dichotomize the event variables across observations means the dependent variable for all experiments will be the probability of conflict occurring in any one day (either zero or one). What explanatory variable to use to explain this probability is dependent on the hypothesis to be tested. Hypothesis 2 asks whether there are events which trigger occurrences of political conflict. Four events are considered as possible triggers to conflict: political repression, political instability, conflict occurring in other countries, and past instances of conflict occurring within that country.

Repression is considered a possible trigger to conflict as a direct result of frustration-aggression theory. Repression increases popular frustration with the regime and hence the possibility of mass conflict. It should be noted that only past governmental actions are considered, thereby eliminating the problem of disentangling the causal order in those cases where conflict and repression occur on the same day. The implicit assumption is that mass political movements take time to assemble their forces in order to confront the government. While this assumption may be questionable in the case of riots, it does have intuitive plausibility in the cases of political demonstrations and strikes.

Political instability, while not necessarily increasing the popular frustration toward the regime, should make potential conflict participants conscious of their grievances toward the regime. This increase in consciousness should decrease the propensity for individuals to displace their frustration toward other objects, increasing the likelihood that they will focus their attention on what they perceive to be the real source of their frustrations—the government.

The inclusion of regional conflict as a potential trigger mechanism for domestic conflict is closely associated with the notion of there being consciousness-raising events that can spark domestic discontent. Whether transmitted through the media, class contact, or other channels, acts in one country may cause other acts in another country. That events may have spillover effects onto other countries is consistent with Rosenau's (1990:298–305) concept of cascading interdependence and has found empirical support in Li and Thompson's (1975) coup contagion hypothesis and Bremer's (1980) study on the contagiousness of international disputes.

There are two reasons for including an explanatory variable composed of lagged occurrences of the dependent variable. First, conflict, like instability and regional conflict, may decrease displacement of frustration related to popular dissatisfaction with the regime, thereby increasing the probability of future conflict (see Figure 7.2). Second, if the lagged dependent variable is not included as an independent variable, there would be no way to disentangle the impact the other explanatory variables have on the probability of conflict and the effect past occurrences of conflict may have on the other explanatory variables. This problem is especially severe given conflict's highly skewed distribution. It is easy to show that repression varies along with conflict, but it is more difficult to show that repression causes conflict or vice versa. The lagged endogenous variable is included to help control for attributing as the cause for conflict those things which are simply its effects.

Determining the proper length of time that can elapse for any of the explanatory variables to trigger mass political conflict is difficult. Increasing the difficulty of the task is that each of the explanatory events may appear on successive days, implying a possibility that it may be a short-term culmination of events that triggers the aggressive response (assumption 1 of frustration-aggression theory). For this reason, explanatory variables for each type of behavior are created using a weighted sum for each corresponding event variable. The weight variables increase by one each time an event takes place in a country but decrease by a certain percentage from one observation to the next.[8] Or, more formally,

$$ES_{jct} = \sum_{t=0}^{-\infty} ES_{jt-1} \times (1 - r) + E_{jct}$$

where

ES_{jct} = weighted sum of event j in country c at time t

ES_{jct-1} = weighted sum at $t - 1$ (if $c_t = c_{t-1}$; else $c_t = 0$)

r = the discount parameter from one observation to the next

E_{jct} = event j in country c at time t

Note that S in ES stands for short-run effects of event E.

By this procedure, the explanatory variables are transformed from dichotomous to continuous variables. Though a series of discount rates (r) are tried, the rate selected to illustrate the short-term effect—10 percent a day—is determined *a priori* as the smallest possible discount rate consistent with the concept being tested in hypothesis 2. After two weeks, it is argued, an event's influence in triggering conflict should no longer be significant. To test hypothesis 2, the effect of trigger event(s), a probit analysis is run using the following equation,

$$P(C) = PCS + PRS + PIS + PRCS$$

where:

$P(C)$ = probability of conflict

PCS = level of conflict occurring in the recent past

PRS = level of repression occurring in the recent past

PIS = level of instability occurring in the recent past

$PRCS$ = level of regional conflict occurring in the recent past

RESULTS

The results of the probit analysis, in Table 7.3, reveal all four variables do positively effect the probability of conflict. Rerunning the tests changing the discount parameter from 10 percent to 50 percent per day makes little difference either to the signs or significance levels of the chi-square scores for each parameter's point estimate. The results support hypothesis 2 that certain events do seem to trigger mass political conflict, though a more

Table 7.3

Probit Analysis Testing the Short-Run Effects of Mass Conflict, Repression, and Regional Mass Conflict on the Probability of Conflict

Log Likelihood for NORMAL -11364.16576

Variable	DF	Estimate	Std Err	ChiSquare	Pr>Chi	Label/Value
INTERCEPT	1	-2.45101322	0.01206	41305.9	0.0001	Intercept
PCS	1	0.4591141	0.01135	1636.204	0.0001	
PRS	1	0.1494437	0.010905	187.8133	0.0001	
PIS	1	0.1540555	0.033637	20.97525	0.0001	
PRCS	1	0.0094542	0.002455	14.82684	0.0001	

sophisticated test, one including longer-term effects, is needed to test for the accumulative effect of repression on conflict.

Hypothesis 3 incorporates predictions as to longer-term effects of repression on conflict. While competing predictions are made concerning positive, negative, or combined effects of repression on conflict, a general test of the relationship can be made by including into a single equation,

$$P(C) = PRL + PR^2L$$

where

$PRL =$ level of repression in the long run
$PR^2L =$ that same level of repression squared

Either the linear or exponential variable for long-term repression may be positively, negatively, or not significantly related to the probability of conflict, for a total of nine possible combinations in all. What each result indicates about the relationship between conflict and repression is summarized in Table 7.4.

To capture longer-run effects, additional level variables are created, following the procedure used in creating the short-run variables but with much smaller discount parameters, indicating a slower rate of decay in the value of the variable from one observation to the next.[9] Though an infinite number of discount parameters are possible, 2 discount parameters are chosen for the test of the hypotheses: a decay rate of 1 percent per day, indicating that an event would lose half of its explanatory value in 69 days; and a decay rate of one-tenth of 1 percent a day, indicating a much slower half life of over 200 days. Also, 2 parameters are used to examine whether there is a difference between the medium and very long-run effects of the explanatory variables (labeled M and L, respectively, in the probit analysis).

Along with linear and squared values of both longer-term levels of repression (PRM, PR^2M; PRL, PR^2L), short-term effects of repression, both linear and squared (PRS, PR^2S), are added to the equation to test hypothesis 3. Short-run effects are included to see whether what occurs in the long run also occurs in the short run. If results differ in the short term versus the long term, this would suggest different time lags for the two effects of repression on conflict and would indicate another dimension besides simply intensity per time unit in which to investigate the relationship. Basically, including linear and squared values for short-, medium-, and long-term effects is an attempt to compare the effectiveness of varying the time dimension versus the intensity dimension in explaining the effect of repression on conflict.

Besides the variables for repression, the factors of short-, medium-, and

Table 7.4
Nine Possible Observed Effects of Repression on Conflict

	Observed Effect		Explanation
	Linear	Squared	
1	+	ns	Repression increases frustration
2	ns	+	Only intense repression increases frustration
3	+	+	Repression increases frustration; intense repression increases frustration exponentially
4	−	ns	Repression inhibits aggression
5	ns	−	Only intense repression inhibits aggression
6	−	−	Repression inhibits frustration; intense repression inhibits aggression exponentially
7	+	−	Repression both inhibits conflict and increases frustration; but at intense levels, inhibition dominant
8	−	+	Repression both inhibits conflict and increases frustration; but at intense levels, frustration dominant
9	ns	ns	Repression has no effect on conflict

long-run effects of instability (*PIS, PIM, PIL*), regional conflict (*PRCS, PRCM, PRCL*), and past level of conflict (*PCS, PCM, PCL*) are added to test hypothesis 3. If any of these additional effects are shown to be significant in the long run, this would indicate there are other reasons for conflict than simply the level of governmental repression present in that society.

The results of the test for hypothesis 3 (Table 7.5) provide strong evidence of a curvilinear (inverted U shape) relationship between past level of repression and the probability of conflict. While all three linear variables for repression (*PRS, PRM, PRL*) are significantly positive, those variables squared (PR^2S, PR^2M, PR^2L) are clearly negative. This is consistent with Gurr's (1969:609–614) finding on the effect of government's negative sanctions on political conflict. At moderate levels, repression increases political conflict, presumably by increasing popular frustration with the regime. But if the repression is intense, the population will divert its frustration toward other objects. This investigation, however, is not sophisticated enough to analyze directly the effects of such displacement.

Table 7.5
Probit Analysis to Test the Linear and Exponential Relationship Between Mass Political Conflict and Repression

```
Log Likelihood for NORMAL -10818.79749
```

Variable	DF	Estimate	Std Err	ChiSquare	Pr>Chi	Label/Value
INTERCEPT	1	-2.76742169	0.022068	15726.53	0.0001	Intercept
PCS	1	0.3122793	0.01424	480.9233	0.0001	
PCM	1	0.0101066	0.003902	6.708794	0.0096	
PCL	1	0.0073119	0.000626	136.5834	0.0001	
PRS	1	0.2165105	0.028764	56.65861	0.0001	
PRM	1	0.0155517	0.00615	6.395279	0.0114	
PRL	1	0.0064242	0.000909	49.89315	0.0001	
PIS	1	0.0962367	0.03741	6.617801	0.0101	
PIM	1	-0.00935609	0.013957	0.44938	0.5026	
PIL	1	0.0069503	0.002649	6.883965	0.0087	
PRCS	1	-0.00343875	0.003753	0.839436	0.3596	
PRCM	1	0.0010876	0.000774	1.972913	0.1601	
PRCL	1	0.0000531	0.000091	0.339061	0.5604	
PR^{2}S	1	-0.02602924	0.005745	20.53053	0.0001	
PR^{2}M	1	-0.00086619	0.000153	32.24455	0.0001	
PR^{2}L	1	-0.00004929	4.399E-6	125.5803	0.0001	

On the negative side, the inclusion of additional variables eliminates regional conflict as a significant trigger to mass conflict, and there is no evidence of a contagion effect in the long run. More important, the significance of long-term variables for conflict (*PCM* + *PCL*) and instability (*PIL*) indicates there are other sources for conflict than simply the level of repression in a society. So there is evidence to caution us not to overstate the conclusions drawn from this preliminary investigation.

Evidence of the effect of time on the relationship between repression and conflict is slightly more complicated. The positive effect of the first-order (linear) effect of the level of repression on conflict (*PRS, PRM, PRL*) and the negative second-order effect (*PR^{2}S, PR^{2}M, PR^{2}L*) suggests it is only the intensity of repression that leads to lower conflict. However, comparing the negative effect of intense repression on the overall level of conflict for the three different time dimensions does reveal a difference between the short- and long-term effects of repression, regardless of intensity.

To determine how important the negative effect of intense repression is to the probability of conflict, we reran the test without including the first power values for the three repression values (*PRS, PRM* + *PRL*). The result of this run (not shown) shows that short-term repression, regardless of how intense, does increase the probability of conflict. On the other hand, if intense levels of repression persist over time, conflict diminishes. This is relative not just to what would have occurred at moderate levels of repression, but to what they would be if repression were never applied

Figure 7.4
Repression and Conflict

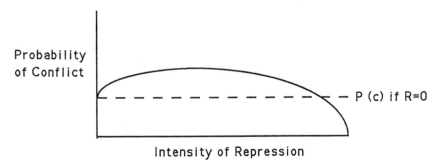

Intensity of Repression

at all. As shown in Figure 7.4, long-term intense levels of repression lower conflict, not just relative to moderate levels of repression, but lower than if repression were never applied at all.

RATIONAL-CHOICE MODEL

We now turn to the test of hypothesis 4, which states that potential participants of mass political conflict calculate the effects of conflict before deciding whether to act. Two simple assumptions are made: that repression is considered a cost of conflict, and that political instability is considered a benefit of it. Repression presumably hurts the people toward whom it is directed, and repression that occurs after mass political conflict is most likely directed against those participants of it. Similarly, it is assumed that political instability occurring after mass political conflict is caused by that conflict, and that the resulting changes are in some manner a benefit to those participants of conflict (e.g., the stepping down of a minister in charge).

The distributed lag variables used to capture the short-run versus long-run effects of various events can also be used to distinguish temporal ordering between different types of events. Specifically, if medium-run conflict exists alongside short-term repression (*PCM* × *PRS*), it is argued the participants in conflict will perceive that the conflict led to the repression. This interactive variable, *PCM* × *PRS*, is constructed to represent the concept labeled $R_t \times C_{t-1}$ in Figure 7.3. To produce the level variable derived from this interactive effect (labeled *learned aversion* in Figure 7.3), an additional variable is created to capture the accumulation of the interactive effect over time. Formally, the level variable is created using the formula,

$$sumPCS \times PCM_t = [.999(PCS \times PCM)_{t-1}] + (PCS \times PCM)_t$$

Table 7.6
Probit Analysis Comparing Frustration-Aggression to the Rational-Choice Model
for Explaining Mass Political Conflict

Log Likelihood for NORMAL -8496.805089

Variable	DF	Estimate	Std Err	ChiSquare	Pr>Chi	Label/Value
INTERCEPT	1	-2.82893411	0.026144	11708.13	0.0001	Intercept
PCS	1	0.3195456	0.017703	325.8111	0.0001	
PCM	1	0.0426033	0.005921	51.77638	0.0001	
PCL	1	0.0051019	0.001306	15.26559	0.0001	
PRS	1	0.2661789	0.034549	59.35609	0.0001	
PRM	1	0.0103456	0.007793	1.762605	0.1843	
PRL	1	0.0057882	0.001108	27.26944	0.0001	
PRL^2	1	-0.01693434	0.00761	4.952434	0.0261	
PRL^2	1	-0.00029527	0.00022	1.793917	0.1804	
PRL^2	1	-0.00005464	6.012E-6	82.60115	0.0001	
PIS	1	0.2054309	0.05025	16.71296	0.0001	
PIM	1	-0.00459238	0.014352	0.102387	0.7490	
PIL	1	0.0055937	0.003122	3.209263	0.0732	
PRCS	1	0.0041739	0.004083	1.045041	0.3067	
PRCM	1	0.0000746	0.000866	0.007404	0.9314	
PRCL	1	0.0001306	0.000106	1.523394	0.2171	
PRS*PCM	1	-0.01296758	0.001767	53.86247	0.0001	
sumPRS*PCM	1	7.4367E-6	2.15E-6	11.96086	0.0005	
PIS*PCM	1	-0.01592972	0.003882	16.84094	0.0001	
sumPIS*PCM	1	-0.00001838	9.663E-6	3.617892	0.0572	

If the value of *sumPRS* × *PCM* is large, this implies that the probability that conflict leads to repression is high. This should deter participants from continuing acts of conflict. Likewise, the accumulative effect of conflict in medium-run conflict times instability in the short run, *sumPCM* × *PIS*, should make dissent more likely. Along with these accumulative effects, the simple interactive effects between the short and medium run, *PCM* × *PRS* and *PCM* × *PIS*, are included to see if what participants learn from conflict differs in the long run from what they learn in the immediate. A probit analysis is run (Table 7.6), adding these four variables (*PCM* × *PRS*, *PCM* × *PIS*, *sumPCM* × *PRS*, and *sumPCM* × *PIS*) to the previous test of the frustration-aggression model (Table 7.5).

The results give little support for the rational-choice model, especially in regards to the effect of repression on conflict. The accumulative effect of responding to conflict with repression (*sumPCM* × *PRS*) is to increase the probability of conflict, exactly opposite of what was predicted from the rational-choice model. This finding suggests that participants of mass political conflict do not calculate the likely response by government before they decide to act. This is consistent with Hibbs's (1973:185) finding that collective protests are unlikely to be deterred by governmental action. However, the negative sign of the interactive variable (*PCM* × *PRS*) suggests that once conflict occurs, the short-run level of conflict may be manipulated by governmental action. This finding is consistent with the notion that the rationale for conflict participants' behavior may change once a conflict episode commences.

Whether one looks at the accumulative (*sumPIS* × *PCM*) or immediate effects (*PIS* × *PCM*), conflict in the medium to long run times instability in the short run decreases the probability of conflict in the present. These results are exactly opposite from what is expected. If instability were considered a benefit of conflict, our rational-choice model (Figure 7.3) predicts that instability following conflict increases future conflict, either through a simple stimulus-response mechanism ($B_t \times C_{t-i}$) or through a longer-term learning function (learned compulsion).

Though counter to the simple assumption made concerning the relationship between conflict and instability, the results may hint at a more sophisticated appraisal of the situation. If the government gives in to the protesters' demands and performs the necessary changes, this may decrease the probability of future conflict by lowering the protesters' frustration with the regime. An alternative explanation, consistent with the rational-choice model, is that instability reflects a cost for participants of mass conflict, as would be the case if the change reflected the coming to power of a more repressive regime. This investigation is unable to distinguish between these two possible explanations.

A DECISION-MAKING MODEL FOR GOVERNMENT

To this point we have only dealt with the psyche and rationale of the participants of political conflict, but the question can be inverted to ask about the behavior of government. If intense levels of repression lead to lower probability of mass conflict, why doesn't the government continually exercise its ability to repress? Part of the answer has already been given in the positive relationship between short-term repression and conflict, regardless of the level of repression. Further evidence can be gleaned by taking the perspective of the government and asking, what should be the proper response to mass political conflict?

To answer this question, we run a test, assuming the government has three possible responses to political conflict: to repress, to change, or to do nothing. To see what is likely to happen if the government represses, two interactive variables between repression and conflict are created, one for the short run (*PRS* × *PCS*) and one for the medium run (*PRM* × *PCM*). Similarly, two interactive variables are created to determine what results if government decides instead to make changes in the executive branch to try to reduce mass conflict (*PIS* × *PCS, PIM* × *PCM*). In running the test forecasting the alternative consequences of government action, variables for the effects of repression and instability are not included since if the government decides to act in response to conflict, it is by definition interactive with the act of conflict.

Table 7.7
Forecast of Alternative Government Action

```
Log Likelihood for NORMAL -11063.29029

Variable    DF    Estimate   Std Err  ChiSquare   Pr>Chi  Label/Value

INTERCEPT   1  -2.57931724  0.015572   27434.63   0.0001  Intercept
PCS         1    0.3211834  0.018116   314.3308   0.0001
PCM         1    0.0877094  0.003285   712.7401   0.0001
PRCS        1  -0.00347035  0.003648   0.905027   0.3414
PRCM        1    0.0024923   0.00052   22.99358   0.0001
PIS*PCS     1    -0.00793   0.017388   0.207996   0.6483
PIM*PCM     1  -0.00389803  0.000573   46.27135   0.0001
PRS*PCS     1    0.0073393  0.005662   1.680094   0.1949
PRM*PCM     1  -0.00139651  0.000125   124.0682   0.0001
```

The results (Table 7.7) reveal an interesting choice for the part of government between using change or repression. There is no clearly determinable short-term relationship between either instability or repression on the probability of conflict. Though both repression and instability are shown to be positively related to conflict when acting by themselves, it seems both repression and instability have a more varied effect on short-term prospects of conflict when they are produced as a response to conflict. However, in the long run, both instability and repression act to lower the probability of conflict. The question, then, is, which policy should the government choose to lower the probability of mass conflict? If there are other costs associated with initiating repressive legislation (e.g., electoral votes), it may make sense to appease the domestic turmoil by giving in to certain demands. On the other hand, by appeasing insurgents' demands, a government may lose support from conservative backers of the status quo.

CONCLUSION

This experiment gives support for analyzing the relationship between repression and mass political conflict in terms of frustration-aggression theory. The episodic character of mass political conflict is consistent with the conception that conflict, once initiated, will continue until the decrease in displacement is overtaken by the increase in catharsis (e.g., a political demonstration wanes after a few days). The observation of events that trigger conflict supports the notion that when the gap between goals and their attainment reaches a critical threshold, conflict follows. Finally, the curvilinear relationship between repression and conflict supports the view that repression can both deter and promote conflict and that it is not time but intensity that is critical in determining which effect will dominate the relationship.

On the negative side, there is little evidence to support the more parsimonious rational-choice model. The cumulative effect of repression following conflict does not decrease the probability of conflict as expected. Nor does the increase in regime instability following conflict increase the likelihood of conflict. However, once in a conflict episode, participants do seem to react to government behavior. Both instability and repression decrease the likelihood of further conflict. This similar response to different government action suggests government may choose alternative paths to regulate conflict.

NOTES

I would like to thank two people without whom this chapter could not have been completed: Rosanna B. Sherick for lending me her data management skills to put the database in order; and Eduard A. Ziegenhagen for his encouragement and criticism during various stages of the chapter's development. Their input is reflected in all that is good about this chapter. All errors and omissions are the sole responsibility of the author.

1. In their seminal work on the subject, Dollard and his colleagues (1939) refer to the relationship between frustration and aggression as a hypothesis, presumably to reflect both its psychoanalytic heritage and its empirical implications. However, here I use it as a model for individual behavior, from which I produce hypotheses about the relationship between mass political conflict and government repression. Therefore, I refer to it as frustration-aggression theory.

2. Political conflict may also channel other forms of individual frustration into frustration toward the regime. This effect is not specified in the model since this study does not investigate what other forms of frustrations are likely to be displaced into frustration toward the regime (e.g., socioeconomic conditions).

3. Still another explanation for the riots emphasizes how the social structure in the affected areas led to institutions in which individuals learned how to behave aggressively (e.g., the role of gangs). While such a learning process may be important in determining conflict (or its displacement), the approach taken here is to subsume such models into the psychological motivation perspective. The important distinction is whether participants rationally anticipate gain from conflict. The analysis is not sophisticated enough to consider all the other alternative ways frustration may be learned and/or vented.

4. In this experiment, repression is operationalized as governmental acts targeted at inhibiting individuals' behavior (political restrictions, censorship, and political execution). For reasons explained later, these events are not scaled according to their severity. The intensity value is simply the number of days a regime enacts incidents of repression over a period of time. The larger percentage of days the government utilizes repression, the greater the intensity of repression. Using this measure for intensity of repression is consistent with our desire to test whether such acts inhibits political protest.

5. There are several reasons for choosing a sample of sixteen European states. Computational costs force a limit on the number of states investigated. Using daily data, there are well over ten-thousand observations per country. On the other hand, a pooled analysis is considered necessary to compare the explanatory variables across state jurisdictions. A region of states is chosen to test whether conflict

in one state increases the likelihood of conflict occurring in other states in the region. Western Europe is selected because the states in the region are fairly homogeneous, sharing a common cultural and political evolution, thereby allowing the study not to get bogged down at this stage with questions of intercultural or political differences. Finally, none of the states in the sample is so large as to require us to differentiate between events occurring in different places of the country.

The use of maximum likelihood estimates makes testing the applicability of a pooled analysis problematic. The usual procedure, testing hypotheses between restricted and unrestricted models, is impossible. Instead, I simply reran all experiments on each of the individual countries as well as in a pooled sample. The results of the individual analysis are, on the whole, very similar to the pooled case. The major difference occurs in those countries which experienced very little political conflict over the period. In such cases, the parameter coefficients are generally in agreement with the pooled analysis, though, not surprisingly, the chi-squares are rarely significant with a high degree of confidence. Therefore, I conclude it is reasonable to pool the data in this instance.

6. The distance between conflict events within each country is censored to that time period between the first and last recorded instances of conflict since no information exists concerning the distance between those events and the event that came before, in the first case, or after, in the last case.

7. Note that the day an event is recorded in the data set is the day the event was coded in the *Times* index, not necessarily the day the event took place. The implicit assumption here is that if the index records two events on subsequent days, it is likely that these events took place one after the other.

8. The level variables are restricted from taking on values between 0 and 0.1. If the calculation for a variable falls below 0.1, the value of the variable becomes 0. This restriction keeps very small values in the explanatory variables from influencing the nonlinear estimates of the slope coefficients in the maximum likelihood procedure. As it turns out, this restriction does not significantly change the results of the experiment.

9. To keep the long-run variables from being overly influenced by short-term events, these variables, once constructed, were lagged six observations so that the previous observation in the case of the two long-term variables is really $t - 6$.

8

TOWARD A DYNAMIC MODEL OF POLITICAL CONFLICT, DEVELOPMENT, AND POLICY: A COMPUTER SIMULATION

Eduard A. Ziegenhagen

The preceding chapters provide opportunities to assess progress toward establishing linkages among model components. This chapter is designed to continue this emphasis in the form of an integrated dynamic model. The model is composed of eight principal components: expectations, system performance, demands, political conflict, insurgency, sanctions, the sanctioning apparatus, and political development. Each is described in turn, and model behavior is presented.

MODEL ARCHITECTURE AND BEHAVIOR

Architecture refers to the structure of the model and its components, in this case determined by icon manipulation and a series of equations, while model behavior represents the product of structure and parameter settings. Model architecture, confined to the principal components noted above, is represented in Figure 8.1. All political systems share these elementary components, and each component has a particular set of relationships to each other determined by its function (Parsons, 1951; Almond, 1965). Demands are most often treated as inputs to such models, although why they are made and how they vary have been treated differently in the literature. Easton, for example, views demands as the expression of the goals of political actors (1965). Most often, the source of demands is attributed to various psychological mechanisms—for example, need hierarchies (Maslow, 1943), absolute and relative deprivation (Runciman, 1966), and frustration-aggression (Dollard et al., 1939; Berkowitz, 1962) and rational-choice paradigms. Regardless of their specific psychological or social psychological nature, demands are most often conceived of as a function

Figure 8.1
Generic Conflict Model

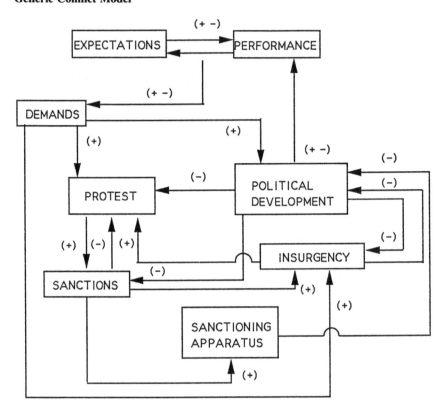

of gaps between expectations of performance and the actual performance of a political system. Expectations are the economic, social, or political returns anticipated by individual or group participants based on social and political norms (Hoselitz and Willner, 1962). System performance, of course, represents whatever tangible or intangible returns are seen as pertinent to expectations.

Expectations generally exceed increases in performance, although they may lag performance during performance decline. Generally, expectations and performance are associated in a pattern of sustained oscillation (Davies, 1962). Demands of the political system are made as gaps between expectations and performance occur. Generally, expectations exceed the ability of a system to meet them, and new expectations tend to be substituted by those that are met. This formulation is consistent with theorists such as Maslow (1943) who argues that persons attempt to satisfy a hierarchy of needs. As lower level needs are satisfied, attempts to satisfy needs at the next level are initiated. Additionally, some expectations are a function of escalating comparative standards such as those of consumption or status. For example, consumption of goods has no identifiable limit. Status expectations also may be limitless due to changing bases for comparison.

Political conflict is a function of demands made of the system. Most often political conflict is manifested by protest behavior, which entails expressions of public disagreement or opposition to the practices and policies of a regime, and insurgency, which involves efforts to eliminate or supplant regime incumbents rather than merely express disapproval. Specific expressions of protest behavior include demonstrations and riots, while insurgent behavior encompasses assassinations and coups. Exactly what proportion of demands is manifested by political conflict has not been established in the literature. Approached from a rational-choice perspective, demands contribute to political conflict only if the anticipated costs of conflict are less than the gains anticipated from participation. If this is not the case, there is no basis for departing from whatever other behavior participants associate with satisfaction of their needs, whether it is passive acceptance of the status quo or participation in approved forms such as economic enterprise or electoral politics. However, when gaps between expectations and performance become severe, or possibly intolerable, anticipated gains outweigh costs, and political conflict can result (Davies, 1962).

Very clearly, political conflict may be inappropriate if other promising means to obtain objectives are available. Rostow (1960) argues that economic growth can result in addressing the basic needs of a population through increases in savings, income, and productivity, without resorting to political conflict or even direct government intervention to address such needs. Even in periods of economic downturn, when persons attempt to avoid sustaining losses rather than realize gains, individuals do not necessarily resort to political conflict. For example, Rawls (1971) contends that political conflict varies in respect to the degree that economic losses are sustained across, rather than within, social strata. If losses are sustained by strata more or less equally, demands for redistribution are less likely to arise.

Some demands are not related to the allocation or distribution of tangible resources. The degree to which particular social groupings are able to maintain or advance their social values, norms, and customs through government intervention varies considerably. Gusfield (1963) and Edelman (1964) describe the behavior of social groups that regard particular national policies as indicators of their status. Attempts to repress languages, religions, and ethnic identities are common in most societies. In such instances, little latitude for compromise exists, a regime's performance is likely to be considered inadequate, and resorting to political conflict may be more likely than in instances of economic dissatisfaction.

The model provides opportunities for incorporating variation in the degree to which demands are likely to be pursued through political conflict by incorporating a conversion parameter. For example, symbolic issues closely related to social worth could carry a greater conversion parameter than economic distribution issues.

The relationship between political conflict and repression is explored in several of the empirical investigations reported above. One is not only interested in whether or not conflict and repression bear a simultaneous relationship but also whether they are linear or curvilinear (see chapters 6 and 7). Political conflict itself entails a wide range of behavior requiring different social and political resources, and it has varying implications for social policy, regime stability, and regime responses. Political conflict lies outside of political expression actively supported by most regimes, although demonstrations are tolerated by a small number of states mostly in Europe or of European political culture. Generally, all regimes employ negative sanctions to regulate political conflict to some extent, and behavior that challenges a regime's existence almost always elicits repressive measures.

Some theorists argue that political conflict is primarily a function of the mobilization of insurgents rather than a gap between demands and system performance. Insurgency entails the mobilization of disaffected participants to act in support of various forms of political conflict by utilizing organizational, communication, and financial capabilities (Tilly, 1978; Gamson, 1974). The need to regulate the behavior of those who wish to supplant incumbents rather than merely alter public policy assumes a high priority for incumbents.

As one would expect, linkages from demands to protest and to insurgent mobilization are positive, as is the link from insurgency to protest. In order to provide for variation in the level of insurgency, initial insurgency parameters can be set and provisions made for beginning differences in the degree to which insurgency supports particular forms of political conflict. For example, if insurgency within a particular political system is based on mobilization to express discontent over economic allocation policy issues, very little support may be forthcoming for protest that is based upon ethnically symbolic issues.

Up to this point, the model is dominated by sustained oscillation between expectations and performance. Yet performance rarely exceeds expectations, and some degree of unmet demands generates political conflict and promotes the growth of insurgency. Many systems are in fact unstable, but most have developed components that are designed to maximize stability by enhancing performance and lessening political conflict and insurgency.

Perhaps most important, systems differ in their ability to meet demands and cope with discontent. For the most part, more developed systems differ from less developed systems by the degree to which their political institutions have emerged to accommodate demands and institutionalize political conflict. The development of social services associated with the welfare state and of bureaucracies to deliver such services constitutes an overt effort to provide for satisfaction of the most basic human needs, but the development of institutions offering opportunities for participation in political life distinguishes more developed systems from those that are less so. For example, the performance of aggregation and articulation functions through interest groups and political parties, participation in the electoral process, and access to decision makers in law making, execution, and adjudication institutions exists in various forms in advanced systems.

Additionally, systems can utilize various strategies for institutionalizing dissent. Governmental responses to various conditions contributing to the likelihood of conflict entail modification of the manner in which demands are processed rather than giving in to demands for change and actually instituting conditions of change. Co-optation of dissidents, modification of the prerequisites for aggregation, and articulation of interests are all means available to regimes without addressing performance and without state intervention in the allocation of societal resources. Taken as a whole, more politically developed systems are better able to lessen the more destructive forms of political conflict than are less developed systems.

Systems also differ in their ability to decrease the gap between expectations and performance. More developed systems are likely to respond to demands by actually increasing performance rather than merely institutionalizing demands. Furthermore, comparatively more developed systems may be able to reduce gaps between expectations and performance. Bringing expectations in closer proximity to performance is common. This can be achieved possibly through enhanced political communication capabilities due to mass media but more likely through communicating institutions such as political parties and interest groups. These sources of information frame issues, define options, and identify alternatives. Consistent with Easton's (1965) perspective, such behavior generates support for regimes and ultimately contributes to system stability. Systems lacking such political infrastructure are likely to be less successful in conforming general expectations to actual performance capabilities of a system and achieving consensus as to what problem-solving options are selected.

Political conflict is also addressed by efforts to limit its expression through punishing those who engage in such behavior. These limitations include the use of negative sanctions, such as restrictions on political organization and communication, and in some instances imprisonment and execution for political acts. Political practitioners in many systems subscribe to the belief that political conflict can be addressed by employing negative sanctions, often in the absence of political infrastructure, although in some instances as an alternative to it.

Some empirical findings support this view, and various relationships between political conflict and sanctioning behavior have been reported, although results are mixed. For example, Alfatooni and Allen (1990), Davis and Ward (1990), and Robinson and London (1991) find that repressive behavior is linked to increased political conflict. However, Hibbs (1973) and Snyder and Tilly (1972) argue that repression lessens political conflict. Less surprisingly, political conflict has been found to increase repressive behavior (Duvall and Shamir, 1980; Jackson et al., 1978; Hibbs, 1973). Another alternative explanation is that repressive behavior and political conflict affect each other. Although relatively few studies investigate this possibility, Davenport (1992), Davis and Ward (1990), Hibbs (1973), and Ziegenhagen (1986) all find support for mutual influence contributing to a cycle of violence hypotheses. If a positive loop links repression to conflict, both increase endlessly. By virtue of historical observation, it is clear that such is not the case. How deescalation occurs is not clear. If a negative rather than a positive loop links repression to conflict, then conflict should decrease with increasing levels of repression. Additionally, if a threshold mechanism—perhaps a tolerance of costs level set by a regime—exists, conflict and repression decline as that threshold is reached (Davenport, 1992). One or the other may decline merely due to the consumption of resources needed to perpetuate the behavior in question.

Sanctioning behavior is incorporated into several simulations, although it is treated differently in each. Richardson (1990) argues that state-sanctioned violence acts on violent conflict reciprocally and indirectly. Indirect linkages are through mobilization and strength of a regime's militant opposition, presumably those most likely to employ violence, and an assessment of the potential for mass violence. That political conflict and the administration of negative sanctions by a regime are related reciprocally seems generally supported. But whether or not to incorporate militant opposition elements and violence potential as structural features or parameter values in the determination of linkages between conflict and sanctions constitutes a strategy choice in determining model architecture rather than a theoretical issue.

The form of the behavior resulting from the structural provisions for political conflict and sanctioning behavior can be best described as dampened oscillation. Dampened oscillation reflects the tendency of regimes to respond to conflict behavior reactively by imposing sanctions after events have occurred. Behaviorally, sanctions lag increases and decreases in conflict; although, if not interrupted, they decrease in amplitude over time as sanctions gradually lessen conflict. In highly repressive systems—that is, those that are more likely to employ continuous and severe sanctions— protest behavior is less likely to be manifested, and if it occurs it is more likely to be reduced quickly through the imposition of severe sanctions (see chapters 6 and 7). Insurgency is less easily controlled as it can be sustained by organizational resources within the regime itself.

As well as can be determined by historical observation and empirical studies, the total elimination of political conflict through sanctions alone is unknown or at least unlikely. Most likely, depending on types of conflict and conflict parameters, only some portion of conflict is vulnerable to effective repression. In some instances the application of sanctions could elicit a reaction from those against whom it is directed. Gurr and Lichbach (1986) argue that the greater the insurgency and the longer insurgents have engaged in political conflict, the less likely conflict will be regulated effectively through the imposition of negative sanctions. For example, only 20 percent of mass conflict or less may be subject to effective application of sanctions, and although it can be reduced, it seems unlikely that it can be completely eliminated. Political conflict may be subject to sanctioning behavior in some instances but is likely to decline in any case between disturbances to the system and to be regenerated by new disturbances. There is some reason to believe that conflict is a cumulative phenomenon, at least to the degree that conflict becomes a component of the political culture of a system. Conflict acquires substantive and instrumental value for dissatisfied political elements (see for example, Sears and McConahay, 1973). Therefore, conflict may persist in the long term even if it is repressed. Furthermore, regime tolerance for political conflict is always high during periods of disturbance without sanctions imposed proportionally in anticipation that conflict will continue to be generated by disturbances to the system.

Application of sanctions to repress political conflict requires a persisting sanctioning apparatus, most often in the form of internal security forces or military organizations that, in fact, focus on repression of political conflict. If sanctions are to be employed, resources must exist to perform such acts, and resources are subject to variation by time. Generally, the growth of sanctioning organizations is related to the degree to which they are involved in sanctioning behavior. The more they are involved in the imposition of sanctions, the greater their demands for state resources, which in turn contributes to the size and growth of the organization. Similar to most organizations, sanctioning organizations tend to be self-perpetuating and attempt to maintain their cumulative organizational growth without regard to occasional decline in the imposition of negative sanctions. Therefore, sanctioning organizations are far more persistent across time than the sanctions they employ and can be sustained by external as well as internal resources. External aid programs to increase military and policing effectiveness are common and are very likely to maintain the sanctioning apparatus although local willingness to utilize internal resources may decline. Perhaps more important, the existence of sanctioning organizations may contribute to the use of sanctions rather than other policy alternatives for coping with political conflict (Davenport, 1992).

The application of sanctions and the existence of omnipresent repressive organizations are not the only options for coping with political conflict but may be closely related to the likelihood that other options will be employed. The nature of political development is explored in voluminous literature, and this task is not attempted here. In most instances it involves popular participation in an electoral system and the relative independence of legislative and judicial bodies from the executive. Those systems that provide for such institutional arrangements are usually acknowledged to be more developed than those that do not (Cutright, 1963; Neubauer, 1967; McCrone and Cnudde, 1969; Bollen, 1980).

Political development is closely related to political conflict and the manner in which it is regulated. Political development is inversely related to the use of negative sanctions for the suppression of political conflict and the persistence of a dominant sanctioning apparatus. A goal-setting mechanism responsive to political development determines the level of political conflict tolerated before sanctions are imposed. Actual levels of political conflict are compared with preferred levels of conflict. If actual conflict levels exceed the topmost levels tolerated, sanctions are imposed to reduce conflict. If actual levels of conflict are below tolerated levels, no sanctions are imposed. Generally, the greater the level of political development, the greater the tolerance of the less violent forms of mass conflict, although no political system tolerates political conflict absolutely. Gurr and Lichbach (1986) advance similar arguments, contending that some regime types may be predisposed toward particular responses to political conflict. Specifically, authoritarian regimes are more likely to employ sanctions, while democratic regimes are less likely to rely as heavily on repressive responses to conflict.

More important, political development institutionalizes mass conflict and lessens the association of destabilizing events to manifestations of conflict. More developed systems differ from less developed systems by their tendency to employ severe negative sanctions and maintain extensive sanctioning institutions, not by their level of mass political conflict (Ziegenhagen, 1986; Davenport, 1992). In some respects, admittedly not very well understood, systems change in their use of negative sanctions irrespective of levels of mass conflict. It is suspected that these changes are a function of political development, specifically the institutionalization of political conflict, which contributes to lower levels. Lower levels of conflict, of course, reduce the need to impose sanctions. The sanctions apparatus also declines as political development progresses and the level of sanctioning behavior is reduced. Concurrently, the tolerance of mass conflict in more developed systems increases, further lessening although not eliminating the predilection to repress political conflict.

Similar to behavior systems, generally, political development does not persist without variation. The most dramatic instance of decline entails the elimination of civilian representative institutions most often by military coups. The expansion of military representation in civilian regimes and the predilection to select repressive responses to political conflict, however, also contribute to political regression. Growth of the sanctioning apparatus itself has a diminishing effect on political development and in some circumstances can lead to its rapid regression. Heavy reliance on sanctions contributes to the growth of the sanctioning apparatus, which can lead to the regression of political development. The relationship between political development and the sanctioning apparatus is dominated by a negative loop.

Political development increases its capacity to regulate the effects of disturbances to the system by responding to demands made of the system. It is noteworthy that demands stimulate both political conflict and political development. Demands may be satisfied not only by the expression of discontent through political conflict and insurgency, but also through the enhancement of the capability or predilection of the political apparatus to satisfy demands.

MODEL BEHAVIOR

A rigorous test of the model is far beyond the confines of this chapter, although several time series tests in combination with sensitivity and scenario analysis can be employed for an early assessment of model behavior. Time series tests provide opportunities to test the model's structure by producing historically observed behavior patterns for a particular system or category of systems. Sensitivity and scenario analysis entail the introduction of parameter values that elicit particular behavior patterns of interest, such as the policy initiatives that are likely to have an impact on particular aspects of system behavior. The initial time series tests involve a comparison of system responses to variation in parameter settings, which distinguish among levels of political development. In this instance a comparison is made of a more developed system with a substantially less developed system as indicated by parameter settings for political development, institutionalization of conflict, and sanctioning apparatus. Stated in somewhat more familiar terms, comparatively less developed systems are likely to be authoritarian and entail the use of sanctions as a response to political conflict to the exclusion of institutionalization. In terms of institutions, they are less likely to be well differentiated by function— that is, law making, law execution, and law adjudication—and they have a comparatively well-developed sanctioning apparatus.

Less politically developed systems secure different results from efforts to regulate protest and insurgency than more developed systems. Effectiveness in the administration of policy responses to political conflict and the transformation of systems themselves vary, particularly in the degree to which they advance or regress developmentally. For experimental purposes, both systems are confronted with the same initial parameter settings for political conflict and insurgency. Results can be seen in Figures 8.2 and 8.3.

The relationship of expectations to system performance differs strikingly

Figure 8.2
Less Developed System: Expectations and Performance

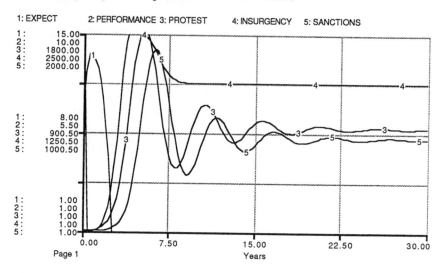

Figure 8.3
More Developed System: Expectations and Performance

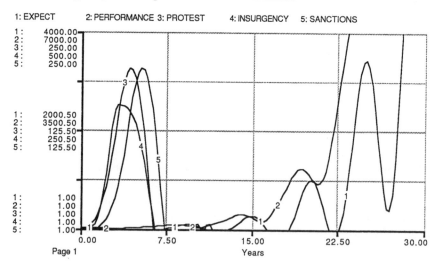

between systems. Poor performance and depressed expectations emerge in the less developed system compared to the oscillation of both in the more developed system. In addition, performance and expectations increase in the more developed system, while both expectations and performance become static in the less developed system. Both systems experience

Figure 8.4
More Developed System: Political Development and Sanctions Apparatus

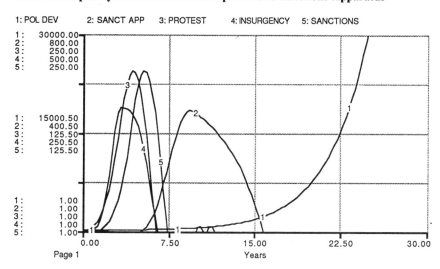

protest and insurgency, but the more developed political system reduces political conflict to well below its initial value and in a shorter time. Both systems utilize sanctions to regulate political conflict, but the less developed system employs sanctions at a higher level and with greater fluctuation than the more developed system. For the less developed system, the sharp rise in sanctions and coordinated repression of protest and insurgency are suggestive of military intervention or coup-like behavior, as political development declines rapidly with the growth of the sanctioning apparatus. Oscillation of protest, insurgency, and sanctions declines but persists at a comparatively high level providing the illusion of stability. This behavior is not present in the more developed system. (See Figure 8.4.)

More differences between system responses can be seen as they are placed under stress of disturbances that are beyond their control. In this instance the disturbance is in the form of a step function representing a change that has an immediate effect and long-term, persisting effects on demands, representing, for example, the sudden impact of an increase in the cost of energy. Results are shown in Figures 8.5, 8.6, and 8.7.

The disturbance begins at year two and persists thereafter for both cases. Political conflict and sanctions increase and oscillate in both systems. In the more developed system, the trend is downward but remains at a substantially higher level than the less developed system. Insurgency declines much more rapidly in the more developed system while it stabilizes at a comparatively high level in the less developed system. However, political development is the most striking difference between systems, as it increases in more developed systems and declines in less developed systems. Ad-

Figure 8.5
Less Developed System: Political Development and Sanctions Apparatus

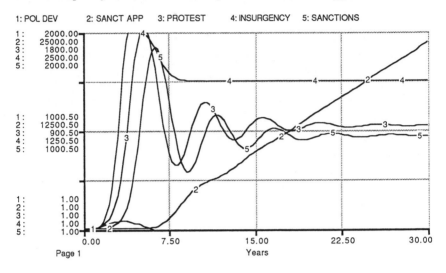

Figure 8.6
Less Developed System: Disturbance at Year 15

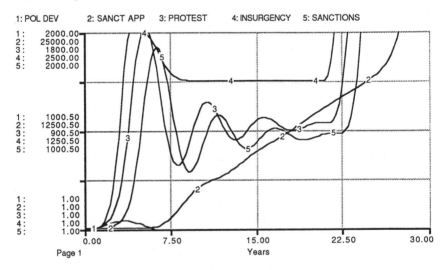

ditionally, the sanctioning apparatus slowly declines in the more developed system and continues to grow in the less developed system.

The less developed system responds to disturbances and accompanying increases in protest and insurgency by greater reliance on repressive policies

Figure 8.7
More Developed System: Disturbance at Year 15

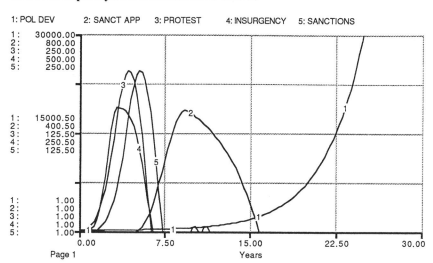

in combination with the advance of institutions charged with the administration of such initiatives. By comparison it is a less successful adaptive strategy than that undertaken by more developed systems. Enhanced levels of political development contribute to long-term positive results in the regulation of conflict and insurgency.

CONCLUSIONS

The model produces initial results consistent with those reported in the literature on political development, conflict, and sanctions policy, although it is too early to assess the usefulness of the model for other than exploratory purposes. Far more sophisticated tests of the model entail use of historical data values for specific political systems. Even then, current results seem to support a modeling strategy based on a dynamic goal-directed system rather than a reactive entity that responds to exogenous influences without the capacity to modify itself to cope with them. System maintenance within some limits of variation becomes an aspect of goal-directed behavior contributing to explanations of why political systems change, at what rate they change, and in what direction.

Political development emerges as a key element in the determination of system functioning. Generally, the more developed the system, the more likely it can cope with disturbances through adaptation as an aspect of the morphogenic process. Democratic systems appear to be highly adaptable. The most essential aspects of democratic systems are probably those which contribute to the capability of the system to adapt and persist in time. In turn, advances in political development are seen as a direct effect of demands made of the system and as an indirect effect of political conflict.

NOTE

This simulation is based upon STELLA II (Systems Thinking, Experimental Learning Laboratory with Animation), High Performance Systems, copyright 1990.

BIBLIOGRAPHY

Abinales, P. N. (1986). "Militarization in the Philippines." *Studies in Third World Societies* 27: 129–174.

Agaogullari, M. A. (1987). "Ultranationalist Right." In I. C. Schick and E. A. Tonak (eds.), *Turkey in Transition, New Perspectives*, pp. 177–217. London: Oxford University Press.

Ake, C. (1969). *A Theory of Political Integration*. Homewood, IL: Dorsey Press.

Aldrich, J. H. and F. D. Nelson (1984). *Linear Probability Logit and Probit Models*. Beverly Hills, CA: Sage Publications.

Alexander, R. J. (1958). "The Army in Politics." In H. E. Davis (ed.), *Government and Politics in Latin America*, pp. 147–165. New York: Ronald Press.

Alfatooni, A. and M. Allen (1991). "Government Sanctions and Collective Political Protest in Periphery and Semiperiphery States: A Time Series Analysis." *Journal of Political and Military Sociology* 19: 29–45.

Almond, G. (1965). "A Developmental Approach to Political Systems." *World Politics* 17: 182–214.

Almond, G. (1970). *Political Development*. Boston: Little, Brown and Co.

Amin, S. (1974). *Accumulation on a World Scale: A Critique of the Theory of Underdevelopment*. New York: Monthly Review Press.

Amin, S. (1976). *Unequal Development: An Essay on the Social Formations of Peripheral Capitalism*. New York: Monthly Review Press.

Apter, D. (1987). *Rethinking Development: Modernization, Dependency, and Post-modern Politics*. Newberry Park, CA: Sage Publications.

Arat, Z. F. (1991). *Democracy and Human Rights in Developing Countries*. Boulder, CO: Lynne Rienner Publishers.

Ashby, H. (1956). *Introduction to Cybernetics*. New York: John Wiley and Sons.

Aulin, A. (1982). *The Cybernetic Laws of Social Progress*. New York: Pergamon Press.

Ayres, H. (1992). "From Coast to Coast, Cities Are Struggling to Control a Swell of Violence." *New York Times*, May 2, 1992, Section 1, p. 10.

Banks, A. (1979). *Cross-National Time-Series Data Archive: Users Manual*, revised. Binghamton, NY: Center for Social Analysis, State University of New York at Binghamton.

Banuazizi, A. (1987). "Social-Psychological Approaches to Political Development." In M. Weiner and S. P. Huntington, (eds.), *Understanding Political Development*, pp. 281–316. Boston: Little, Brown and Co.

Baran, P. (1957). *The Political Economy of Growth*. New York: Monthly Review Press.

Baran, P. (1966). *La Economica Politica del Crecimiento*. Mexico: F.C.E.

Ben-Eli, M. (1979). "Amplifying Regulation and Variety Increase in Evolving Systems." *Journal of Cybernetics* 9: 285–296.

Bergesen, A. (1980). "Cycles of Formal Colonial Rule." In T. Hopkins and I. Wallerstein (eds.), *Processes of the World System*, pp. 119–126. Beverly Hills, CA: Sage Publications.

Berkowitz, L. (1962). *Aggression: A Social Psychological Analysis*. New York: McGraw-Hill.

Birand, M. A. (1987). *The General's Coup in Turkey, An Inside Story of 12 September 1980*. London: Brassey's Defence Publishers.

Black, C. (1966). *The Dynamics of Modernization*. New York: Harper & Row.

Bollen, K. (1980). "Issues in the Comparative Measurement of Political Democracy." *American Sociological Review* 45: 370–390.

Boswell, T. and W. J. Dixon (1990). "Dependency and Rebellion: A Cross-National Analysis." *American Sociological Review* 55: 540–559.

Bousquet, N. (1980). "From Hegemony to Competition: Cycles of the Core?" In T. Hopkins and I. Wallerstein (eds.), *Processes of the World System*, pp. 46–83. Beverly Hills, CA: Sage Publications.

Bremer, S. (1980). "The Contagiousness of Coercion: The Spread of Serious International Disputes, 1900–1976." *International Interactions* 9: 29–55.

Bremer, S., J. Singer, and J. Stuckey (1972). "Capability Distribution, Uncertainty, and Major Power War, 1820–1965." In B. Russett (ed.), *Peace, War and Numbers*, pp. 19–48. Beverly Hills, CA: Sage Publications.

Brinton, C. (1965). *The Anatomy of Revolution*. New York: Vintage Press.

Brown, J. (1987). "The Military and Politics in Turkey." *Armed Forces and Society* 13: 235–253.

Brown, J. (1988). "The Politics of Disengagement in Turkey: The Kemalist Tradition." In C. P. Danopoulos (ed.), *The Decline of Military Regimes*, pp. 131–146. Boulder, CO: Westview Press.

Buzan, B. (1983). *People, States and Fear: The National Security Problem in International Relations*. Chapel Hill: University of North Carolina Press.

Bwy, D. (1968). "Dimensions of Social Conflict in Latin America." *American Behavioral Science* 11: 39–50.

Cardoso, F. H. (1977). "The Consumption of Dependency Theory in the U.S." *Latin American Research Review* 12: 7–24.

Cardoso, F. H. and E. Faletto (1979). *Dependency and Development in Latin America*. Berkeley: University of California Press.

Chilcote, R. (1984). "Toward the Democratic Opening in Latin America: The Case of Brazil." *Monthly Review* 35: 15–24.

Chiro, D. (1977). *Social Change in the Twentieth Century*. New York: Harcourt Brace Jovanovich.

Cnudde, C. F. and D. E. Neubauer (1969). "New Trends in Democratic Theory." In C. F. Cnudde and D. E. Neubauer (eds.), *Empirical Democratic Theory*, pp. 511–534. Chicago: Markham Publishing Co.

Cohen, Y., R. Brown, and A. Organski (1981). "The Paradoxical Nature of State Building: The Violent Creation of Order." *American Political Science Review* 75: 901–910.

Coleman, J. (ed.) (1968). *Education and Political Development*. Princeton, NJ: Princeton University Press.

Collier, D. (ed.) (1979). *The New Authoritarianism in Latin America*. Princeton, NJ: Princeton University Press.

Coser, L. (1956). *The Function of Social Conflict*. Glencoe, IL: The Free Press.

Coser, L. (1967). *Continuities in the Study of Social Conflict*. New York: The Free Press.

Cox, R. W. (1987). *Production, Power, and World Order*. New York: Columbia University Press.

Cramer, J. S. (1991). *The Logit Model: An Introduction for Economists*. New York: Edward Arnold.

Cronin, J. E. (1980). "Stages, Cycles, and Insurgencies: The Economics of Unrest." In T. Hopkins and I. Wallerstein (eds.), *Processes of the World System*, pp. 101–118. Beverly Hills, CA: Sage Publications.

Cutright, P. (1963). "National Political Development: Measurement and Analysis." *American Sociological Review* 28: 253–264.

Davenport, C. (1992). "Examining the Cycle of Violence: A Competitive Investigation of Rival Hypotheses." Unpublished paper.

Davies, J. (1962). "Toward a Theory of Revolution." *American Sociological Review* 27: 5–19.

Davies, J. (1969). "The J-Curve of Rising and Declining Satisfactions as a Cause of Some Great Revolutions and a Contained Rebellion." In T. Gurr (ed.), *The History of Violence in America*, pp. 690–730. New York: Praeger.

Davis, D. and M. Ward (1990). "They Dance Alone: Deaths and the Disappeared in Contemporary Chile." *Journal of Conflict Resolution* 34: 449–475.

Decalo, S. (1976). *Coups and Army Rule in Africa*. New Haven: Yale University Press.

Deutsch, K. (1961). "Social Mobilization and Political Development." *American Political Science Review* 55: 493–514.

Deutsch, K. (1963). *The Nerves of Government: Models of Political Communication and Control*. Glencoe, IL: The Free Press.

Dixon, W. J. and B. E. Moon (1989). "Domestic Conflict and Basic Needs Outcomes: An Empirical Assessment." *Comparative Political Studies* 22: 178–198.

Dodd, C. H. (1990). *The Crisis of Turkish Democracy*. Huntington, England: Eothen Press.

Dollard, J., L. W. Doob, N. E. Miller, O. H. Mowrer, and R. R. Sears (1939). *Frustration and Aggression*. New Haven: Yale University Press.

Dominguez, J. I., N. S. Rodley, B. Wood, and R. Falk (eds.) (1979). *Enhancing Global Human Rights*. New York: McGraw-Hill.

Doran, C., R. Pendley and W. Phillips (1973). "A Test of Cross-National Event Reliability." *International Studies Quarterly* 17: 175–201.

Dos Santos, T. (1970). "The Structure of Dependence" *American Economic Review* 25: 231–236.

Duncan, H. (1968). *Symbols in Society*. New York: Oxford University Press.

Duvall, R., S. Jackson, B. Russett, D. Snidal, and D. Sylvan (1981). "A Formal Model of Dependencia Theory: Structure and Measurement." In R. Merritt and B. Russett (eds.), *From National Development to Global Community*, pp. 312–350. Winchester, MA: Allen and Unwin.

Duvall, R. and M. Shamir (1980). "Indicators from Errors: Cross-National, Time-Series Measures of the Repressive Dispositions of Governments." In C. Taylor (ed.), *Indicator Systems for Political, Economic and Social Analysis*, pp. 135–182. Cambridge, England: Ogeschager and Hann.

Easton, D. (1965). *A Systems Analysis of Political Life*. New York: John Wiley and Sons.

Eberwein, W. (1987). "Domestic Political Processes." In S. Bremer (ed.), *The Globus Model: Computer Simulation of Worldwide Political and Economic Developments*, pp. 159–282. Boulder, CO: Westview Press.

Eckstein, H. H. (1964–1965). "On the Etiology of Internal Wars." *History and Theory* 4: 113–163.

Economic Commission for Latin America (ECLA) (1963). *The Economic Development of Latin America in the Post-War Period*. New York: United Nations.

Edelman, M. (1964). *The Symbolic Uses of Politics*. Urbana: University of Illinois Press.

Emmanuel, A. (1972). *Unequal Exchange: A Study of the Imperialism of Trade*. New York: Monthly Review Press.

Erikson, E. (1962). *Young Man Luther: A Study in Psychoanalysis and History*. New York: Norton.

Eroglu, C. (1987). "The Establishment of Multiparty Rule: 1945–71." In I. C. Schick and E. A. Tonak (eds.), *Turkey in Transition, New Perspectives*, pp. 101–143. London: Oxford University Press.

Etzioni, A. (1961). *A Comparative Analysis of Complex Organizations*. New York: The Free Press.

Feierabend, I. and R. Feierabend (1972). "Systemic Conditions of Political Aggression: An Application of Frustration-Aggression Theory." In I. Feierabend et al. (eds.), *Anger, Violence and Politics: Theories and Research*, pp. 136–183. Englewood Cliffs, NJ: Prentice-Hall.

Feierabend, I., R. Feierabend, and B. Nesvold (1969). "Social Change and Political Violence: Cross National Patterns." In H. Graham and T. Gurr (eds.), *Violence in America*. New York: Praeger.

Fidel, K. (1970–1971). "Military Organization and Conspiracy in Turkey." *Studies in Comparative International Development* 6: 19–43.

Finer, S. E. (1982). "The Morphology of Military Regimes." In R. Kolkowicz and A. Korbonski (eds.), *Soldiers, Peasants and Bureaucrats, Civil-Military Relations in Communist and Modernizing Societies*, pp. 281–310. London: George Allen and Unwin.

Finer, S. E. (1988). *The Man on Horseback, the Role of Military in Politics*, second enlarged edition. Boulder, CO: Westview Press.

Flanigan, W. and E. Fogelman (1970). "Patterns of Political Violence in Comparative Historical Perspective." *Comparative Politics* 3: 1–20.

Frank, A. G. (1967). *Capitalism and Underdevelopment in Latin America: Historical Studies in Chile and Brazil*. New York: Monthly Review Press.

Frank, A. G. (1969). *Latin America: Underdevelopment or Revolution*. New York: Monthly Review Press.

Galtung, J. (1971). "Structural Theory of Imperialism." *Journal of Peace Research* 8: 81–117.

Gamson, W. (1974). *The Strategy of Social Protest*. Homewood, IL: Dorsey Press.

Geller, D. (1982). "Economic Modernization and Political Instability in Latin America." *Western Political Quarterly* 35: 33–49.

Gemmell, N. (1982). "Economic Development and Structural Change: The Role of the Service Sector." *Journal of Developmental Studies* 19: 37–66.

Germani, G. and K. Silvert (1967). "Politics, Social Structure and Military Intervention in Latin America." In P. G. Snow (ed.), *Government and Politics in Latin America, A Reader*, pp. 299–318. New York: Holt Reinhart and Winston.

Goldstein, J. and J. Freeman (1990). *Three-Way Street: Strategic Reciprocity in World Politics*. Chicago: Chicago University Press.

Gordon, D. M. (1980). "Stages of Accumulation and Long Economic Cycles." In T. Hopkins and I. Wallerstein (eds.), *Processes of the World System*, pp. 9–45. Beverly Hills, CA: Sage Publications.

Gow, D. and K. White (1978). *Guide to Econometrics*. New York: McGraw–Hill.

Greene, W. H. (1990). *Econometric Analysis*. New York: Macmillan.

Gude, E. W. (1969). "Batista and Betancourt: Alternative Responses to Violence." In H. D. Graham and T. R. Gurr (eds.), *Violence in America: A Staff Report*, pp. 731–748. Washington, DC: U.S. Government Printing Office.

Gurr, T. (1967–1968). "Psychological Factors of Civil Violence." *World Politics* 20: 245–278.

Gurr, T. (1969). "A Comparative Study of Civil Strife." In H. D. Graham and T. Gurr (eds.), *Violence in America: Historical and Comparative Perspectives*, pp. 572–626. New York: Signet.

Gurr, T. (1970). *Why Men Rebel*. Princeton, NJ: Princeton University Press.

Gurr, T. (1972). "The Calculus of Civil Conflict." *Journal of Social Issues* 28: 27–47.

Gurr, T. (1980). "On the Outcomes of Violence." In T. Gurr (ed.), *Handbook of Political Conflict: Theory and Practice*, pp. 238–296. New York: The Free Press.

Gurr, T. (1986a). "Persisting Patterns of Repression and Rebellion: Foundations for a General Theory of Political Coercion." In M. P. Karns (ed.), *Persistent Patterns and Emergent Structures in a Waning Century*, pp. 149–168. New York: Praeger Special Studies.

Gurr, T. (1986b). "The Political Origins of State Violence and Terror: A Theoretical Analysis." In M. Stohl and G. A. Lopez (eds.), *Government Violence and Repression*, pp. 45–71. Westport, CT: Greenwood Press.

Gurr, T. (1988). "War, Revolution, and the Growth of the Coercive State." *Comparative Political Studies* 21: 45–65.

Gurr, T. and M. Lichbach (1986). "Forecasting Internal Conflict: A Competitive Evaluation of Empirical Theories." *Comparative Political Studies* 19: 3–38.

Gusfield, J. (1963). *Symbolic Crusade: Status Politics and the American Temperance Movement.* Urbana: University of Illinois Press.

Hale, W. (1990). "The Turkish Army in Politics, 1960–73." In A. Finkel and N. Sirman (eds.), *Turkish State, Turkish Society*, pp. 53–77. London: Routledge.

Halebsky, S. (1976). *Mass Society and Political Conflict.* London: Cambridge University Press.

Harris, G. S. (1965). "The Role of the Military in Turkish Politics." *Middle East Journal* (Winter-Spring): 54–66 (Part I), 169–176 (Part II).

Harris, G. S. (1985). *Turkey: Coping with Crisis.* Boulder, CO: Westview Press.

Hayward, F. (1973). "Political Participation and Its Role in Development: Some Observations Drawn from the African Context." *Journal of Developing Areas* 7: 591–611.

Henderson, C. W. (1991). "Conditions Affecting the Use of Political Repression." *Journal of Conflict Resolution* 35: 120–142.

Heper, M. and A. Evin (eds.) (1988). *State Democracy and the Military, Turkey in the 1980s.* Berlin: Walter de Gruyter.

Herman, E. (1982). *The Real Terror Network: Terrorism in Fact and Propaganda.* Boston: South End Press.

Hibbs, D. (1973). *Mass Political Violence: A Cross-National Causal Analysis.* New York: John Wiley and Sons.

Himes, J. (1980). *Conflict and Conflict Management.* Athens: The University of Georgia Press.

Hopkins, T. (1978). "World-System Analysis: Methodological Issues." In B. H. Kaplan (ed.), *Social Change in the Capitalist World Economy*, pp. 199–217. Beverly Hills, CA: Sage Publications.

Hoselitz, B. and A. Willner (1962). "Economic Development, Political Strategies and American Aid." In M. Kaplan (ed.), *The Revolution in World Politics*, pp. 355–380. New York: John Wiley and Sons.

Huntington, S. P. (1957). *The Soldier and the State.* London: Cambridge University Press.

Huntington, S. P. (1965). "Political Development and Political Decay." *World Politics* 17: 386–430.

Huntington, S. P. (1968). *Political Order in Changing Societies.* New Haven: Yale University Press.

Huntington, S. P. (1987). "The Goals of Development." In M. Weiner and S. P. Huntington (eds.), *Understanding Political Development*, pp. 3–32. Boston: Little, Brown and Co.

Hyter, T. (1971). *Aid as Imperialism.* Baltimore: Penguin Books.

Jackman, R. W. (1975). *Politics and Social Equality: A Comparative Analysis.* New York: John Wiley & Sons.

Jackman, R. W. (1976). "Politicians in Uniform: Military Governments and Social Change in the Third World." *American Political Science Review* 70: 1078–1097.

Jackman, R. W. (1978) "The Predictability of Coups d'Etat: A Model with African Data." *American Political Science Review* 72: 1262–1275.

Jackson, S., B. Russett, D. Snidal, and D. Sylvan, (1978). "Conflict and Coercion in Dependent States." *Journal of Conflict Resolution* 22: 627–657.

James, P. (1986). "Externalization of Conflict: Testing a Crisis-Based Model." *Canadian Journal of Political Science* 80: 921–945.

Janowitz, M. (1964). *The Military in the Development of New Nations: An Essay in Comparative Analysis.* Chicago: University of Chicago Press.

Johnson, C. (1966). *Revolutionary Change.* Boston: Little, Brown and Co.

Johnson, J. J. (1962). "The Latin American Military as a Politically Competing Group in Transitional Society." In J. J. Johnson (ed.), *The Role of the Military in Underdeveloped Countries*, pp. 91–129. Princeton, NJ: Princeton University Press.

Johnson, J. J. (ed.) (1962). *The Role of the Military in Underdeveloped Countries.* Princeton, NJ: Princeton University Press.

Johnson, T. H., R. O. Slater, and P. McGowan (1984). "Explaining African Military Coup d'Etat, 1960–1982." *American Political Science Review* 78: 622–640.

Karakartal, B. (1985). "Turkey: The Army as Guardian of Political Order." In C. Clapham and G. Philip (eds.), *The Political Dilemmas of Military Regimes*, pp. 46–63. London: Croom Helm.

Karpat, K. H. (1981). "Turkish Democracy at Impasse: Ideology Party Politics and the Third Military Intervention." *International Journal of Turkish Studies* 2: 1–43.

Karpat, K. H. (1988). "Military Interventions: Army-Civilian Relations in Turkey Before and After 1980." In M. Heper and A. Evin (eds.), *State Democracy and the Military, Turkey in the 1980s*, pp. 137–155. Berlin: Walter de Gruyter.

Karpat, K. H. (1970). "The Military and Politics in Turkey, 1960–1964: A Socio-Cultural Analysis of a Revolution." *American Historical Review* 75: 1654–1683.

Kelejian, H., W. Oates, and E. Wallace (1981). *Introduction to Econometrics: Principles and Applications.* New York: Harper & Row.

Kennedy, P. A. (1989). *A Guide to Econometrics.* Cambridge, MA: MIT Press.

Keyder, C. (1987). "Economic Development and Crisis: 1950–1980." In I. C. Schick and E. A. Tonak (eds.), *Turkey in Transition, New Perspectives*, pp. 293–308. London: Oxford University Press.

King, G. (1989). "Event Count Models for International Relations: Generalizations and Applications." *International Studies Quarterly* 33: 123–147.

Koutsoukis, K. (1978). "Socioeconomic Change and Cabinet Composition in Greece." *The Greek Review of Social Research* 32: 74–79.

Koutsoukis, K. (1982). *Political Leadership in Modern Greece.* Athens: Athena Publications.

Lang, K. (1975). *Military Institutions and the Sociology of War: A Review of the Literature with an Annotated Bibliography.* Beverly Hills, CA: Sage Publications.

Lasswell, H. (1941). "The Garrison State and Specialists on Violence." *American Journal of Sociology* 46: 455–468.

Lasswell, H. and M. Kaplan (1950). *Power and Society: A Framework for Political Inquiry.* New Haven, CT: Yale University Press.

Li, R. and W. Thompson (1975). "The Coup Contagion Hypothesis." *Journal of Conflict Resolution* 19: 63–88.

Lichbach, M. (1987). "Deterrence or Escalation? The Puzzle of Aggregate Studies of Repression and Dissent." *Journal of Conflict Resolution* 31: 266–297.

Lieuwen, E. (1961). *Arms and Politics in Latin America*. New York: Praeger.

Lieuwen, E. (1962). "Militarism and Politics in Latin America." In J. J. Johnson (ed.), The *Role of the Military in Underdeveloped Countries*, pp. 131–163. Princeton, NJ: Princeton University Press.

Linz, J. J. and A. Stepan (eds.) (1978). *The Breakdown of Democratic Regimes*. Baltimore: Johns Hopkins University Press.

Lipset, S. (1959). "Some Social Requisites of Democracy: Economic Development and Political Legitimacy." *American Political Science Review* 53: 69–105.

Lipset, S. (1985). *Consensus and Conflict*. New Brunswick, NJ: Transaction Books.

Lissak, M. (1964). "Selected Literature on Revolutions and Coup d'Etat in the Developing Nations." In M. Janowitz (ed.), *The New Military, Changing Patterns of Organization*, pp. 339–362. New York: Russell Sage Foundation.

Londregan, J. B. and K. T. Poole (1990). "Poverty, the Coup Trap and the Seizure of Executive Power." *World Politics* 42: 151–183.

Lopez, G. A. and M. Stohl (1989). *Dependence, Development and State Repression*. Westport, CT: Greenwood Press.

Lutwak, E. (1979). *Coup d'Etat: A Practical Handbook*. Cambridge, MA: Harvard University Press.

McCamant, J. (1984). "Governance Without Blood: Social Science's Antiseptic View of Rule: or the Neglect of Political Repression." In Michael Stohl (ed.), *The State as Terrorist: The Dynamics of Governmental Violence and Repression*, pp. 105–142. Westport, CT: Greenwood Press.

Mardin, S. (1978). "Youth and Violence in Turkey." *Archives Europeen de Sociologie* 19: 229–254.

Maslow, A. (1943). "A Theory of Human Motivation." *Psychological Review* 370–396.

Mason, D. T. (1989). "Nonelite Response to State-Sanctioned Terror." *Western Political Quarterly* 42: 467–492.

McCrone, D. and C. Cnudde (1969). "Toward a Communications Theory of Democratic Political Development: A Causal Model." In C. Cnudde and D. Neubauer (eds.), *Empirical Democratic Theory*. Chicago: Markham.

McGowan, P. and T. H. Johnson (1984). "African Military Coup d'Etat and Underdevelopment: A Quantitative Historical Analysis." *Journal of Modern African Studies* 22: 633–666.

McPhail, C. and D. Miller (1973). "The Assembling Process: A Theoretical and Empirical Examination." *American Sociological Review* 38: 721–735.

Meier, G. M. (1984). *Leading Issues in Economic Development*. New York: Oxford University Press.

Mlinar, Z. and H. Teune (1978). *Developmental Logic of Social Systems*. Beverly Hills, CA: Sage.

Modelski, G. (1987a). *Exploring Long Cycles*. Boulder, CO: Lynne Rienner.

Modelski, G. (1987b). *Long Cycles in World Politics*. Seattle: University of Washington Press.

Montesquieu, C. (1989). *The Spirit of the Laws*. New York: Cambridge University Press.

Moore, B., Jr. (1978). *Injustice: The Social Basis of Obedience and Revolt*. White Plains, NY: M. E. Sharpe.

Muller, E. N. (1985). "Income Inequality, Regime Repressiveness, and Political Violence." *American Sociological Review* 50: 47–61.

Muller, E. N. and M. A. Seligson (1987). "Inequality and Insurgency." *American Political Science Review* 81: 425–451.

Muller, E. N. and E. Weede (1990). "Cross-National Variation in Political Violence." *Journal of Conflict Resolution* 34: 624–651.

Nardin, T. (1971). *Violence and the State*. Beverly Hills, CA: Sage Publications.

Needler, M. C. (1963). *Latin American Politics in Perspective*. New York: Van Nostrand Reinhold Company.

Needler, M. C. (1966). "Political Development and Military Intervention in Latin America." *American Political Science Review* 60: 616–626.

Neubauer, D. (1967). "Some Conditions of Democracy." *American Political Science Review* 61: 1002–1009.

Nieburg, H. (1979). "Agonistics: Rituals of Conflicts." *In The Annals: Collective Violence*, pp. 56–78. American Academy of Political and Social Sciences.

Nieburg, H. L. (1963). "The Uses of Violence." *Journal of Conflict Resolution* 7: 43–54.

Nieburg, H. L. (1969). *Political Violence: The Behavioral Process*. New York: St. Martin's Press.

Nordlinger, E. (1972). *Conflict Regulation in Divided Societies*. Cambridge, MA: Harvard University Press.

Oberschall, A. (1973). *Social Conflict and Social Movements*. Englewood Cliffs, NJ: Prentice-Hall.

O'Donnell, G. A. (1979). *Modernization and Bureaucratic Authoritarianism: Studies in South American Politics*. Berkeley, CA: Institute of International Studies.

O'Kane, R. H. (1981). "A Probabilistic Approach to the Causes of Coup d'Etat." *British Journal of Political Science* 11: 287–308.

O'Kane, R. H. (1983). "Toward an Examination of the General Causes of Coup d'Etat." *European Journal of Political Research* 11: 27–44.

O'Kane, R. H. (1987). *The Likelihood of Coups*. Brookfield, VT: Gower Publishing Company.

Olson, M. (1963). "Rapid Growth as a Destabilizing Force." *Journal of Economic History* 23: 529–552.

Opp, K. and W. Roehl (1990). "Repression, Micromobilization, and Political Protest." *Social Forces* 69: 521–547.

Ozbudun, E. (1981). "The Turkish Party System: Institutionalization, Polarization, and Fragmentation." *Middle Eastern Studies* 17: 228–240.

Palma, G. (1978). "Dependency: A Formal Theory of Underdevelopment or a Methodology for the Analysis of Concrete Situations of Underdevelopment?" *World Development* 6: 881–924.

Parsons, T. (1951). *The Social System*. Glencoe, IL: The Free Press.

Perlmutter, A. and V. Bennett (1980). *The Political Influence of the Military: A Comparative Reader*. New Haven: Yale University Press.

Pevsner, L. C. (1984). *Turkey's Political Crisis, Background Perspectives, Prospects*. New York: Praeger.

Pindyck, R. S. and D. Rubinfeld (1991). *Econometric Models and Economic Fore-casts*. New York: McGraw-Hill.

Pirages, D. (1976). *Managing Political Conflict*. Lagos, Nigeria: Nelson Ltd.

Piven, F. F. and R. A. Cloward (1977). *Poor People's Movements: Why They Succeed; How They Fail*. New York: Pantheon Books.

Piven, F. F. and R. A. Cloward (1971). *Regulating the Poor*. New York: Pantheon Books.

Portes, A. (1976). "On the Sociology of National Development: Theories and Issues." *American Journal of Sociology* 82: 55–85.

Przeworski, A. and H. Teune (1985). *The Logic of Comparative Social Inquiry*. Malabar, CA: Robert E. Krieger.

Putnam, R. D. (1967). "Toward Explaining Military Intervention in Latin American Politics." *World Politics* 20: 83–110.

Pye, L. W. (1962). "Armies in the Process of Modernization." In J. J. Johnson (ed.), *The Role of the Military in Underdeveloped Countries*, pp. 69–89. Princeton, NJ: Princeton University Press.

Rae, D. (1968). "A Note on the Fractionalization of Some European Party Systems." *Comparative Political Studies* 1: 413–418.

Rasler, K. (1986). "War, Accommodation and Violence in the United States, 1890–1970." *American Political Science Review* 80: 921–945.

Rawls, J. (1971). *A Theory of Justice*. Cambridge, MA: Harvard University Press.

Richardson, J. (1987). "Violence and Repression: Neglected Factors in Development Planning." *Futures* 6: 651–668.

Richardson, J. (1990). "Understanding Violent Conflict in Sri Lanka: How Theory Can Help." G. C. Mendis Memorial Lecture. Unpublished address.

Roberts, K. (1985). "Democracy and the Dependent Capitalist State in Latin America." *Monthly Review* 37: 12–26.

Robinson, R. and J. London (1991). "Dependency, Inequality and Political Violence: A Cross National Analysis." *Journal of Political and Military Sociology* 19: 119–156.

Rose, R. (ed.) (1976). *The Dynamics of Public Policy: A Comparative Analysis*. Beverly Hills, CA: Sage Publications.

Rosenau, J. N. (1990). *Turbulence in World Politics: A Theory of Change and Continuity*. Princeton, NJ: Princeton University Press.

Rosh, R. (1988). "Third World Militarization: Security Webs and the States They Ensnare." *Journal of Conflict Resolution* 32: 671–698.

Rostow, W. (1960). *The Stages of Economic Growth*. Cambridge: Cambridge University Press.

Rummel, R. (1963). "Dimensions of Conflict Behavior Within and Between Nations." *General Systems Yearbook* 8: 1–50.

Runciman, W. (1966). *Relative Deprivation and Social Justice*. Berkeley: University of California Press.

Rustow, D. A. (1959). "The Army and the Founding of the Turkish Republic." *World Politics* 11: 513–552.

Samim, A. (1987). "The Left." In I. C. Schick and E. A. Tonak (eds.), *Turkey in Transition, New Perspectives*, pp. 147–176. London: Oxford University Press.

Sears, D. and J. McConahay (1973). *The Politics of Violence*. New York: Houghton Mifflin.

Seidman, R. B. (1978). *The State, Law and Development*. London: Crown Helm Ltd.

Simmel, G. (1955). *The Web of Group Affiliations and Conflict*. New York: The Free Press.

Snyder, D. (1978). "Collective Violence: A Research Agenda and Some Strategic Considerations." *Journal of Conflict Resolution* 22: 500–530.

Snyder, D. and E. Kick (1979). "Structural Position in the World System and Economic Growth, 1955–1970: Multiple-Network Analysis of Transnational Interactions." *American Journal of Sociology* 84: 1096–1126.

Snyder, D. and C. Tilly (1972). "Hardship and Collective Violence in France, 1830–1960." *American Sociological Review* 37: 520–532.

Sorokin, P. (1957). *Social Change and Cultural Dynamics*. Boston: Porter Sargent.

State Institute of Statistics (1950–1990). *Statistical Yearbook of Turkey*, various issues. Ankara: State Institute of Statistics.

Steinbruner, J. (1974). *The Cybernetic Theory of Decision: New Dimensions of Political Analysis*. Princeton, NJ: Princeton University Press.

Stepan, A. (1971). *The Military in Politics: Changing Patterns in Brazil*. Princeton, NJ: Princeton University Press.

Stohl, M. (1975). "War and Political Violence: The Case of the U.S. from 1890–1960." *Journal of Conflict Resolution* 19: 379–416.

Stohl, M. and G. Lopez (1986). "Preface." In M. Stohl and G. A. Lopez (eds.), *Government Violence and Repression*, pp. vii–viii. Westport, CT: Greenwood Press.

Strauch, R. (1983). "A Critical Assessment of Quantitative Methodology as a Policy Analysis Tool." In Martin Shubik (ed.), *The Mathematics of Conflict*, pp. 29–54. New York: Elsevier Science Publishing Co.

Sunar, I. and S. Sayari (1986). "Democracy in Turkey: Problems and Prospects." In G. O'Donnell, P. C. Schmittere, and L. Whitehead (eds.), *Transitions from Authoritarian Rule*, pp. 165–186. Baltimore: Johns Hopkins University Press.

Tanter, R. (1969). "International War and Domestic Turmoil: Some Contemporary Evidence." In H. Graham and T. Gurr (eds.), *The History of Violence in America: A Report to the National Commission on the Causes and Prevention of Violence*, pp. 550–569. New York: Bantam.

Taylor, C. and D. Jodice (1983). *World Handbook of Political and Social Indicators*, third edition. New Haven: Yale University Press.

Teune, H. (1978). "The Developmental Ecology of Political Intervention." In Z. Mlinar and H. Teune (eds.), *The Social Ecology of Change*, pp.149–167. Beverly Hills, CA: Sage Publications.

Theil, H. (1961). *Economic Forecasts and Policy*. Amsterdam: North Holland Publishing Company.

Tilly, C. (1978). *From Mobilization to Revolution*. Reading, MA: Addison-Wesley.

Tilly, L. and C. Tilly (1981). *Class Conflict and Collective Action*. Beverly Hills, CA: Sage Publications.

Ullman, R. H. (1978). "Human Rights and Economic Power: The United States versus Idi Amin." *Foreign Affairs* 57: 529–543.

United Nations (1990). *World Population Prospects*. New York: United Nations.

Vaner, S. (1987). "The Army." In I. C. Schick and E. A. Tonak (eds.), *Turkey in Transition, New Perspectives*, pp. 236–265. London: Oxford University Press.

Walker, S. and I. Lang (1988). "The Garrison State Syndrome in the Third World: A Research Note." *Journal of Political and Military Sociology* 16: 105–116.

Wallerstein, I. (1974). *The Modern World System*. New York: Academic Press.

Wallerstein, I. (1976). "Semi-Peripheral Countries and the Contemporary World Crisis." *Theory and Practice* 3: 461–484.

Walton, J. and C. Ragin (1990). "Global and National Sources of Political Protest: Third World Responsiveness to the Debt Crisis." *American Sociological Review* 55: 876–890.

Ward, M. and U. Widmaier (1982). "The Domestic-Foreign Conflict Nexus: New Evidence and Old Hypotheses." *International Interactions* 9: 75–98.

Wayman, F. (1975). *Military Involvement in Politics: A Causal Model*. Beverly Hills, CA: Sage Publications.

Wehr, P. (1979). *Conflict Regulation*. Boulder, CO: Westview Press.

Weiker, W. F. (1980). *The Turkish Revolution 1960–61*. Westport, CT: Greenwood Press.

Weiker, W. F. (1981). *The Modernization of Turkey from Ataturk to the Present Day*. New York: Holmes and Meier Publishers.

Weiner, M. (1987). "Introduction." In M. Weiner and S. P. Huntington (eds.), *Understanding Political Development*, pp. v–vii. Boston: Little, Brown.

Weiner, M. and S. Huntington (1987). *Understanding Political Development*. Boston: Little, Brown.

Weiner, M. and J. LaPalombara (1966). "The Impact of Parties on Political Development." In J. LaPalombara and M. Weiner (eds.), *Political Parties and Political Development*, pp. 399–435. Princeton, NJ: Princeton University Press.

Wolpin, M. (1986). "State Terrorism and Repression in the Third World." In M. Stohl and G. Lopez (eds.), *Government Violence and Repression*, pp. 97–164. Westport, CT: Greenwood Press.

Zashin, E. (1972). *Civil Disobedience and Democracy*. New York: The Free Press.

Ziegenhagen, E. A. (1986). *The Regulation of Political Conflict*. New York: Praeger.

Ziegenhagen, E. A. and K. A. Koutsoukis (1992). *Political Conflict in Southern Europe: Regulation, Regression and Morphogenesis*. New York: Praeger.

Zimmerman, E. (1983). *Political Violence, Crisis and Revolutions: Theories and Research*. Cambridge, MA: Schenkman.

Zolberg, A. R. (1968a). "Military Intervention in the New States of Tropical Africa." In H. Bienen (ed.), *The Military Intervenes: Case Studies in Political Development*, pp. 71–98. New York: Russell Sage.

Zolberg, A. R. (1968b). "The Structure of Political Conflict in the New States of Tropical Africa." *American Political Science Review* 62: 70–87.

Zolberg, A. (1981). "Origins of the Modern World System: A Missing Link." *World Politics* 33: 252–281.

Zuk, G. and W. Thompson (1982). "The Post-Coup Military Spending Question:

A Pooled Cross-Sectional Time-Series Analysis." *American Political Science Review* 76: 60–74.

Zwick, J. (1984). "Militarism and Repression in the Philippines." In M. Stohl and G. A. Lopez (eds.), *The State as Terrorist*, Westport, CT: Greenwood Press.

Author Index

Subject Index

ABOUT THE CONTRIBUTORS

EDUARD A. ZIEGENHAGEN is a professor of political science at the University Center, State University of New York at Binghamton. He is the author of *Techniques for Political Analysis* with George Bowlby, *The Regulation of Political Conflict,* and *Political Conflict in Southern Europe* with Kleomenis Koutsoukis.

ZEHRA F. ARAT is an associate professor of political science at the State University of New York at Purchase. She is the author of *Democracy and Human Rights in Developing Countries* and "Democracy and Economic Development: Modernization Theory Revisited."

ALI ÇARKOĞLU is a visiting professor of political science at the University Center, State University of New York at Binghamton. He is the author of *Rational Expectations, The Natural Rate Hypothesis and the Stabilization Debate in Turkey: 1965–1986* and *Macroeconomic Effects of Property Rights in Labor Managed Firms*, as well as reports on the applications of economic theory to marketing issues for various public and private organizations in Turkey and Britain.

CINDY M. CHRISTIAN is an assistant professor of political science at the Texas Technological University at Lubbock. She is the author of "Testing the Reliability and Validity of the Conflict and Peace Data Bank and United Nations Roll Call Votes" with Gesel Durham, and "A Closed Cybernetic Model of Decision-Making: U.S. Foreign Policy in Latin America."

CHRISTIAN ALEXANDER DAVENPORT is an assistant professor of political science at the University of Houston. He is the author of *The Dynamics of State Repression,* "The Autonomist Theory of Social Conflict" with A. M. Sharakiya, and "Transformation of Class Structure in the United States" with James Petras.

MICHAEL DILLON is a doctoral candidate in political science at the University Center, State University of New York at Binghamton. He is the author of "A Formal Model of Rational Cooperation," and his dissertation is focused on cooperation among major European powers since 1945.

HAN-JYUN HOU is a member of the faculty of National Chung-Hsin University of Taiwan. His dissertation entails an exploration of the relationship of political conflict to political repression and the development of political institutions employing a computer simulation.

KLEOMENIS S. KOUTSOUKIS is an associate professor of political science at Panteion University, Athens, Greece, and director of the Center for Hellenic Studies. He is the author of *The Process of Political Development in Greece: 1922–1971, Political Leadership in Modern Greece, Political and Socioeconomic Development in Greece: An Empirical Approach,* and *Political Conflict in Southern Europe* with Eduard A. Ziegenhagen.